ILLUSTRATED
DICTIONARY
—— *of* ——
DREAM SYMBOLS

ILLUSTRATED DICTIONARY

—— *of* ——

DREAM SYMBOLS

A Biblical Guide to Your Dreams and Visions

Dr. Joe Ibojie

DESTINY IMAGE™ EUROPE srl

Via Maiella, 1
66020 San Giovanni Teatino (Ch) - Italy

"Changing the world, one book at a time."

This book and all other Destiny Image™ Europe books are available at Christian bookstores and distributors worldwide.

To order products, or for any other correspondence:

DESTINY IMAGE™ EUROPE srl

Via Acquacorrente, 6
65123 - Pescara - Italy
Tel: +39 085 4716623 - Fax: +39 085 9431270
E-mail: info@eurodestinyimage.com

Or reach us on the Internet: www.eurodestinyimage.com.

Previously published in two volumes by Destiny Image Europe:
Dreams and Visions ISBN 13: 978-88-89127-13-1
The Illustrated Bible-Based Dictionary of Dream Symbols ISBN 13: 978-88-89127-14-8

This addition published under license,
ISBN 13: 978-0-7684-1212-3

For Worldwide Distribution, Printed in the U.S.A.

3 4 5 6 7 8 9 10 11 / 14 13 12 11

Endorsements

Illustrated Dictionary of Dream Symbols stands tall among other books you might read on the subject of dreams and visions. It teaches the reader to understand and appreciate the voice of God in the night season of life through practical principles inherent in the Word of God. The author, Joe Ibojie, ministered in Cali, Colombia, and profoundly imparted to the Colombian Christians. The anointing of God was clearly evident in Joe's ministry as he taught and ministered with deep and dynamic revelation to Church leaders in Colombia. I recommend this book to all believers, young and old, including pastors and Church leaders. This book will create a new hunger in the Body of Christ and will cause them to listen to the voice of God and be guided by the Holy Spirit in a completely new way.

Apostle Randy Macmillan
Founder of Mission South America
Norfolk, Virginia, USA

This book and its Bible-based dictionary are mighty tools in the hand of those in the Body of Christ who are seeking to recognize the voice of God in their life. God has blessed Dr. Ibojie not only with a powerful anointing and gift himself, but also with the grace to help others unlock the inner potential within themselves through powerful keys of wisdom and insight. This book is a treasure chest filled with God's revelation and hidden mysteries that have been waiting to be uncovered since before the foundation of the earth. *Illustrated Dictionary of Dream Symols* shall bless, strengthen, and guide any believer in search of the purpose, promise, and destiny of God for their lives.

Thank God for this Christ-centered, Bible-based message that will restore the awareness that God continually longs to communicate His love, desires, and will to His children. *"He who watches over Israel will never slumber nor sleep"* (Ps. 121:4). While you are sleeping, He is still speaking. Let he who has an ear (and the desire to hear) listen to what the Spirit is saying to the Church.

Bishop Ron Scott Jr.
President, Kingdom Coalition International
Hagerstown, Maryland, USA

The prophet Joel declares that "in the last days" the Holy Spirit's outpouring will include an increase in dreams and visions as a form of prophetic gifting. How many of us have had dreams and visions without realizing that God may be speaking to us in parables? It stands to godly reason that if the Lord is indeed speaking to us while we sleep, then He will also give the gift of interpretation so that we may understand what He is saying.

In *Illustrated Dictionary of Dream Symbols*, Joe Ibojie presents sound scriptural principles and practical advice that can help us to this end. As Joe repeatedly makes clear, such understanding is not formula-based, nor is it human reason, but "interpretation is of the Lord." Therefore, we must diligently seek Him.

Joe Ibojie is a medical doctor who is also an ordained minister of the gospel. He has an effective prophetic ministry with a Daniel-type anointing in the interpretation of dreams. That this book is clearly rooted in the Word of God is evidenced by his encyclopedic knowledge and Scripture use. I am sure many readers will gain much spiritual benefit from a careful reading of this book.

Gordon Shewan
Senior Pastor, All Nations Christian Fellowship
Aberdeen, Scotland, UK

This is a comprehensive study of the reality of spiritual dreaming. The significance of the prophetic language of dreams and how God's eternal purpose is expressed in our dreams is well established. Dr. Ibojie has studied the Scripture and uses biblical keys to unlock understanding into this supernatural area of divine communication. He is a meticulous teacher of the Word of God and a wise master builder, and his explanation of the interpretation of dreams is a foundational teaching that will greatly assist the believer in understanding the significance of dreams, without moving into error.

This study is balanced, well-written, and very motivational. It will be a blessing to the Body of Christ and is a must-read for all teachers of prophecy, elders of the congregation, and students of dreams.

Emmanuel Ziga
President, Grace for All Nations Ministries International
Seattle, Washington, USA

Father God desires to speak to His people. The Lord is doing much of His communication in visions and dreams, but it has been difficult for many to determine what is from God and what is not. The Lord has given Dr. Joe a divine insight into the way He speaks to us through such heavenly encounters. This book is a practical guide that helps answer many questions, including God's purposes and types of dreams and visions and what they typically mean. There is also a wonderful chapter on how to hear the voice of God. We have found *Illustrated Dictionary of Dream Symbols* to be the best book we have read in regard to dreams and visions. Our prayers are for this book to be a blessing to many hearing the call of destiny from God as it's expressed to us in visions and dreams.

Robert and Joyce Ricciardelli
Directors, Visionary Advancement Strategies
Seattle, Washington, USA
www.vision2advance.com

I have been privileged to minister with Joe on a frequent basis. However, I am more privileged to know him not just as a person with Daniel-type anointing or as a prophetic voice (although he is frequently both of these to me), but as one of my closest friends. A true servant of God, Joe is a man with a passion to see God's kingdom extend wherever he goes and to whomever he meets. Writing this book is simply an extension of that passion and it has come out of years of experience. He has worked it out on a practical level and seen people transformed and set free to a life of liberty and purpose in the Holy

Spirit. Others have been built up, encouraged, and edified because they gained a clearer understanding of God's purposes and plans in their lives through a godly and, I believe, biblical interpretation of their dreams.

Illustrated Dictionary of Dream Symbols is a book to be revisited time and again. It corrects much of the flaky teaching about dreams that is often propagated and seeks to anchor everything in the truth and steadfast surety of Scripture. This is a book that every prophetic person in the Church should have and should study, weigh, and test it against Scripture. This book should be placed not on a shelf, but on a nightstand!

Pastor Phil Sanderson
All Nations Christian Fellowship
Aberdeen, Scotland, UK

Dr. Joe Ibojie is a true man of God who walks in real integrity and ministers under the anointing and inspiration of the Holy Spirit. Accurate prophetic revelation flows as Dr. Joe interprets dreams. I see this book as a manual to equip and inspire you in this area. The timing is just right for the release of this book, which is sure to unlock incredible truths that lie within your dreams and visions. As you read, God will open up your understanding on this little-heard truth and reveal a whole new avenue of hearing God's voice. Highly recommended as a must-read for every dreamer!

Duncan Wyllie
Senior Pastor, Kairo Christian Outreach Center
Peterhead, Scotland, UK

I have worked closely with Dr. Joe Ibojie as a member of the pastoral team of All Nations Church and the Greater Church in Aberdeenshire. It has been my privilege to have had access to this book's genius and to monitor its progress from conception to completion. Joe has an extraordinary understanding of the meaning of dreams and the ministry of angels. He is a man of unusual gifting, passion, and tenderness, and his writing portrays the gracious nature of his character. The impact of his insights has had a profound effect on me. On numerous occasions, I have observed firsthand the liberty, joy, and peace that many individuals have received through Joe's ability to interpret, with certainty, the mysteries of their dreams. He is becoming a popular speaker in church conferences as his gifting is becoming better known and sought after by Christians. I am persuaded that *Illustrated Dictionary of Dream Symbols* will equip and enable many readers to develop a similar understanding of their own dreams. This book should generate a persuasion throughout the Church of the significance of dreams and their place in the myriad ways that God reveals Himself to mankind.

Reverend Hector Mackenzie
Bible Teacher, Director, Christian Solidarity Worldwide
All Nation Christian Fellowship
Aberdeen, Scotland, UK

Illustrated Dictionary of Dream Symbols is a wonderful tool to help train and equip today's believers in the revelatory realm of dreams, as well as their interpretation and application. Dr. Joe Ibojie presents a vibrant book that is both inspiring and challenging.

Catherine Brown
Founder, Gatekeepers Prayer & Mission
Glasgow, Scotland, UK
www.gatekeepers.org.uk
www.millionhoursofpraise.com

I've always had very vivid dreams, and it's only now that I've started to unravel them with the help of *Illustrated Dictionary of Dream Symbols*. For the first time during prayer, I've started to receive pictures as well. This book has truly blessed me immensely.

Jess Howells
Editor
Kent, England, UK

I have always been skeptical about this "dream thing", but there is a certain balance in this book that brings about an enjoyment in dream interpretation. I am proud of this hard work for the Kingdom. I have enjoyed and learned from reading this book by my beloved son Dr. Joe Ibojie. If the Bible talks about it, we cannot afford to be silent. Thanks for this insight!

Bishop Fred Addo
International Praise Cathedral, Kaduna, NIGERIA

On our flight from Amsterdam to Florida, I sat beside Joe Ibojie. Joe obviously thought he would opt for the reading method of passing time, as he had a few books tucked under his arm. One of these books was his draft of a dictionary of dream symbolism. He was going through it, cross-referencing each definition with the Bible and adding annotations where necessary. In no time at all the conversation turned to dreams and all books were put to the side. The next eight hours passed so quickly that we could hardly believe it when we landed in Miami. In fact, throughout the following two weeks, as Joe and I shared a room and ministered together, the conversation would always turn to dreams and visions. Little did I know that the content of most of our friendly chats since then would make it to the pages of his wonderful book. Not that my contribution was anything more than asking Joe difficult questions, but I was pleased to see that his answers to these questions are contained in this book.

I have been privileged to minister with Joe on a frequent basis, but I am more privileged to know him not just as a person with Daniel-type anointing or as a prophetic voice (although he is frequently both these things to me), but as one of my closest friends. He is a true servant of God and a man with a passion to see God's Kingdom extend to wherever he goes and whomever he meets. Writing this book is simply an extension of this passion and has come out of years of experience—of working it out on a practical level, of seeing people transformed and set free to a life of liberty and purpose in the Holy Spirit, and of seeing people built up, encouraged, and edified, because they have come to a clearer understanding of God's purposes and plans in their life through a godly and, I believe, biblical interpretation of their dreams.

Pastor Phil Sanderson
All Nations Christian Fellowship
Aberdeen, Scotland, UK

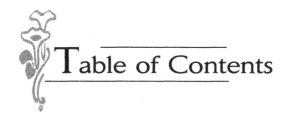

Table of Contents

PART III: UNDERSTANDING SYMBOLS

PART IV: SYMBOLS

PART V: DICTIONARY OF DREAM SYMBOLS

PART VI: OTHER SYMBOLIC OVERTONES

Foreword
by Bishop John Francis

There are some people who have been raised up to speak to the nations of the world, who have insight that only God can give. I believe Dr. Joe Ibojie is one of those voices through which God gives revelation and insight concerning our destiny.

This book, *Illustrated Dictionary of Dream Symbols,* will bless you and change your life as it helps you to gain insightful knowledge of what God is speaking to you through dreams and visions. As you read, the eyes of your understanding will be enlightened, and God will open the doors that have been closed in your life.

I highly recommend this book to every preacher, every Christian, and anyone who has ever had a dream or vision and who really wants to understand his or her spiritual encounters with God.

Bishop John Francis, Senior Pastor
Ruach Ministries, London

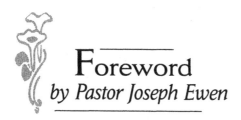

Foreword
by Pastor Joseph Ewen

When leaders of Scotland's Charismatic Church put on a "Prophetic Ministries" seminar several years ago, I did not realize that a prophetic word given to Joe Ibojie sowed the seeds that would lead him to greater heights in the prophetic realm, and, eventually, to the writing of this book.

We have traveled together a few times and ministered in various prophetic seminars. On one such occasion—while in America teaching on the prophetic at Crow Reservation in Montana—Joe said to me, "It's your fault because you prophesied over me!" All I can say is that I'm willing to take the blame and give God all the glory for the power of the prophetic word in Joe's life.

He is an outstanding man of God who has grown in stature in the prophetic ministry over the years. He has gained great understanding in the Holy Spirit of what it means to be prophetic, and of what our dreams can mean to us. Paul prayed for the Ephesians, *"may [God] give you the Spirit of wisdom and revelation, so that you may know Him better"* (Eph. 1:17).

This book on understanding dreams is a testimony to this prayer in Joe's life. He is able to take such knowledge and explain it in a way that we can all understand what our dreams mean. This is not a book just to read and pass on; it is one to go back and make reference to as you learn to interpret your dreams. We all dream, whether we realize it or not. Some dream more than others; so keep this book on the shelf (or on your nightstand) because you will need it again.

Joe writes as he speaks, and you can feel his passion in the pages, along with his eagerness to share what God has given him. He is also a firm believer in being part of the local church, and he contends for prophetic words being released to every believer. *"For you can all prophesy in turn so that everyone may be instructed and encouraged"* (1 Cor. 14:31). Our heart is to see people realize their potential, be able to encourage each other, and reach out to the world.

Many people, both inside and outside of the Church, would love to have their dreams interpreted. Joe's book is a great tool to help us serve the Body of Christ and reach out to the lost as we learn to hear God in this unique way.

Pastor Joseph Ewen
Founder and Leader of Riverside Church Network
Banff, Scotland, UK

Foreword
by Catherine Brown

…Write down the revelation and make it plain on tablets so that a herald may run with it. For the revelation awaits an appointed time; it speaks of the end and will not prove false. Though it linger, wait for it; it will certainly come and will not delay (Habakkuk 2:2-3).

The first time I met Dr. Joe Ibojie was in Aberdeen city on an extremely cold evening when the sky was dark with impending snow. By contrast, Joe's countenance was bright and sunny and in all of our ensuing dialogue, whether in person, by telephone or e-mail, I have found Joe's love for Christ and for life to be a constant source of joy.

Joe and his wife, Cynthia, and their four delightful children warmly welcomed me into their hearts and their home. It was at their family home that I had my first taste of African food—delicious! As a medical practitioner, Joe's life is full and busy. Not only this, but he and Cynthia have recently become pastors of The Father's House, a Christian fellowship in Aberdeen. I believe in "meeting the man behind the ministry," and I am delighted to commend Dr. Joe Ibojie to you as a loving husband, father, doctor, teacher, brother, and friend as well as a gifted Christian writer. He is a genuine and humble Christian leader. I am sure you will be blessed by his character and desire to serve the Lord.

I have enjoyed ministering with Joe. He is enthusiastic and energetic and is an anointed teacher on the subject of dreams and their interpretation. Joe's inspiration is ever our Lord Jesus Christ.

It was a wonderful experience to journey with Joe as he worked on his first two books, *Illustrated Dictionary of Dream Symbols* being the companion to *Dreams and Visions: How to Receive, Interpret, and Apply Your Dreams.* I have thoroughly enjoyed learning more about dreams and their interpretation as we have fellowshiped, studied the Scriptures, and prayed together. Joe's teaching is motivational.

Illustrated Dictionary of Dream Symbols is written in clear language, with detailed descriptions throughout its narrative that assist the reader on the journey of discovering the gift of interpretation. Dr. Joe enables the reader to become conversant with the parabolic language of symbols through Holy Spirit-inspired articulation. We rejoice that our Lord in His infinite grace and mercy chooses to communicate with His children. Ultimately, the gift of God's revelation ought to draw us deeper into a loving relationship with Christ, His Church, and those who do not yet know Him

Illustrated Dictionary of Dream Symbols is not intended to be a standalone resource; in other words, interpretation of symbols is not to be seen as a prescriptive exercise. Without prayerful application and understanding, our attempts at interpretation would be little more than presumptive. We may rest in the reality that interpretations belong to God (see Gen. 40:8). Joe encourages the reader to approach dream interpretation from a worshipful posture, giving careful consideration to the context and content of each dream or revelatory experience (such as a vision). Interpretation cannot be seen as a formula, but rather we ought to receive it as a gift from God, whereby the Holy Spirit imparts wisdom and understanding, fusing them with our faith, and opens our surrendered hearts and minds to receive Divine Counsel in a way that we can readily apply the interpretation of the dream symbols to our modern lifestyles.

Illustrated Dictionary of Dream Symbols is a useful resource to help train and equip the Church to demonstrate God's love to the many who have not yet received salvation.

Jesus spoke in the language of parables and symbols to His disciples and to the multitudes who followed Him. Our Lord used numerous images to describe what the Kingdom of Heaven is like, such as a field (see Matt. 13:24), a mustard seed (see Matt. 13:31), treasure hidden in a field (Matt. 13:44), and a net let down into the lake that catches all kinds of fish (see Matt. 13:47). Jesus asked His disciples, *"Have you understood all these things?" They replied "yes." Jesus then responded, "Therefore every teacher of the law who has been instructed about the kingdom of heaven is like the owner of a house who brings out of his storeroom new treasures as well as old"* (Matt. 13:52).

My prayer for you, dear reader, is that you will gain understanding by the Holy Spirit from *Illustrated Dictionary of Dream Symbols* and that you will enjoy this new treasure that the Lord has poured out from Heaven's storeroom through his servant, Dr. Joe Ibojie.

We live to glorify our heavenly Father. Don't be disappointed if it takes a little time and effort to grow in your gifting. Jesus is patient and gracious as He trains us in His ways. Be blessed!

Catherine Brown, servant of Christ
Author of *The Normal, the Deep and the Crazy* and
Confessions of a Fasting Housewife

Gatekeepers Prayer & Mission
Million Hours of Praise
Glasgow, UK

DREAMS AND VISIONS

PART I

CHAPTER 1

An Introduction to Dreams and Visions

Dreams and visions are natural to man. In fact, one can say they are part and parcel of the journey on earth. They are valuable survival tools in a world constantly distancing itself from God. The Bible says that the steps of a good man are ordered from God; I believe that dreaming is one sure way of getting fresh mandate from Him. Ultimately, we need to hear God for ourselves on a personal level. Revelation is a by-product of intimacy with God and revelatory "gifting" is the potential, or capability, to receive revelation. As Psalm 25:14 says, *"The Lord confides in those who fear Him; He makes His covenant known to them."*

Only by the Holy Spirit can one get a true and correct interpretation of dreams, visions, and mysteries of God. From Genesis to Revelation, the true meaning of the parables, dreams, mysteries, and "the handwriting of God" were divinely "sealed." That's why magicians, enchanters, wise men, and religious leaders in Egypt and Babylon could not interpret or understand these revelations. Up to this day, no other power besides God can tell the true meaning of a dream, no matter how simple the dream might seem.

In this book, I quote extensively from authorized Bible translations because I believe that the Word of God can speak for itself. Where appropriate, I have given a few of my personal experiences, but only to bring biblical truth to a practical relevance. By and large, the contents of this book are based on what is recorded in Scripture.

Any other books on understanding dreams as written by non-Christians offer un-Christian methods of interpretation; unlike the interpretations offered by this book, such are not inspired by the Holy Spirit. These authors are not filled with the Holy Spirit, so they are unable to understand spiritual things. Therefore, they offer "soulish" conclusions at best, which often mislead and misdirect those seeking true interpretation. This book endeavors to provide you with a necessary understanding to approach your own dreams through the Holy Spirit, and it does so by providing biblical illustrations and meanings of dreams and symbols, and by exploring the godly art of dream interpretation.

Dreams

Dreams come from God in the form of a parable language or illustrated stories. These personalized encoded messages are full of symbols that express the mysteries of God. As a result of the symbolism, dreams need some form of interpretation before a proper understanding can be gained. Interpretation can come to the dreamer either spontaneously, after praying to God about the dream, or through a person gifted in dream interpretation. Many people still hesitate to seek the meaning of their dreams, although it is biblical to do so; yet dream interpretation should be a carefully guided effort. Wrong interpretation has the potential to lead a person into bondage.

God utilizes very individualistic language in communicating to us in dreams. He takes it from our life experiences, specific personal traits, and biblical examples. God also uses events in our lives that no one knows about except Him, and sometimes incorporates these into His communications. So, a person gifted in dream interpretation can help with one's understanding, but correct interpretation must come from the dreamer due to a dream's specific, individualistic traits.

Contrary to the view that some people do not receive dreams, I believe that God speaks to everyone through them in one way or another. However, most people are unable to recall their dreams and, therefore, cannot appreciate their importance. Many people wonder why they do not receive many dreams. Some even claim that they do not dream at all, while others are simply at a loss at what to do with their endless amounts of dreams. These puzzles have no simple answers. But everyone needs to understand this incredible form of divine communication, so that regardless of what category you belong to, you can avail yourself of a dream's inherent potential.

During a dream encounter, your soul finds respite in an atmosphere devoid of the world's mind-set of tension; this is true whether you remember the dream or not. Dreams that cannot be remembered do have some value because they are sown into the dreamer's spirit. By the time you are 70 years old, you will have spent a lot of time in dreamland. During a dream encounter, God can impart to our spirits, just as He did when giving divine wisdom to a dreaming Solomon (see 1 Kings 3). Dreams, therefore, are more than just information packages; all the gifts of the Holy Spirit can be received through them.

God uses dreams to reveal Himself to the heart of man. Having a dream is similar to experiencing the spiritual atmosphere of the Garden of Eden; there are no limitations in time or in the dreamer's capabilities. However, good and bad impartation can occur in dreams because both good and evil spirits exist in dreamland, just as they did in the Garden of Eden.

God's major purpose for giving us dreams is so that we respond appropriately on earth to what He is doing in Heaven. The first, most important response to a dream is to pray for all its elements, events, and persons (both friends and perceived enemies); you should do that even before gaining an understanding of the dream's meaning. The next useful step is to record the dream and pay attention to what God might be saying—whether it's warning, encouraging, or corrective.

Most misunderstandings or fears evoked by a dream usually result from the dreamer's failure to realize that most events in a dream are *potential* circumstances. In other words, these situations can eventually occur, but are not inevitable. A dream that warns of danger is so that a person can avert the danger; a dream that speaks of good promises needs to be prayed through so as to result in its fulfillment.

One type of dream that can mislead is when the dreamer has forgotten some vital parts; partial information is dangerous. So, recording our dreams is of utmost importance. You should write down your dream in a notebook, because writing not only records the dream, but also allows God to throw in more insight for its understanding. Recording the date, time, and place when the dream was received is also important. Dreams fade if not recorded because God writes them in spiritual ink that fades.

God will increase the number of dreams you receive if you keep proper records of the dreams that you have had. He honors such efforts by unfolding greater insight and more revelation. As you study your dreams, God will reveal more of Himself to you through them. Delays in recording dreams may result in losing its essential elements, which may become irretrievable as the vanishing ink fades away.

A dream with a more clear promise brings a greater responsibility to act on it, and there is also greater enemy opposition against its fulfillment. The interpretation in dreams must be properly studied, as both the dream and its interpretation may need further understanding. Do not try to adjust what you see in the dream to what you know in the natural. Sometimes the person you know is superimposed onto the one whom you do not know.

A dream may occur or be remembered in fragments. In most of these cases, God usually wants to focus on the parts that one can remember. Fragmented dreams may also indicate poor reception, as due to a dreamer's sin or a lack of prayer. God may also be protecting the dreamer by concealing some aspects of a dream. When you do have dream recall, it's through a prompting of the Holy Spirit. Sometimes God gives dream revelation for you alone, so that you can offer it up in prayer—it's *not* for public pronouncement.

One of God's purposes in sending us dreams and visions is ultimately to align us with His plans. He speaks to us where we are to lead us further into Christ. The purpose of dreams and visions is to break through our rational thought patterns to show us what we have yet to hear or believe. There must be a willingness to obey what God says to us in dreams and visions, so that we can realize the overall end-time purposes of God.

In Scripture, some dreams affected the entire destiny of mankind; to these dreamers of old, their reveries were just ordinary dreams at the time of receiving them. Therefore, one should wonder about the possible relevance of dreams we get today.

Dream or Vision?

True dreams sent by God come in the form of multimedia packages—a mixture of images, metaphors, similes, poems, dreams, and remarkable story lines during sleep. Dreams are only received when one is asleep, which is not the same as a vision. Dreaming is not restricted only to night season; dreams are received in the spirit and then get translated into the mind for comprehension. Our mind has a pictorial depository where dream imagery is received and processed. Sanctifying the mind prepares it to receive dreams without corruption, despite background noise of the world's events.

A vision, however, is the visual perception of revelation or supernatural occurrence through our spiritual eyes; these are often more real and more literal than dreams. One can receive a vision even when the mind is awake.

Differences Between Dreams and Visions

DREAMS	VISIONS
To receive dreams, the mind has to be asleep: Genesis 15:12-13: *"As the sun was setting, Abram fell into a **deep sleep,** and a thick and dreadful darkness came over him. Then the Lord said to him, 'Know for certain that your descendants will be strangers in a country not their own, and they will be enslaved and mistreated four hundred years.'"*	Visions are received with varying degrees of mind alertness, through trances, apparitions, and divine sights. An open vision is received with the natural eyes wide open.
Dreams are always experienced on a personal basis.	Visions can be experienced in a group setting: Acts 22:6-9: *"About noon as I came near Damascus, suddenly a bright light from heaven flashed around me. I fell to the ground and heard a voice say to me, 'Saul! Saul! Why do you persecute Me?' 'Who are You, Lord?' I asked. 'I am Jesus of Nazareth, whom you are persecuting,' He replied. **My companions saw the light, but they did not understand the voice of Him who was speaking to me.**"*

DREAMS	VISIONS
Dreams are received by the spirit of man, and are mostly spirit-to-spirit encounters. What seems to be bodily involvement in our dreams is due to visions within dreams. Daniel 7:1: *"In the first year of Bels-hazzar king of Babylon, Daniel **had a dream, and visions passed through his** mind as he was lying on his bed. He wrote down the substance of his dream."* This is the so-called dream/vision category, common in the ministry of Seer.	Visions may involve varying degrees of the physical or natural realm, such as tangible bodily experiences. Acts 22:10-11: *"'What shall I do, Lord?' I asked. 'Get up,' the Lord said, 'and go into Damascus. There you will be told all that you have been assigned to do.' My companions led me by the hand into Damascus, **because the brilliance of the light had blinded me."***
Dreams are *more symbolic.*	Visions are *more literal.*
Most dreams need to be *interpreted* symbolically.	Visions need to be carefully *evaluated* before proclamation.
Dreams are often more *divinely coded on purpose for the dreamer* with personal symbolism. Twilight dreams are less ambiguous because they require prompt response.	Visions are *more real, often clearer, and may require little interpretation.* They may, sometimes, demand immediate or prompt response.

Dreams and Vision Interplay

Dreams and visions can interplay in a dreamer's life in many ways. A dreamer can have many manifestations: either external or internal visions; visions in a dream; visions in a vision; a dream within a dream; or a dream in a vision. On the whole, various combinations of this interplay occur. Although dreams are purely spiritual experiences (or spirit-to-spirit encounters), visions are spiritual encounters with differing involvement of various levels of the natural realm.

The prophet Daniel aptly described the dream and vision interplay in Daniel 7:1. Unlike a vision, a dream is welded to a dreamer's heart and has the potential of stirring up the deepest part of a human heart. Bodily involvement is also not primarily common in pure dreams.

Most times, what seems to be bodily movement in dreams is a result of dreams with visions within them.

For most dreamers, the majority of spiritual encounters within dreams also contain visionary components. Therefore, what can occur appears to be bodily involvement when dreaming, or even a carryover of pain from a dream/vision category when the dreamer awakens. *A pure dream should have no carryover of bodily pains because it's a spirit-to-spirit affair.* On the other hand, visions have a varying degree of involvement with the natural realm. For instance, Paul was blinded for three days after his conversion, and Jacob walked with a limp for the rest of his life after his visionary encounter.

God Himself spoke of the subtle differences between dreams and visions when He spoke of Moses: *"When a prophet of the Lord is among you, I reveal Myself to him in visions, I speak to him in dreams"* (Num. 12:6). The fact that God says, *"I speak to him"* indicates intimacy or a further deepening of relationship. On the other hand, *"I will reveal Myself"* means showing God's nature or displaying His attributes. Therefore, dreams connect with God's heart, whereas visions reveal His nature. No wonder it is only by revelation that we experience the true nature of God.

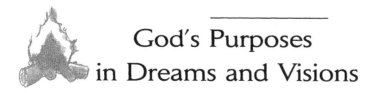

CHAPTER 2

God's Purposes in Dreams and Visions

Ultimately, God uses dreams to align our hearts, thoughts, and intentions to His eternal purpose. He may use dreams in a variety of ways: to answer our questions; to appoint us to a new mission; to command changes in how we live; to commune with us concerning secrets of His heart; to promise us something yet to come; to teach us vital truths that we might have missed, and so forth.

Many misconceptions about dreams result from precepts of worldly wisdom. Humanistic ideology states that dreams only tell us unresolved aspects of a dreamer, such as anxieties, bitterness, jealousy, unforgiveness, secret yearnings, and untapped ambitions. This school of thought further claims that all these occur in dreams because the person has not recognized them while awake, or is perhaps even unwilling to admit to them. The fact is that God relates these aspects in our dreams both to correct our excesses and to guide us into truth. He brings them into our dreams for the purpose of aligning us with His eternal purpose. As the Bible says:

For God [does reveal His will; He] speaks not only once but more than once, even though men do not regard it [including you, Job]. [One may hear God's voice] in a dream, in a vision of the night, when deep sleep falls on men while slumbering upon the bed, then He opens the ears of men and seals their instruction [terrifying them with warnings], that He may withdraw man from his purpose and cut off pride from him [disgusting him with his own disappointing self-sufficiency]. He holds him back from the pit [of destruction], and his life from perishing by the sword [of God's destructive judgments] (Job 33:14-18 AMP).

The message of a dream or vision can come in many ways: as prophecy (most common); a word of knowledge; a gift of discernment; a gift of healing; a gift of wisdom; or as a gift of interpretation. Solomon was given wisdom in a dream. He woke up and was wiser and began to demonstrate divine wisdom and respect for human life. God can radically rewrite our lives through the dreams we receive. Dreams have the power to expand, confirm, enlighten, enrich, and deepen your understanding of God's Word:

- ◆ Through dreams, we get more details and specific direction for achieving a given task. Dreams can also give hidden insight of wisdom specific to the situation.

- ◆ It is important to know that God does not send dreams to embarrass, condemn, or confuse us.

- ◆ Through dreams and visions, God grants us insightful under-standing of our own hearts. The apostle Peter's wrong mindset that Gentiles were unclean (which came from his Jewish upbringing) was revealed to him through visions he received from God:

  "Surely not, Lord!" Peter replied. "I have never eaten anything impure or   unclean."
  The voice spoke to him a second time, "Do not call anything impure that God has made clean." This happened three times, and immediately the sheet was taken back to heaven (Acts 10:14-16).

  In modern terms, these visions sound like what many would describe as "pizza dreams," which supposedly come from eat-ing junk food too late at night. But these dreams were divinely inspired, even though Peter did not understand the message until much later.

- ◆ God uses dreams and visions to give us insight into circum-stances of life and the true reason behind our experiences. Abra-ham's dream of his descendants going into slavery in Egypt was foretold and explained as follows:

Know for certain that your descendants will be strangers in a country not their own, and they will be enslaved and mistreated four hundred years (Genesis 15:13).

♦ God exposes satan's plans and gives us insight into hell's assignments.

♦ God designs some dreams to be therapeutic; He reveals hidden hurts from the dreamer's past and gives healing.

In Damascus there was a disciple named Ananias. The Lord called to him in a vision, "Ananias!" "Yes, Lord," he answered. The Lord told him, "Go to the house of Judas on Straight Street and ask for a man from Tarsus named Saul, for he is praying. In a vision he has seen a man named Ananias come and place his hands on him to restore his sight." "Lord," Ananias answered, "I have heard many reports about this man and all the harm he has done to Your saints in Jerusalem. And he has come here with authority from the chief priests to arrest all who call on Your name." But the Lord said to Ananias, "Go! This man is My chosen instrument to carry My name before the Gentiles and their kings and before the people of Israel. I will show him how much he must suffer for My name." Then Ananias went to the house and entered it. Placing his hands on Saul, he said, "Brother Saul, the Lord—Jesus, who appeared to you on the road as you were coming here—has sent me so that you may see again and be filled with the Holy Spirit." Immediately, something like scales fell from Saul's eyes, and he could see again. He got up and was baptized (Acts 9:10-18).

♦ Some dreams and visions have significant intercessory calls, and may require the dreamer to stand in the gap through prayer.

During the night Paul had a vision of a man of Macedonia standing and begging him, "Come over to Macedonia and help us." After Paul had seen the vision, we got ready at once to leave for Macedonia, concluding that God had called us to preach the gospel to them (Acts 16:9-10).

♦ Through dreams, God gives the voice of proclamation and deliverance. That is so we can be the voice of agreement that allows God's transformation and renewal to come to a situation, as in Amos 3:7: *"Surely the Sovereign Lord does nothing without revealing His plan to His servants the prophets."*

During the night I had a vision—and there before me was a man riding a red horse! He was standing among the myrtle trees in a ravine. Behind him were red, brown and white horses. I asked, "What are these, my lord?" The angel who was talking with me answered, "I will show you what they are." Then the man standing among the myrtle trees explained, "They are the ones the Lord has sent to go throughout the earth." And they reported to the angel of the Lord, who was standing among the myrtle trees, "We have gone throughout the earth and found the whole world at rest and in peace." Then the angel of the Lord said, "Lord Almighty, how long will You withhold mercy from Jerusalem and from the towns of Judah, which You have been angry with these seventy years?" So the Lord spoke kind and comforting words to the angel who talked with me. Then the angel who was speaking to me said, "Proclaim this word: This is what the Lord Almighty says: 'I am very jealous for Jerusalem and Zion, but I am very angry with the nations that feel secure. I was only a little angry, but they added to the calamity.' Therefore, this is what the Lord says: 'I will return to Jerusalem with mercy, and there My house will be rebuilt. And the measuring line will be stretched out over Jerusalem,' declares the Lord Almighty. Proclaim further: This is what the Lord Almighty says: 'My towns will again overflow with prosperity, and the Lord will again comfort Zion and choose Jerusalem'" (Zechariah 1:8-17).

◆ Through dream symbolism, God can design a dream in such a way that it is not acted on until the time comes for its understanding; only then can the appropriate action be taken. Some dreams unfold in stages because their message is for both current and future fulfillment:

Although Joseph recognized his brothers, they did not recognize him. Then he remembered his dreams about them and said to them, "You are spies! You have come to see where our land is unprotected" (Genesis 42:8-9).

Other Functions of Dreams

◆ Dreams contain superior wisdom and intelligence because of the Spirit of God.

◆ They show where we are wrong.

Meanwhile, Saul was still breathing out murderous threats against the Lord's disciples. He went to the high priest and asked him for letters to the synagogues in Damascus, so that if he found any there who belonged to the Way, whether men or women, he might take them as prisoners to Jerusalem. As he neared Damascus on his journey, suddenly a light from heaven flashed around him. He fell to the ground and heard a voice say to him, "Saul, Saul, why do you persecute Me?" "Who are You, Lord?" Saul asked. "I am Jesus, whom you are persecuting," He replied. "Now get up and go into the city, and you will be told what you must do" (Acts 9:1-6).

◆ They show us where we have not yet taken on a Christ-like attitude (see Peter's vision in Acts 10:14-16).

◆ They warn us concerning danger (see Mary and Joseph hiding Jesus in Matthew 2:11-15).

◆ They predict future events.

Joseph had a dream, and when he told it to his brothers, they hated him all the more. He said to them, "Listen to this dream I had: We were binding sheaves of grain out in the field when suddenly my sheaf rose and stood upright, while your sheaves gathered round mine and bowed down to it." His brothers said to him, "Do you intend to reign over us? Will you actually rule us?" And they hated him all the more because of his dream and what he had said. Then he had another dream, and he told it to his brothers. "Listen," he said, "I had another dream, and this time the sun and moon and eleven stars were bowing down to me" (Genesis 37:5-9).

◆ They reveal the deeper meaning of our lives.

◆ Dreams are places where our spirit, our soul, and sometimes even the real purpose of our lives, return to rest: in an atmosphere not dominated by our mind.

How God Uses Dreams and Visions in Scripture

The Bible is full of many instances where God used dreams and visions as channels through which He reached out to humanity. *"Long ago God spoke in many different ways to our fathers through the prophets [in dreams, in visions, and even face to face] telling them little by little about His plans"* (Heb. 1:1 TLB). God spoke to Abraham in dreams, telling him of the many years his descendants would be slaves and strangers in a country not their own:

> *As the sun was setting, Abram fell into a deep sleep, and a thick and dreadful darkness came over him. Then the Lord said to him, "Know for certain that your descendants will be strangers in a country not their own, and they will be enslaved and mistreated four hundred years. But I will punish the nation they serve as slaves, and afterward they will come out with great possessions"* (Genesis 15:12-14).

This part of Abraham's covenant was cut in a dream because, at that time, his mind would have been incapable of comprehending the truth of this revelation. Similarly, Joseph (of the coat of many colors) saw his destiny in a dream and yet did not totally understand its content. When the dream's fulfillment came many years later, its magnitude was beyond his wildest imagination, and the Bible records that *"he remembered his dreams about them"* (Gen. 42:9).

In a vision asking for his help, the apostle Paul received a call to Macedonia. As a result of this vision, the gospel entered Europe (see Acts 16:7-10). The Bible records that he concluded, *"God had called us to preach the gospel to them."* This vision was pivotal to the advancement of God's kingdom into Europe. Whenever the meaning of a dream or vision has been confirmed, we should take up our responsibility.

Joseph's Dreams

Let's take a look at Joseph in Genesis 37:1-10 and explore God's purposes for him through the anatomy of the dreams.

> *Jacob lived in the land where his father had stayed, the land of Canaan. This is the account of Jacob. Joseph, a young man of seventeen, was tending the flocks with his brothers, the sons of Bilhah and the sons of Zilpah, his father's wives, and he brought their father a bad report about them. Now Israel loved Joseph more than any of his other sons, because he had been born to him in his old age; and he made a richly ornamented robe for him. When his brothers saw that their father loved him more than any of them, they hated him and could not speak a kind word to him. Joseph had a dream, and when he told it to his brothers, they hated him all the more. He said to them, "Listen to this dream I had: We were binding sheaves of grain*

out in the field when suddenly my sheaf rose and stood upright, while your sheaves gathered round mine and bowed down to it." His brothers said to him, "Do you intend to reign over us? Will you actually rule us?" And they hated him all the more because of his dream and what he had said. Then he had another dream, and he told it to his brothers. "Listen," he said, "I had another dream, and this time the sun and moon and eleven stars were bowing down to me." When he told his father as well as his brothers, his father rebuked him and said, "What is this dream you had? Will your mother and I and your brothers actually come and bow down to the ground before you?" (Genesis 37:1-10).

In breaking down both dreams to look at their individual meanings, we find the following information:

First Dream

SYMBOLS	MEANING	POINTS OF NOTE
Sheaves of grains out of the field.	Joseph and his brothers.	*Background setting.* Joseph's dreams were given within the context of a kindred feud in Jacob's household. As Joseph struggled with animosity in the family, God revealed his future, and allegorized it with his current struggles in the family.
Joseph's sheaf of grain.	Joseph would be elevated above his brothers.	
Field.	Their life situation.	
"Suddenly my sheaf rose and stood upright..."	Joseph's elevation.	Indicates the suddenness of Joseph's rising from being a prisoner to becoming a prime minister.
Bowing.	Obeisance and respect for high authority.	

15

Second Dream

SYMBOLS	MEANING	POINTS OF NOTE
Me.	Literally referring to Joseph.	Confirmation and further exposition of the first dream.
Stars.	Important personalities.	Tilted focus: the brothers were so carried away by their obeisance to Joseph in the dreams that they failed to see that God regarded them as "stars." The second dream, therefore, was meant to speak encouragement to the brothers and reveal their importance in God's plans. They were to become the patriarchs.
Moon and Sun.	Rulers of the known world.	Joseph's father and mother did not bow before him, but the rulers of the known world did, once he became prime minister of the greatest kingdom on earth at the time. Joseph had a narrow perspective of the promised ruler role that God showed him in the first dream. To correct this imbalance, God used the moon and the sun to indicate that his rule would cover nations of the known world.

These two dreams were not the same, but each presented different aspects of the same subject and emphasized different points. The second dream confirmed the first as established in Heaven and addressed issues that arose in the minds of Joseph and his brothers after the first dream.

Dreams God Gave to Unbelievers in the Bible

Here are some key dreams that God gave to unbelievers, which affected the course of history.

- ◆ **Abimelech the Canaanite king:** In Genesis 20:1-7, Abimelech had a dream in which God told him that Sarah was Abraham's wife.

- ◆ **Laban, the Aramean, Rebekah's brother:** In Genesis 31:22-24, he pursued Jacob but was apprehended by God in a dream to *"Be careful not to say anything to Jacob, either good or bad."*

- ◆ **Pharaoh of Egypt:** In Genesis 41:1-7, God gave him a dream of the global famine that would follow seven years of prosperity.

- ◆ **The Midianite, an enemy soldier:** In Judges 7:9-15, Gideon was encouraged by the dream and its interpretation, which he heard while on a divinely inspired spy mission to the enemy's camp. God did this to bring His people to victory at a critical moment in their history.

- ◆ **Pilate's wife:** In Matthew 27:19, *"While Pilate was sitting on the judge's seat, his wife sent him this message:'Don't have anything to do with that innocent man, for I have suffered a great deal today in a dream because of him.'"*

Figurative Use of the Word "Dream" in the Bible

Ecclesiastes 5:7:

For in the multitude of dreams and many words there is also vanity. But fear God (NKJV).

Much dreaming and many words are meaningless. Therefore stand in awe of God (NIV).

Dreaming instead of doing is foolishness and there is ruin in a flood of empty words: fear God instead (TLB).

The entirety of Ecclesiastes 5 addresses the issues of human attitudes toward God. In this instance, using the word *dream* is not related to prophetic dreams or messages from God. Rather, it speaks of the foolishness entailed in too much planning without work.

Jude 1:8

Yet these false teachers go on living their evil, immoral lives, degrading their bodies and laughing at those in authority over them, even scoffing at the glorious ones (those mighty powers of awful evil who left their first estate) (TLB).

Likewise also those dreamers defile the flesh, reject authority and speak evil of dignitaries (NKJV).

Using the term *dreamers* indicates that they were not being realistic. In other words, they were merely daydreaming.

Isaiah 29:7-8

Then the hordes of all the nations that fight against Ariel, that attack her and her fortress and besiege her, will be as it is with a dream, with a vision in the night—as when a hungry man dreams that he is eating, but he awakens, and his hunger remains; as when a thirsty man dreams that he is drinking, but he awakens faint, with his thirst unquenched. So will it be with the hordes of all the nations that fight against Mount Zion.

This is a figurative use of the word *dream* being used as a simile, which is a phrase that makes comparisons explicit by using the formula of *like* or *as*. This Scripture means that dreams happen in a supernatural way and may not always be taken literally as being as real in the natural.

Dreams and Visions That Affected Our Destiny

In looking at scriptural examples of dreams that affected mankind's destiny, I hope to jog your mind as to the possible relevance of your own dreams. Remember, these particular people of old had what they believed to be ordinary dreams, but these reveries ended up greatly impacting mankind.

Joseph: The Earthly Father of Jesus

Obedience enhances the seer's ability to hear the voice of God. Joseph stands as a giant for his role as the earthly father of Jesus. But he's also an exemplary figure for his art of hearing God, his unwavering faith in God, and his unswerving commitment to obeying His commandments. Joseph had an extraordinary ability to receive messages from God with profound lucidity, which he then followed with prompt obedience. More than this, his swift obedience was necessary.

Joseph's dreams were mainly direct speeches from divine messengers, which had no ambiguity and allowed for his prompt obedience. After receiving dreams with remarkable angelic interactions and dream phrases, he acted promptly. By doing so, he secured humanity's destiny. He epitomizes the dreamer with an excellent spirit who receives messages from God and pays attention to them.

From the outset, Joseph was destined to a role in the background away from the limelight. A carpenter of probably little significance, his only prized possession was the young lady to whom he was betrothed. Like any young man, he looked forward to marriage with great expectation. No doubt, he quietly waited for this blossoming lily in the garden of his heart. At this point, however, like lightning in the sky, his boat was rocked by an emotional avalanche of the news of Mary's pregnancy. Although hard to believe, she was pregnant and not by him! Bewildered by the circumstance, Joseph was at a crossroads. The ground itself must have shifted beneath his feet. Nevertheless, Joseph kept his cool and stayed committed.

He agonized and sobbed, but even then remembered kindness. In an act of kindness, he decided to keep the news from becoming public so as to save Mary's life. At the close of the day, he retired to the comfort of his bed. Sleep fell and overwhelmed him, putting off his weary body and mind from further agitation. In the serenity and tranquillity of this night, Heaven visited humanity. An angel came to Joseph in a dream and gave him understanding as to the true reason behind his "troubles."

This is how the birth of Jesus Christ came about: His mother Mary was pledged to be married to Joseph, but before they came together, she was found to be with child through the Holy Spirit. Because Joseph her husband was a righteous man and did not want to expose her to public disgrace, he had in mind to divorce her quietly. But after he had considered this, an angel of the Lord appeared to him in a dream and said, "Joseph son of David, do not be afraid to take Mary home as your wife, because what is conceived in her is from the Holy Spirit. She will give birth to a son, and you are to give Him the name

Jesus, because He will save His people from their sins (Matthew 1:18-21).

Joseph obeyed God and married Mary. He lived with her, but kept his distance. He resisted his carnal urges, subdued the lusts of his flesh, tamed his tongue, and looked after Mary and her pregnancy. He restrained himself so that humanity might have Jesus, according to the promise that He would be born of a virgin woman and that His purity would remain undefiled. The devil could not find any hold on Jesus, just because one man—Joseph—had the ability to rule his emotions and flesh; in doing so, he gave hope and purpose by providing disciplined parentage for Jesus on earth.

After the birth of Jesus, King Herod became jealous. Jesus' life was in jeopardy. Again Joseph had another dream:

When they had gone, an angel of the Lord appeared to Joseph in a dream. "Get up," he said, "take the child and His mother and escape to Egypt. Stay there until I tell you, for Herod is going to search for the child to kill Him." So he got up, took the child and His mother during the night and left for Egypt, where he stayed until the death of Herod. And so was fulfilled what the Lord had said through the prophet: "Out of Egypt I called My son" (Matthew 2:13-15).

However, that did not mark the end of Joseph's dreams. When the time came to leave Egypt, he had yet another dream:

After Herod died, an angel of the Lord appeared in a dream to Joseph in Egypt and said, "Get up, take the child and His mother and go to the land of Israel, for those who were trying to take the child's life are dead." So he got up, took the child and His mother and went to the land of Israel (Matthew 2:19-21).

But when he heard that Archelaus was reigning in Judea in place of his father Herod, he was afraid to go there. Having been warned in a dream, he withdrew to the district of Galilee, and he went and lived in a town called Nazareth. So was fulfilled what was said through the prophets: "He will be called a Nazarene" (Matthew 2:22-23).

A dreamer's ability to receive revelation with clarity is connected to the purity of his lifestyle and his obedience to what God says. The life of Joseph also clearly reveals that angelic involvement is a defense in a dreamer's ministry.

Other Examples in Scripture

◆ **Peter's Vision: Salvation Is Extended to the Gentiles**

God said to Peter, *"Do not call anything impure that God has made clean"* (Acts 10:15). This was a landmark revelation—first to Peter and then to the entire Jewish people—that salvation belonged not only to Jews, but also to the Gentiles.

◆ **Paul's Conversion**

Paul was chosen to carry the gospel to the Gentiles, therefore shaping our destiny. Ananias later received a vision from God confirming this: *"This man is My chosen instrument to carry My name before the Gentiles and their kings and before the people of Israel"* (Acts 9:15).

◆ **Abrahamic Covenant—Through Whom "All the Families of the Earth Will Be Blessed"**

After this, the word of the Lord came to Abram in a vision: "Do not be afraid, Abram. I am your shield, your very great reward." But Abram said, "O Sovereign Lord, what can You give me since I remain childless and the one who will inherit my estate is Eliezer of Damascus?" And Abram said, "You have given me no children; so a servant in my household will be my heir." Then the word of the Lord came to him: "This man will not be your heir, but a son coming from your own body will be your heir" (Genesis 15:1-4).

"In the fourth generation your descendants will come back here, for the sin of the Amorites has not yet reached its full measure." When the sun had set and darkness had fallen, a smoking firepot with a blazing torch appeared and passed between the pieces. On that day the Lord made a covenant with Abram and said, "To your descendants I give this land, from the river of Egypt to the great river, the Euphrates... (Genesis 15:16-19).

CHAPTER 3

Types of Dreams and Visions

In order to understand dreams and visions more successfully, it is useful to take a look at the various types that can occur. This allows us to better judge our own interpretations and conclusions. Most dreams are symbolic, with God using metaphors for one object or person to represent another.

True and False Dreams

The Bible has two broad categories of dreams: true dreams and false dreams. A false dream is a product of the dreamer's own delusion. Scripture says that any dream God has not sent is a false, made-up story and delusion of the human mind. In the Book of Jeremiah, God says, "I did not send them" and "their made-up dreams are flagrant lies." Consequently, you cannot receive a dream as true unless it is sent by God. If God has sent the dream, then it is a true dream with a message from Him.

False Dreams: Made-Up Delusions From the Heart

"I have heard what the prophets say who prophesy lies in My name. They say 'I had a dream! I had a dream!' How long will this continue in the hearts of these lying prophets, who prophesy the delusions of their own minds?" (Jeremiah 23:25-26)

'Listen to the dream I had from God last night' they say. And then they proceed to lie in My name, how long will this continue? If they

are 'prophets' they are prophets of deceit, inventing everything they say. By telling these false dreams they are trying to get My people to forget Me in the same way as their fathers did, who turned away to idols of Baal. Let these false prophets tell their dreams and let My true messengers faithfully proclaim My every word. There is a difference between chaff and wheat! Does not My word burn like fire? ...Is not it like a mighty hammer that smashes the rock to pieces? So I stand against these prophets who get their messages from each other, these smooth-tongued prophets who say 'This message is from God.' Their made-up dreams are flagrant lies that lead My people into sins. I did not send them and they have no message at all for My people," says the Lord (Jeremiah 23:25-32 TLB).

For thus says the Lord of hosts, the God of Israel: Do not let your prophets and your diviners who are in your midst deceive you, nor listen **to your dreams which you cause to be dreamed** (Jeremiah 29:8 NKJV).

The Lord of heaven's armies, the God of Israel, says: "Do not let the false prophets and mediums that are there among you fool you. Do not listen to the dreams that they invent, for they prophesy lies in My name. I have not sent them," says the Lord (Jeremiah 29:8 TLB).

The phrase "your dreams which you cause to be dreamed" refers to dreams invented because of people pressuring them to declare dreams—regardless of whether or not they actually had one. In the days of Jeremiah, prophets were sent on vision or dream quests and were expected to receive dreams or visions, as evidence of their being true prophets. As a result, many made up stories merely to save face.

Then the Lord said to me, "The prophets are prophesying lies in My name. I have not sent them or appointed them or spoken to them. They are prophesying to you false visions, divinations, idolatries **and the delusions of their own minds** (Jeremiah 14:14).

Then the Lord said: "The prophets are telling lies in My name. I did not send them or tell them to speak or give them any message. They prophesy **visions and revelations they have never seen nor heard;** *they speak foolishness concocted out of their own lying hearts* (Jeremiah 14:14 TLB).

24

Then the Lord said to me, "the false prophets prophesy lies in My name. I sent them not, neither have I commanded them, nor have I spoken to them. They prophesy to you a false or pretended vision, a worthless divination, conjuring or practicing magic, trying to call forth the responses supposed to be given by idols, and the deceit of their own minds (Jeremiah 14:14 AMP).

Ask the Lord for rain in the springtime, it is the Lord who makes the storm clouds; He gives showers of rain to men, and plants of the field to everyone. **The idols speak deceit, dreamers see visions that lie. They tell dreams that are false.** *They give comfort in vain. Therefore the people wander like sheep oppressed for lack of a shepherd* (Zechariah 10:1-2).

Visions

A vision is a visual perception of revelation or supernatural occurrence with the spiritual eyes. One can receive a vision even when the mind is awake. Great interplay exists between the natural and the supernatural, often with varying degrees of bodily activities and involvement of the physical realm. These bodily activities can sometimes result in healing, physical tiredness, or even physical afflictions after a visionary encounter. Most times visions need little interpretation, but they do require careful proclamation and applications. They speak not only of God's nature, but also offer more remarkable impartation to recipients than dreams.

Open Visions

These occur when you watch an open scene with your eyes open, yet you "see" the scene in the spirit.

I, Daniel, was the only one who saw the vision, the men with me did not see it, **but such terror overwhelmed them that they fled and hid themselves.** *So I was left alone, gazing at this great vision; I had no strength left, my face turned deathly pale and I was helpless. Then I heard him speaking, and as I listened to him, I fell into a deep sleep, my face to the ground. A hand touched me and set me trembling on my hands and knees* (Daniel 10:7-10).

25

Divine Sight

This is an open vision in which the natural surroundings blend into the overall scene. With divine sight, you cannot tell if the image is real or spiritual.

> *Now Moses was tending the flock of Jethro his father-in-law, the priest of Midian, and he led the flock to the far side of the desert and came to Horeb, the mountain of God. There the angel of the Lord appeared to him in flames of fire from within a bush. Moses saw that though the bush was on fire it did not burn up. So Moses thought, "I will go over and see this strange sight—why the bush does not burn up." When the Lord saw that he had gone over to look, God called to him from within the bush, "Moses! Moses!" And Moses said, "Here I am." "Do not come any closer," God said. "Take off your sandals, for the place where you are standing is holy ground." Then He said, "I am the God of your father, the God of Abraham, the God of Isaac and the God of Jacob." At this, Moses hid his face, because he was afraid to look at God (Exodus 3:1-6).*

Closed Visions

There are two specific types of closed visions. With your eyes closed, the image of the vision is "seen" in your mind as either:

1. Pictorial or static vision.

2. Panoramic vision (like a movie) in which there is motion.

Interactive Dreams and Visions

Interactive dreams or visions occur when an exchange happens between the dreamer and God in the encounter. In order for interaction to take place, the dreamer must be able to retain some degree of appropriate consciousness of his or her true, natural situation while in the dream or vision.

Interactive Visions

In my experience, interactive visions are more common than interactive dreams, but your experience may be different. Perhaps this is because visions involve varying degrees of the natural realm; therefore, it is easier to retain the degree of natural consciousness required for interaction to occur in visionary encounters. Peter had an interactive vision in Acts 10:9-20 in which God unfolded His plan of salvation to the Gentiles. Another example occurs when God appeared to Ananias and commanded him to lay hands on Saul to restore his sight (see Acts 9:19-16).

Interactive Dreams

The frequency of interactive dreams reflects the glory of God available to society and the grace of God in the dreamer's life when the encounter occurs. The Lord warned King Abimelech of Sarah's true nature as Abraham's wife as a means of giving him grace from Abraham's deception in disguising their true relationship.

> *Now Abraham moved on from there into the region of the Negev and lived between Kadesh and Shur. For a while he stayed in Gerar, and there Abraham said of his wife Sarah, "She is my sister." Then Abimelech king of Gerar sent for Sarah and took her. But God came to Abimelech in a dream one night and said to him, "You are as good as dead because of the woman you have taken; she is a married woman." Now Abimelech had not gone near her, so he said, "Lord, will you destroy an innocent nation? Did he not say to me, 'She is my sister,' and didn't she also say, 'He is my brother?' I have done this with a clear conscience and clean hands." Then God said to him in the dream, "Yes, I know you did this with a clear conscience, and so I have kept you from sinning against Me. That is why I did not let you touch her. Now return the man's wife, for he is a prophet, and he will pray for you and you will live. But if you do not return her, you may be sure that you and all yours will die" (Genesis 20:1-7).*

My Personal Experience

In an interactive dream, God once asked me to put Isaiah 54 into a song. I replied that He knew that I'm not a good singer and requested that He allow me to put only a few verses into a song. God insisted, however, that my song had to include the entire chapter. In the dream's next scene, I was heading home to inform my wife of the encounter. On the way, I met a gathering of Christians who were singing praises to God. I decided to join them and, to my surprise, they were all singing Isaiah 54. At the very moment I joined in, they were singing the second verse, which was being projected onto a big screen in the front of a hall. This is how the Scripture read: "Enlarge the place of your tent, stretch your tent curtains wide, do not hold back; lengthen your cords, strengthen your stakes." At this point, I woke up.

Twilight Dreams and Visions

These are dreams or visions, including trances, which are received in twilight states. They come in various forms. Some are "breaking news"-type encounters; others are of a summary type; and many are trances. All of these manifestations are common to the ministry of a seer.

Breaking News

These dreams and visions are characteristically short, sharp, and clear, and are given mainly for the purpose of guidance. In the last days, God will increase His communication through various types of dreams. But He will particularly increase the number and lucidity of dreams received in the twilight state. God commonly uses "breaking news" dreams at critical periods in a dreamer's life to align him to God's purposes. Joseph, the earthly father of Jesus, had many such dreams in the period surrounding the future Messiah's birth.

God also uses "breaking news" dreams to break through our natural defenses to convey an urgent message. On the whole, an increase in "breaking news spiritual encounters" of various sorts will occur in the last days. These manifestations are full of dream phrases, which give clear, unambiguous instructions or warnings; they are commonly associated with angelic messages and speak of "things that are happening" or what will happen shortly, hence the term "breaking news."

For example, of Jesus' future birth, the Bible states:

But after he [Joseph] *had considered this* [divorcing Mary]*, an angel of the Lord appeared to him in a dream and said, "Joseph son of David, do not be afraid to take Mary home as your wife because what is conceived in her is from the Holy Spirit. She will give birth to a son, and you are to give Him the name Jesus, because He will save His people from their sins* (Matthew 1:20-21).

Further examples of breaking news dreams/visions can be found in Jacob's dream (see Gen. 31:10-14), Laban's dream (see Gen. 31:24), and further dreams to Jesus' earthly father (see Matt. 2:12-13).

Summary Dreams

God uses these dreams to recap the many dreams that may occur in a night. Summary dreams are common with high-volume dreamers or seers. These short dreams contain the main highlights of a night's spiritual encounters. I have had many of these dreams, and I tended to overlook them, but God revealed their purpose. Once, I was on a church retreat and I was going to speak the next morning. The night before I was scheduled to speak, however, I had many dreams that I couldn't remember. I woke up in the middle of the night and prayed about those dreams, even though I didn't remember them. As I drifted back to sleep, God told me in a dream that He was going to summarize that night's dreams for me, and that He had actually done this in the past even though I hadn't taken notice. The Lord then proceeded to give me main points of the night's encounters.

Trances

A trance is a state of partial or complete detachment from one's physical surroundings. Trances are classic examples of twilight spiritual encounters. They can occur at any time and mimic the feeling of being between sleeping and being awake. Like "breaking news" dreams, trances are short, sharp, and clear and are usually rich in phrases and often involve angels. As in the Bible, they often speak to the person in unambiguous terms, mostly addressing imminent or ongoing issues that demand prompt action:

> *About noon the following day as they were on their journey and approaching the city, Peter went up on the roof to pray. He became hungry and wanted something to eat, and while the meal was being prepared, he fell into a trance* (Acts 10:9-10).

> *"When I returned to Jerusalem and was praying at the temple, I fell into a trance and saw the Lord speaking. 'Quick!' He said to me. 'Leave Jerusalem immediately, because they will not accept your testimony about Me'"* (Acts 22:17-18).

Proclamation Dreams and Visions

In certain dreams and visions, we can become the voice of agreement for God to proclaim His plans on earth. Proclamation dreams and visions can also occur through the voice of an angel, a divine messenger, or even God Himself. Most proclamations speak of decreed events, so we are well advised to take them seriously. Once proclaimed, the event happens almost instantaneously in the spirit realm, although its natural manifestation may follow later (see Zech. 1:8-17).

Another common form of proclamation is when God uses a respected spiritual leader or worldwide leader to declare an insightful spiritual statement relevant to the dreamer's life. Sometimes the dreamer makes the proclamation and declares profound insights into a situation. On the surface, such proclamations may be totally out of context with a dream's setting, but they can be deeply relevant to certain situations in the dreamer's circumstances.

My Personal Experience

In one dream, I got out of a car while wearing an army general's uniform. However, I didn't realize that I had the uniform on until I got out of the car. I then declared to two people having an argument that, "If only you knew that there was urgency in the spirit," then they would have to be more focused. At this particular time, God was speaking to me about the need to speed up what He had asked me to do.

In another dream, I was about to board a plane to attend a medical conference. (In my secular life, I work as a medical doctor.) Before boarding the plane, I had to pass through a security checkpoint. The security officer called me "Prophet Ibojie." When I asked the officer why he said that, he replied that I was wearing the badge of a prophet. I then realized that I had the badge on, and, as I looked behind me, I saw my medical files on the floor.

The Importance of Proclamation Dreams

Proclamation dreams are important because they can be prophetic declarations to a situation marked by indecision or confusion. Another scriptural example can be found in the vision that Zechariah saw:

> *Then the angel who was speaking to me left, and another angel came to meet him and said to him: "Run, tell that young man, 'Jerusalem will be a city without walls because of the great number of men and livestock in it. And I Myself will be a wall of fire around it,' declares the Lord, 'and I will be its glory within. Come! Come! Flee from the land of the north,' declares the Lord, 'for I have scattered you to the four winds of heaven,' declares the Lord. 'Come, O Zion! Escape,*

you who live in the Daughter of Babylon!' For this is what the Lord Almighty says: 'After he has honored Me and has sent Me against the nations that have plundered you—for whoever touches you touches the apple of His eye—I will surely raise My hand against them so that their slaves will plunder them. Then you will know that the Lord Almighty has sent me. Shout and be glad, O Daughter of Zion. For I am coming, and I will live among you,' declares the Lord. 'Many nations will be joined with the Lord in that day and will become My people. I will live among you and you will know that the Lord Almighty has sent Me to you. The Lord will inherit Judah as His portion in the holy land and will again choose Jerusalem. Be still before the Lord, all mankind, because He has roused Himself from His holy dwelling" (Zechariah 2:3-13).

Predictive and Corrective Dreams

Predictive dreams offer foresight. They can be:

◆ *Prophetic dreams*: Numbers 12:6; Deuteronomy 13:1-2; and First Samuel 28:6.

◆ *Blessing and destiny dreams*: Genesis 28:10-12; 37:5-11; and First Kings 3:5.

◆ *Turning point dreams:* the butler's dream in Genesis 40:9-15.

Corrective dreams are insightful and can take the following forms:

◆ *Warning and correction dreams:* Job 33:14-18; Daniel 4:4-27; Genesis 20:3; and Matthew 27:19.

◆ *Encouragement and confirmation dreams:* Judges 7:13-15.

◆ *Guidance dreams:* Acts 16:10.

Dreams/Visions That Call to Service and Commission

Certain dreams or visions can register God's call and/or commissioning to a person's divine destiny in the Lord. Two examples of this are when Saul (Paul) was brought out of his lifetime career of persecuting Christians, and when Isaiah accepted his prophetic call with the purification of his lips.

"Who are You, Lord?" Saul asked. "I am Jesus, whom you are perse-cuting," He replied. "Now get up and go into the city, and you will be told what you must do" (Acts 9:5-6).

In the year that King Uzziah died, I saw the Lord seated on a throne, high and exalted, and the train of His robe filled the temple. Above Him were seraphs, each with six wings: With two wings they covered their faces, with two they covered their feet, and with two they were flying. And they were calling to one another: "Holy, holy, holy is the Lord Almighty; the whole earth is full of His glory." At the sound of their voices the doorposts and thresholds shook and the temple was filled with smoke. "Woe to me!" I cried. "I am ruined! For I am a man of unclean lips, and I live among a people of unclean lips, and my eyes have seen the King, the Lord Almighty." Then one of the seraphs flew to me with a live coal in his hand, which he had taken with tongs from the altar. With it he touched my mouth and said, "See, this has touched your lips; your guilt is taken away and your sin atoned for." Then I heard the voice of the Lord saying, "Whom shall I send? And who will go for Us?" And I said, "Here am I. Send me!" He said, "Go and tell this people: 'Be ever hearing, but never understanding; be ever seeing, but never perceiving'" (Isaiah 6:1-9).

Healing and Deliverance in Dreams

Many dreamers have received emotional healing in dreams, and testimonies of physical healing are plentiful. Several instances in Scripture depict dreamers either being strengthened physically or receiving encouragement in dreams. Some possible reasons why the dream atmosphere is conducive for such occurrences include:

◆ In dreams, God bypasses our logic, our preconceived notions, and other obstacles of the conscious mind to connect with our spirit, which is the center of man. Perhaps, like a mirror, a dream may have most relevance when it reflects what is wrong with us. However, this can be where we misunderstand our dreams the most.

◆ Dreams are where our spirit and soul return to find balance and real purpose in life, in an atmosphere not dominated by our mind.

♦ In our dreams and visions, God may show us where we have yet to take on a Christ-like attitude in life. See Peter's vision in Acts 10:14-16.

♦ God can give divine impartation in dreams to overcome our issues, problems, or fears.

♦ In dreams, God can take us back in time to reveal what needs to be properly dealt with.

♦ God can impart the required grace, mercy, and power for healing afflictions.

♦ A dreamer can become the voice of proclamation in a dream to decree a healing or deliverance on earth.

Emotional healing takes place in dreams or visions when (and if) we submit to it. In Acts 10:9-16, for example, God delivered the apostle Peter from the mindset that only the Jews were qualified for salvation. In terms of healing, there should be deliverance from hurts that occurred in our negative experiences, as well as from ungodly soul ties and unconfessed, habitual sins. Deliverance is also necessary from other destructive influences, including the spirits of Jezebel, divination, and witchcraft. Healing is also necessary from unforgiveness, bitterness, and a critical or judgmental spirit.

Until healing occurs, the enemy has an open door to terrorize a person, and this extends to dreams as demonic activities or nightmares. Once God heals the trauma, the memory is also healed and nightmares may disappear. This has been my testimony. One can say that fear damages the pictorial center and, quite possibly, also our word depository, which then plays up in our dreams as negative experiences.

Theophanic Dreams

These are dreams in which God appears and comes in the fullness of His glory and with awesome reverential fear. His appearance is so powerful that the dreamer is compelled to listen. An example of a theophanic dream can be found with that of Abimelech speaking to God in Genesis 20:1-7.

33

Dialoguing With God in Dreams

This dialogue often takes the form of a series of dreams in which the dreamer awakens between dreams and intercedes in response to the preceding dream. God then replies to the dreamer's response with another dream so as to continue the discussion.

On many occasions, I have had dialogue with God in my dreams. I once had a series of seven dreams in about an hour, and all the dreams were on the same subject. In this encounter, God gave me progressive revelations in response to my intercession. Dialoguing in dreams can span a period of minutes, hours, days, weeks, or months. Therefore, it is most important that the dreamer record all his dreams.

We should ask God to give further information on anything revealed to us in dreams. Most of the time, God wants to continue speaking to us on these issues. Also, the majority of recurring dreams are God's progressive revelations on issues that the dreamer does not properly understand or has not adequately dealt with; the repetition is usually to address the dreamer's inner uncertainty or confusion.

One biblical example is found when Joseph (of the coat of many colors) had two dreams consisting of different details, yet they were on the same subject. Joseph's two dreams constituted a pair of dialoguing dreams. After the first dream, Joseph and his brothers responded to the dream. Then, God continued His discourse by releasing the second dream (see Chapter 2). Also, the repetition of Joseph's dreams indicates God's emphasis on the subject.

Abraham's dream in Genesis 15 is a combination of an interactive and dialoguing dream. In this visitation, God reassures Abraham about the future promise of his descendants. This encounter includes an interactive vision (verses 1-9), an interlude (verses 10-11), and the furtherance of his discussion with God (verses 12-18).

"This Is That" Phenomenon

A seer may not instantly gain full understanding of all that he receives. And there are many reasons why this may happen. Oftentimes, God will prompt him to recall relevant revelations when the need arises. Observe how God dealt with Samuel in regard to Israel's future leader, Saul.

Now the day before Saul came, the Lord had revealed this to Samuel: "About this time tomorrow I will send you a man from the land of Benjamin. Anoint him leader over My people Israel; he will deliver My people from the hand of the Philistines. I have looked upon My people, for their cry has reached Me." When Samuel caught sight of Saul, the Lord said to him, "This is the man I spoke to you about; he will govern My people" (1 Samuel 9:15-17).

The Value of "This Is That" Phenomenon

Through the "this is that" phenomenon, Jesus' disciples recalled the Old Testament writing, *"Zeal for Your house will consume Me,"* as was previously prophesied in Psalm 69:9.

When it was almost time for the Jewish Passover, Jesus went up to Jerusalem. In the temple courts He found men selling cattle, sheep and doves, and others sitting at tables exchanging money. So He made a whip out of cords, and drove all from the temple area, both sheep and cattle; He scattered the coins of the money-changers and overturned their tables. To those who sold doves He said, "Get these out of here! How dare you turn My Father's house into a market!" His disciples remembered that it is written: "Zeal for Your house will consume Me" (John 2:13-17).

The following prophetic Scripture from the prophet Joel was recalled by the apostle Peter in Acts 2:15-21 as he addressed the crowd on the Day of Pentecost:

Even on My servants, both men and women, I will pour out My Spirit in those days. I will show wonders in the heavens and on the earth, blood and fire and billows of smoke. The sun will be turned to darkness and the moon to blood before the coming of the great and dreadful day of the Lord. And everyone who calls on the name of the Lord will be saved; for on Mount Zion and in Jerusalem there will be deliverance, as the Lord has said, among the survivors whom the Lord calls (Joel 2:29-32).

Most dreamers may have experienced this phenomenon without recognizing it. Commonly, many feel familiarity with a place where they have never been in the natural. Truth be told, the majority of such cases are due to a quickening of spiritual familiarity from their own spirit.

Premonitory Deep and Heavy Sleep

Some seers are hit with a premonition of imminent, deep, heavy sleep when God wants to break through daily routines. The Lord does this to convey an urgent message in a dream, vision, or trance—because in order to receive a dream, one's mind needs to be asleep, whether it is day or night.

Over the years, I have learned to discern when this unusual sense of premonition comes upon me. I have never found it to be crippling or disabling. Actually, this sleep is quite pleasant, even though deep and heavy. If resisted, the urge will usually go away quite easily, but when complied with, it can lead to outstanding revelation within minutes.

Many instances of this phenomenon occur in the Bible. Most take place within the context of visionary encounters. Abraham's covenant was cut in a vision, and then later concluded in a dream. Genesis 15:12 says, *"As the sun was setting, **Abram fell into a deep sleep,** and a thick and dreadful darkness came over him."* In this sleep, God revealed what Abraham's mind was unable to comprehend at the time of his dream.

Falling Into Deep Sleep Within the Context of Visionary Encounter

God sends such deep sleep in order to bypass the mind, connect with the spirit of man, and avoid the seer's mind-set. This is necessary to impress the spirit with what the mind may be incapable of comprehending at the time.

> *Then I heard him speaking, and as I listened to him, I fell into a deep sleep, my face to the ground* (Daniel 10:9).

> *So the man gave names to all the livestock, the birds of the air and all the beasts of the field. But for Adam no suitable helper was found. So the Lord God **caused the man to fall into a deep sleep; and while he was sleeping,** He took one of the man's ribs and closed up the place with flesh. Then the Lord God made a woman from the rib He had taken out of the man, and He brought her to the man* (Genesis 2:20-22).

Apparitions

This is a visionary manifestation of the supernatural in the physical realm, and it's perceived by natural senses. Apparitions were very common in biblical days. Although still quite common in modern times, many people experience them without realizing it. An apparition can be a tangible experience or an actual happening of a supernatural event in the physical realm.

Sometimes, they are barely more than mere sight; and at other times, they are a tangible sense of an actual experience in the physical realm. Apparitions are an example of interplay between spiritual and natural in visionary encounters. Most of them are interactive. Observe the phenomenon of apparitions in the following Bible passages:

King Belshazzar gave a great banquet for a thousand of his nobles and drank wine with them. While Belshazzar was drinking his wine, he gave orders to bring in the gold and silver goblets that Nebuchadnezzar his father had taken from the temple in Jerusalem, so that the king and his nobles, his wives and his concubines might drink from them. So they brought in the gold goblets that had been taken from the temple of God in Jerusalem, and the king and his nobles, his wives and his concubines drank from them. As they drank the wine, they praised the gods of gold and silver, of bronze, iron, wood and stone. Suddenly the fingers of a human hand appeared and wrote on the plaster of the wall, near the lampstand in the royal palace. The king watched the hand as it wrote. His face turned pale and he was so frightened that his knees knocked together and his legs gave way (Daniel 5:1-6).

That night Jacob got up and took his two wives, his two maidservants and his eleven sons and crossed the ford of the Jabbok. After he had sent them across the stream, he sent over all his possessions. So Jacob was left alone, and a man wrestled with him till daybreak (Genesis 32:22-24).

After six days Jesus took with Him Peter, James and John the brother of James, and led them up a high mountain by themselves. There He was transfigured before them. His face shone like the sun, and His clothes became as white as the light. Just then there appeared before them Moses and Elijah, talking with Jesus. Peter said to Jesus, "Lord, it is good for us to be here. If You wish, I will put up three shelters—one for You, one for Moses and one for Elijah." While he was still speaking, a bright cloud enveloped them, and a voice from the cloud said, "This is My Son, whom I love; with Him I am well pleased. Listen to Him!" When the disciples heard this, they fell face down to the ground, terrified. But Jesus came and touched them. "Get up," He said. "Don't be afraid." When they looked up, they saw no one except Jesus (Matthew 17:1-8).

When they had crossed, Elijah said to Elisha, "Tell me, what can I do for you before I am taken from you?" "Let me inherit a double portion of your spirit," Elisha replied. "You have asked a difficult thing," Elijah said, "yet if you see me when I am taken from you, it will be yours— otherwise not." As they were walking along and talking together, suddenly a chariot of fire and horses of fire appeared and separated the two of them, and Elijah went up to heaven in a whirlwind. Elisha saw this and cried out, "My father! My father! The chariots and horsemen of Israel!" And Elisha saw him no more. Then he took hold of his own clothes and tore them apart (2 Kings 2:9-12).

Now when Joshua was near Jericho, he looked up and saw a man standing in front of him with a drawn sword in his hand. Joshua went up to him and asked, "Are you for us or for our enemies?" "Neither," he replied, "but as commander of the army of the Lord I have now come." Then Joshua fell face down to the ground in reverence, and asked him, "What message does my Lord have for His servant?" The commander of the Lord's army replied, "Take off your sandals, for the place where you are standing is holy." And Joshua did so (Joshua 5:13-15).

CHAPTER 4

How Dreams Are Received, Remembered, and Recorded

How to Prepare to Receive Your Dreams

Since we see dreams with the eyes of the heart, we should not switch off the light in our hearts. God is the light of our human hearts—He is the Father of light—and if you fill your heart with God, then light will shine in. The Bible says, *"Every good and perfect gift is from above, coming down from the Father of the heavenly lights, who does not change like shifting shadows"* (James 1:17). Therefore, we should commit the last moment of each day to meditating on God's Word and preparing the spiritual soil of our heart for whatever dreams God may give us.

Make provision for keeping a record of your nightly encounter with God. Be sure you have a pen and notebook on hand. (Some people may find it easier to record dreams using a small tape recorder.) Meditate on the meaning of your dreams after they have been recorded and capture the essence of what God is saying to you. *"It is the glory of God to conceal a matter; to search out a matter is the glory of kings"* (Prov. 25:2).

Most people find that fasting and prayer heightens sensitivity to the Spirit. Fasting prepares you to receive revelation faster and at a deeper level! Adding the reading of God's Word to your fasting releases faith, which is our eye for operating in the supernatural. Peter's fasting and prayers cleared the way for him to receive a groundbreaking vision of the Gentiles' salvation:

About noon the following day as they were on their journey and approaching the city, Peter went up on the roof to pray. He became hungry and wanted something to eat, and while the meal was being prepared, he fell into a trance (Acts 10:9-10).

Before retiring to bed each night, it is also a good idea to meditate on God's goodness and kindness.

Praise the Lord, O my soul; all my inmost being, praise His holy name. Praise the Lord, O my soul, and forget not all His benefits— who forgives all your sins and heals all your diseases, who redeems your life from the pit and crowns you with love and compassion, who satisfies your desires with good things so that your youth is renewed like the eagle's. The Lord works righteousness and justice for all the oppressed. He made known His ways to Moses, His deeds to the people of Israel: The Lord is compassionate and gracious, slow to anger, abounding in love. He will not always accuse, nor will He harbor His anger forever; He does not treat us as our sins deserve or repay us according to our iniquities. For as high as the heavens are above the earth, so great is His love for those who fear Him; as far as the east is from the west, so far has He removed our transgressions from us. As a father has compassion on his children, so the Lord has compassion on those who fear Him (Psalm 103:1-13).

How to Remember Your Dreams

Most dreams vanish with the intrusion of daily thoughts. A dream and its vital details may also be lost if the dreamer is not at peace. Most dreams can be lost within a minute or two of waking up, so it's important to spend quiet time to let dreams speak into the stillness of our mind. We need this quiet time to recall our dreams. Before a day's busyness starts, we should allow time for dreams to drift into the image center of our mind.

Stillness is not lack of activity, but calmness in the inner being. Remember, dreams can be hindered by the effect of alcohol, bitterness, anger, resentment, medication, and even physical exhaustion. Also, attempting to interpret a dream before its full recollection and recording is a common cause for losing vital parts of a dream. Another simple cause for lack of recall is when a dreamer does not give much attention to his dreams. We should recall our dreams immediately upon awaking, just as the prophet Zechariah did:

Then the angel who talked with me returned and wakened me, as a man is wakened from his sleep. He asked me, "What do you see?" I answered, "I see a solid gold lampstand with a bowl at the top and seven lights on it, with seven channels to the lights" (Zechariah 4:1-2).

Dreams are received in the spirit when the mind is asleep and unable to receive translation. The mind participates best when it is awake. Dreams literally line up in the spirit, wait for the mind to wake up, and then get translated in the first few minutes of one's being awake. Many times, however, dreamers may think their way through things while dreaming. Therefore our mind is largely, but not totally, bypassed in dreaming. Dreams are most likely to be lost or forgotten in the first few minutes of waking. *"Like a dream he flies away, no more to be found, banished like a vision of the night"* (Job 20:8). Dreams are written in spiritual ink that quickly fades, so we must transcribe them into the more durable ink of human memory. We should always write down what we receive, whether it is clear or not:

In the first year of Belshazzar king of Babylon, Daniel had a dream, and visions passed through his mind as he was lying on his bed. He wrote down the substance of his dream (Daniel 7:1).

One of the most common causes of not remembering dreams is the intrusion of the voice of a person's mind. We must learn to put off our mind's voice, with its echoes of life's failures, successes, challenges, and unanswered prayers, all of which speak quite loudly. Dreams are best captured before pressures of life's routines start flooding into our consciousness.

A sudden noise upon waking up, such as from an alarm clock, is another common cause for failing to recall dreams. Noise drives away the stillness required for a dream to drift from one's spirit into the mind's image center.

How to Record Your Dreams

The Bible clearly instructs us to write down whatever we receive from God, whether in dreams or other forms of revelation. If we do not record dreams and visions, they are of little use.

In the fourth year of Jehoiakim son of Josiah king of Judah, this word came to Jeremiah from the Lord: "Take a scroll and write on it all the words I have spoken to you concerning Israel, Judah and all the other nations from the time I began speaking to you in the reign of Josiah till now. Perhaps when the people of Judah hear about every disaster I plan to inflict on them, each of them will turn from his wicked way; then I will forgive their wickedness and their sin (Jeremiah 36:1-3).

Go now, write it on a tablet for them, inscribe it on a scroll, that for the days to come it may be an everlasting witness (Isaiah 30:8).

Then the Lord replied: "Write down the revelation and make it plain on tablets so that a herald may run with it" (Habakkuk 2:2).

The revelation of Jesus Christ, which God gave him to show His servants what must soon take place. He made it known by sending His angel to His servant John, who testifies to everything he saw—that is, the word of God, and the testimony of Jesus Christ (Revelation 1:1-2).

A dream is often like one scene in a movie. Therefore, it's important to record all your dreams so that you can build up a broader picture over a period of time. From time to time, go over your dream recordings to gain a wider perspective of what God is saying: you might see an element that was missed from just a single dream:

"All this," David said, "I have in writing from the hand of the Lord upon me, and He gave me understanding in all the details of the plan" (1 Chronicles 28:19).

In the process of writing down his revelations, David learned that God gave him more insightful understanding of what was being revealed. Recording dreams also brings in more details that might otherwise have been lost. Revelation should always be recorded to ensure that we have a hard copy of what God has said. This is important for several reasons:

◆ Future circumstances may suggest that we have misheard God.

◆ We can confront our circumstances with hopeful expectation of the substance of our revelation, as opposed to letting our natural circumstances seemingly deny it.

◆ Revelation that is recorded will not be easily forgotten amidst the storms of life.

♦ Recorded revelations may be made available to be reviewed by others.

A dreamer may wake up in the middle of the night to record a dream or vision. This may occur because God or an angel has directly awakened the person. *"Then the angel who talked with me returned and wakened me, as a man is wakened from his sleep"* (Zech. 4:1). A dreamer may also awake in the middle of the night by acquiring the discipline to do so. *"At this I awoke and looked around. My sleep had been pleasant to me"* (Jer. 31:26).

How Dreams Are Received

The "Antenna"

God has to give revelation before anyone can receive it. A person's capability of receiving revelation can be likened to a television antenna. The functioning of a television antenna depends on many factors—including its positioning, correct tuning, and availability of airwave signals. Similarly, a human "antenna" is also dependent on many factors in order to receive revelation. Different sizes of television antennas can be likened to varying degrees of giftedness needed to receive dreams and visions.

The Bible reveals that the spirits of the prophets are subject to the prophets (see 1 Cor. 14:32). The same is true for using the gift of receiving dreams and revelation. The extent to which a gifted dreamer receives is dependent on what the dreamer does with this valuable gifting. Human "antennas" are primarily geared to receive from God, but they can also tap into a counterfeit channel in the spiritual realm and get hijacked by satan. Many spiritually gifted people are recruited into the devil's service, such as in the New Age movement.

We must be cautious about what we receive and then truly discern where it is coming from. Satan controls a powerful network of information that can sometimes appear as God's revelation. Remember, revelation is a fresh, divine spotlight on an aspect of God's eternally established truth to humanity. If we misuse dreams, it might result in God's withholding further revelation, so we must believe that God speaks through dreams and visions and not treat them with triviality.

From the outset, it is vital to be able to identify factors that will ensure you receive correct revelation. For example, a proper security system must be in place to guarantee that reception of spiritual signals is put toward godly purposes. Tuning the frequency of human antennas involves training the human spirit to receive from God. This is done by studying the Word of God and by living a life of prayer and sacrificial service through regular fasting and growing in intimacy with God. All of these elements will increase the amount and clarity of dreams we receive.

God Imparts Dreams Into the Spirit of Man

God releases dreams and visions to our spirit. This impartation is enhanced by the state of our spirit, which is determined by factors like spiritual wisdom, a sanctified conscience, and communion with God:

♦ *Spiritual wisdom* is the practical application of the Word of God and such wisdom always come from Heaven. *"But the wisdom that comes from heaven is first of all pure; then peace-loving, considerate, submissive, full of mercy and good fruit, impartial and sincere"* (James 3:17). In other words, wisdom is comprehensive insight into the ways and purposes of God, as enunciated in His Word.

♦ *A sanctified conscience* is one washed by the blood of Jesus, which transcends the limits of the intellect. It also operates by the laying down of a personal agenda and preferring the interest of others to our own.

♦ *Communion with God* is the basis for which wisdom and conscience are birthed and maintained in God. We need constant communion between our spirit and the Spirit of God. Understanding this will enhance the planting of dreams in the spirit.

Another factor that enhances an automatic sowing of dreams into the spirit *is being submitted to God.* As the writer of Hebrews reminds us, this is pivotal: *"How much more should we submit to the Father of our spirits and live"* (Heb. 12:9b). Submission to God enhances the sowing of revelation in the human spirit.

Hindrances to Receiving Dreams

♦ *When God withholds further revelation:* An ultimate objective of dreaming is to call the dreamer to action. If this action is not taken, then the value and purpose of giving the dream goes unrealized, and the reception of further dreams is

44

hindered. When this happens, God withholds further dreams and visions.

◆ *When there is no peace in your spirit:* Our spirit must be in a condition to release to the mind and receive what God is giving. Therefore, we must live in the peace of God, and maintain the unity of the Spirit through the bond of peace.

◆ *When we grieve the Holy Spirit:* When the Holy Spirit withdraws from us, we do not receive revelation.

Do not let any unwholesome talk come out of your mouths, but only what is helpful for building others up according to their needs, that it may benefit those who listen. And do not grieve the Holy Spirit of God, with whom you were sealed for the day of redemption. Get rid of all bitterness, rage and anger, brawling and slander, along with every form of malice. Be kind and compassionate to one another, forgiving each other, just as in Christ God forgave you (Ephesians 4:29-32).

◆ *When revelation is not planted in the right place:* The planting of dreams and visions in the human spirit is also hindered when we go to bed in anger. The Bible says, *"'In your anger do not sin': Do not let the sun go down while you are still angry, and do not give the devil a foothold"* (Eph. 4:26-27).

◆ *When we live a prideful life:* God resists the proud and exalts the humble. If you are full of pride, God does not give revelation. He may protect us from becoming too proud by sealing parts of the dream.

◆ *When we use alcohol or drugs:* These substances can depress reception and remembrance of dreams. They also affect release of dreams to the image center and the processing of revelation in the human mind. Drugs and chemicals cannot cause one to have dreams. But they do result in a chemical imbalance that produces hallucinations, which are quite different from dreams. A hallucination is defined as a "false perception with a characteristically compelling sense of the reality of something not really present" *(Reader's Digest Universal Dictionary)*.

Blurred images and distorted, fragmented dreams show signs of a planting in our souls that has somehow been hindered.

The Mind Will Ultimately Process the Dream

At first, our carnal mind is incapable of understanding revelation, although it can begin to process it. When dreams and visions are planted in our spirit, our mind gets bypassed; thus, emotion, sentiments, mindsets, human will, worldly ambition, goals, and expectations are also bypassed. Properly processing dreams and visions means eventually having to involve our soul. Therefore, dreams and visions are eventually released from our spirit into our consciousness.

The dynamics of translating revelation from man's spirit to his mind is influenced by the dreamer's faith. Release of dreams to the mind is enhanced by faith in God. Without faith, a revelation will remain inactive in the spirit. Once a revelation has been processed, its meaning and understanding is correlated to the dreamer's natural circumstances; this stage is influenced by the peace and liberty that come from God's indwelling presence. Without faith, any release from the spirit of man is fragmented. Without the Holy Spirit's presence, there is no godly liberty and understanding. The Bible says that where the Spirit of God is, there is liberty (see 2 Cor. 3:17).

Normal Seasonal Variation in the Reception of Dreams

Whether you are a high-volume or low-volume dreamer, everyone has seasons of intense dreaming, and then seasons when dreams are scarce. Times of normal, seasonal lows in receiving and remembering dreams are characterized by:

- ◆ Peace and liberty, which the dreamer maintains from the Holy Spirit's presence, even though he is receiving very scanty dreams.

- ◆ God speaking through other means (such as the still small voice). The dreamer uses this period to develop further sharpness in other abilities.

- ◆ Inner assurance, so that the dreamer does not suffer from emptiness and unholy fear.

- ◆ Lack of anxiety or frustration.

- ◆ Usually quite a brief period.

If a seasonal low in receiving dreams is rather prolonged, the dreamer should go back to former spiritual disciplines that may have lapsed unintentionally. Some seasons of poor reception are due to issues in the dreamer's life; this could arise from a need to study the Word of God. In my practical experience, when my dreams are getting blurred, scanty, and difficult to remember, my first instinctive reaction is to study Scripture a little more:

◆ The Word of God gives you wisdom and is the light on your path. Without light, you cannot see.

◆ Meditating on the Word of God sharpens your imagination and enhances your ability to see in the Spirit. Holy imagination entails visualizing Bible scenes as you read the Scriptures. This practice prepares the soil of the mind to receive pictorial revelation.

◆ The Word of God is sharper than a two-edged sword and rightly divides between what is of the spirit and what is of the soul, marrow, and bone (between wholesome and unwholesome), and between attitudes and thoughts of the heart.

A lack of worshiping God could also be a hindrance. Worship brings the glory of God's presence to manifestation, and this glory has the power to dispel any form of darkness. Sin is also a hindrance to receiving revelation from God, and it seals the heavens from the dreamer. Mishandling previous revelation—especially by manipulation—will make God withhold any further revelation.

When God Seals the Antenna of the Prophet/Seer

God may withhold revelation beyond the normal, seasonal lows (as mentioned above). In many biblical instances, God sealed (or blocked) the antenna from receiving revelation due to people who persisted on sinning without repentance:

> *Be stunned and amazed, blind yourselves and be sightless, be drunk, but not from wine, stagger, but not from beer. The Lord has brought over you a deep sleep: He has sealed your eyes [the prophets]. He has covered your heads [the seers]. For you the whole vision is nothing but words sealed in a scroll. And if you give the scroll to someone who can read, and say to him, "Read this, please," he will answer, "I can't, it is sealed." Or if you give the scroll to someone who cannot read, and say, "Read this, please," he will answer, "I don't know how to read" (Isaiah 29:9-12).*

As it is written: "God gave them a spirit of stupor, eyes so that they could not see and ears so that they could not hear, to this very day" (Romans 11:8).

The boy Samuel ministered before the Lord under Eli. In those days the word of the Lord was rare; there were not many visions (1 Samuel 3:1).

Her [Jerusalem] gates have sunk into the ground; their bars he has broken and destroyed. Her king and her princes are exiled among the nations, the law is no more, and her prophets no longer find visions from the Lord (Lamentations 2:9).

And these also stagger from wine and reel from beer: Priests and prophets stagger from beer and are befuddled with wine; they reel from beer, they stagger when seeing visions, they stumble when rendering decisions (Isaiah 28:7).

The Evil Revelatory Delay

Satan can interfere with transmission from the spirit to the natural consciousness (the mind), which is where understanding and remembrance occur. The devil often interferes through the nearly incessant intrusion of our mind's voice. The devil can do this in two main ways:

1. He can input information into the human mind and make it appear as revelation, with the intention of causing confusion and deception.

2. He can hinder a dreamer's ability to translate what the spirit receives for its understanding in the human mind. A block in translation is a major way the devil hinders the remembrance of dreams. Visions are less affected in this way.

When the work of satan is responsible for poor reception and remembrance of dreams, I call this "revelatory siege" and it's usually characterized by:

◆ Frustration

◆ Anxiety

◆ Lack of peace

◆ Insecurity

◆ A feeling of emptiness

During this period of "delay"—when reception is hindered and translation of spiritual experience to human memory is blocked—God will often give revelation through other means.

Different Amounts of Dreaming

High, Medium, and Low Volume Dreamers

Revelatory giftedness is the potential to receive revelation. However, what is eventually received, and how this occurs, depends on one's relationship with God, because the Lord confides in those who fear Him. Additionally, some people are gifted to receive variable volumes of revelations. The essential point is how the dreamers put giftedness into use. God is able to meet each dreamer's needs within his level of giftedness.

There are high, medium, and low volume dreamers:

- **High volume** dreamers receive as many as two or more dreams in a single night on a consistent basis. The majority of what a high volume dreamer receives may address issues pertaining to routines of life that most people would not imagine God to be interested in.

- **Medium volume** dreamers receive an amount in-between the other two categories.

- **Low volume** dreamers receive about one dream in a week, or one dream in a few weeks, on a fairly regular basis.

- **Others, or so-called non-dreamers,** include those who claim to be non-dreamers because they cannot recall any dreams. Everyone dreams, although some people may have completely lost the ability to recall dreams, particularly if they fail to pay attention to their dreams over a long time. They then lose or severely weaken their innate potential for recalling dreams.

It is God's prerogative to give revelation before anyone can receive it. But since most dreamers operate below their gifted potential, there is always room for advancement when the person pays attention to dreams and moves closer to God. This is also how it becomes possible to increase the scope of our dreams' coverage to include non-personal issues.

Most people will have lengthy dreams when they are born-again (new Christians). However, the percentage of lengthy dreams may be reduced as one grows in relationship with God. Most likely, this happens because we allow life's impurities to be washed away. As we attain more Christ-likeness, we can communicate more closely with God and get sharper, clearer, and shorter dreams. Many mature Christians can still have lengthy dreams from time to time, if God deems it necessary. Multiple dreams in one night often refer to different aspects of a message or different scenes of the same story; this is a common occurrence in the life of high volume dreamers.

Repeated Dreams

This refers to dreams repeated more than once within a short time, and which commonly occur in a single night. There may be minor variations in elements or symbolic actions within the dreams, but the plot remains the same (see Joseph's dream in Genesis 37:1-15 and Pharaoh's dreams in Genesis 41:1-8).

Dreams are repeated for the following reasons:

◆ For divine insights into other aspects that might have been missed.

◆ Misunderstanding or partial understanding of a previous dream's message.

◆ Decreed events, which God has ordained to happen. Joseph said dreams can recur when the event is settled in Heaven. Such dreams will soon happen.

The reason the dream was given to Pharaoh in two forms is that the matter has been firmly decided by God, and God will do it soon (Genesis 41:32).

◆ No responses or inappropriate responses to previous dreams.

Recurring Dreams

Recurring dreams are those that are repeated more than twice over a long period of time. These often indicate an issue that needs to be resolved or is in the process of resolution.

Dreams can recur because of the following:

◆ Hurts or unhealed wounds of the past.

50

- Emotional scars that need healing.

- Bondages or negative strongholds that need to be pulled down.

- Divine insights into other aspects of the matter that might have been missed.

- Persistent misunderstanding or partial understanding of a message from a previous dream.

- No responses or inappropriate responses to previous dreams.

Once a recurring dream has been correctly interpreted and its meaning acted upon, then the dream will usually cease. If the dream recurs again, then the original interpretation was probably incorrect or incomplete.

Sleep, Sleeplessness, and Your Dream

Sleep is the temporary suspension of exercise in the power of the body and soul. A dream is the visual revelation received when one is asleep, so one must be sleeping to dream. Sleeplessness is the lack of regular sleep periods. Receiving a dream encounter only takes a few seconds or minutes. One can receive a lengthy dream in just a few seconds (as often happens in twilight states) because dream encounters are outside of time.

Factors such as stress, anxiety, sorrow, or being traumatized can impinge on one's ability to get regular sleep, so these factors will also adversely affect a person's dream-life. A person's state of mind will influence the dramatization of the dream message and so affect it that proper understanding becomes colored and the message's true substance becomes compromised.

Nightmares and Night Terror

The true definition of a nightmare is a dream that arouses feelings of acute fear, dread, or anguish. A nightmare, therefore, is a subjective term that reflects an individual dreamer's perception and judgment. What is a nightmare to one person may not be a nightmare to another; perhaps this explains why children are more prone to call dreams "nightmares." Under the following circumstances, dreams are regarded as nightmares by a majority of dreamers:

◆ Dreams that have become more graphic as a result of not listening to previous warnings in dreams. God often waits patiently for our response. If we fail to respond to the dream, it may be repeated over and over again. If we continue to ignore it, we may be frightened by a terrible nightmare to show us how serious the situation has become.

◆ Dreams of spiritual warfare could easily be regarded as nightmares because they are often God's expositions on happenings of wars in the spirit realm. They warn the dreamer about hell's assignments and reveal a divine strategy for victory.

◆ Dreams that warn of impending dangers could easily be regarded as nightmares. Most such dreams address personal weaknesses, focus on the likelihood of poor judgment that may lead to bad decisions, or warn of the danger of wrong associations or influences—the list is endless. King Nebuchadnezzar had a terrifying dream that told him about his kingdom's future.

In the second year of his reign, Nebuchadnezzar had dreams; his mind was troubled and he could not sleep. So the king summoned the magicians, enchanters, sorcerers and astrologers to tell him what he had dreamed. When they came in and stood before the king, he said to them, "I have had a dream that troubles me and I want to know what it means" (Daniel 2:1-3).

Job was warned in dreams about what would come across his path, even though he did not understand them, *"For God does speak—now one way, now another—though man may not perceive it"* (Job 33:14). The dreams gradually became a nightmare to him: *"When I think my bed will comfort me and my couch will ease my complaint, even then you frighten me with dreams and terrify me with visions"* (Job 7:13-14).

How Visions Are Received

Visions are received predominantly in the spirit, with varying degree of involvement of the natural realm. Thus, a person can receive a vision with the natural eyes wide open but see the vision in the spirit. In apparitions, however, the supernatural happenings can be perceived with the natural senses and even experienced tangibly.

The Interplay of Visions and the Physical Nature

As previously explained, visions are spiritual encounters with differing points of involvement in the physical realm. In some scriptural examples, people who had visions were left with residual, physical evidence of the encounter. Unlike dreams—in which encounters are on a purely individual basis—visions can be corporate because of its involvement in the natural realm. In Genesis, Jacob had a visionary encounter with an angel that left him with a physical deformity:

> *So Jacob was left alone, and a man wrestled with him till daybreak. When the man saw that he could not overpower him, **he touched the socket of Jacob's hip so that his hip was wrenched as he wrestled with the man*** (Genesis 32:24-25).

Paul described a visionary experience in which he was not sure whether or not he was in the body:

> *I know a man in Christ who fourteen years ago was caught up to the third heaven. **Whether it was in the body of out of the body I do not know**—God knows. And I know that this man—whether in the body or apart from the body I do not know, but God knows—was caught up to paradise. He heard inexpressible things, things that man is not permitted to tell* (2 Corinthians 12:2-4).

Visions and the Third Heaven

The frequency of visions received in a particular place reflects the openness of the "third Heaven" over that location. The immediate surroundings of the throne and abode of God are the third Heaven. (The second Heaven refers to the zone of spiritual warfare, which is the abode of satan and his agents; while the first heaven refers to earth).

In Genesis, Jacob saw the open heaven:

> *He had a dream in which he saw a stairway resting on the earth, with its top reaching to heaven, and the angels of God were ascending and descending on it. There above it stood the Lord, and He said: "I am the Lord, the God of your father Abraham and the God of Isaac. I will give you and your descendants the land on which you are lying"* (Genesis 28:12-13).

Jesus also spoke of open heavens in John 1:51, *"I tell you the truth, you shall see heaven open, and the angels of God ascending and descending on the Son of Man."* The heavens also opened during the baptism of Jesus Christ:

> *Then Jesus came from Galilee to the Jordan to be baptized by John. But John tried to deter Him, saying, "I need to be baptized by You, and do You come to me?" Jesus replied, "Let it be so now; it is proper for us to do this to fulfill all righteousness." Then John consented. As soon as Jesus was baptized, He went up out of the water. At that moment heaven was opened, and He saw the Spirit of God descending like a dove and lighting on Him. And a voice from heaven said, "This is My Son, whom I love; with Him I am well pleased"* (Matthew 3:13-17).

An opening of the heavens bypasses hindrances of the second Heaven to connect God's abode with the earthly realm. The third Heaven can be opened over a geographical location, on a permanent or temporary basis; one could also be opened over the head of an individual, but usually only temporarily. Scripture speaks of *"your heavens which are over your head"* (Deut. 28:23 NKJV). Angelic activities and visitations are increased under open heavens, as is the possibility of falling into a trance or other visionary encounters:

> *...Peter went up on the roof to pray. He became very hungry and wanted to eat, and while the meal was being prepared, he fell into a trance. He saw heaven opened...* (Acts 10:9-11).

An open Heaven invites you to come up to the third Heaven realm, which is where blessings are poured on mankind. A heavenly portal is a permanent opening of the third Heaven over a place. Heavenly portals exist in many locations on earth, but usually in places of very high contention in the spirit realm, such as Jerusalem, Mount Sinai, and Bethel.

Keys to "Open Heaven" Activation

Temporary opening of a "third Heaven" over a location is facilitated by what we do. If we want this to happen we should be doing the following:

◆ Exercising our spiritual senses on a constant basis:

But solid food belongs to those who are of full age, that is, those who by reason of use have their senses [spiritual] exercised to discern both good and evil (Hebrews 5:14 NKJV).

◆ Ensuring that every experience in our spiritual life is Bible-guided. We should exercise the practice of waiting upon God to activate the seer anointing.

◆ Strengthening our spirit-man. Many people collapse when their inner strength cannot withstand pressure from the outside.

I have not stopped giving thanks for you, remembering you in my prayers. I keep asking that the God of our Lord Jesus Christ, the glorious Father, may give you the Spirit of wisdom and revelation, so that you may know Him better. I pray also that the eyes of your heart may be enlightened in order that you may know the hope to which He has called you, the riches of His glorious inheritance in the saints (Ephesians 1:16-18).

◆ Ensuring that we see with eyes of faith, as "the eyes of our understanding" are actually eyes of our faith. For most people, prophetic experiences may be initiated in their mind, as in a daydream. Therefore, we must sanctify our imagination to enhance this process; then, by faith, we must position ourselves where God can initiate a spiritual experience. In seeking spiritual experience with God, it is also important to keep our hearts and motives pure. We must learn to control our minds and learn to quiet our souls before the Lord. Paul admonished us to look at what is not seen, for our natural senses will not cease to see physical circumstances around us. As spiritual people, however, we should be careful what we hear or see because that affects our spiritual senses and, ultimately, our spiritual experiences.

◆ Applying the blood of the Lamb: *"He did not enter by means of the blood of goats and calves; but He entered the Most Holy Place once for all by His own blood, having obtained eternal redemption"* (Heb. 9:12).

◆ Praying and fasting:

If My people, who are called by My name, will humble themselves and pray and seek My face and turn from their ways, then will I hear from heaven and will forgive their sin and will heal their land (2 Chronicles 7:14).

The king went to Gibeon to offer sacrifices, for that was the most important high place, and Solomon offered a thousand burnt offerings on that altar. At Gibeon the Lord appeared to Solomon during the night in a dream, and God said, "Ask for whatever you want Me to give you" (1 Kings 3:4-5).

◆ Giving tithes and offerings: Cornelius' charitable giving is a classic story of how an offering on earth can initiate a response from Heaven, and thereby create an open connection:

...He distinctly saw an angel of God, who came to him and said, "Cornelius!" Cornelius stared at him in fear. "What is it, Lord?" he asked. The angel answered, "Your prayers and gifts to the poor have come up as a memorial offering before God" (Acts 10:3-4).

"Bring the whole tithe into the storehouse, that there may be food in My house. Test Me in this," says the Lord Almighty, "and see if I will not throw open the floodgates of heaven and pour out so much blessing that you will not have room enough for it" (Malachi 3:10).

◆ Meditating on the Word of God:

And we have the word of the prophets made more certain, and you will do well to pay attention to it, as to a light shining in a dark place, until the day dawns and the morning star rises in your hearts (2 Peter 1:19).

And if the Spirit of Him who raised Jesus from the dead is living in you, He who raised Christ from the dead will also give life to your mortal bodies through His Spirit, who lives in you (Romans 8:11).

A Closed (Brass) Heaven

When there is no open Heaven, then there is no answer from God. When the Lord shuts the heavens over a place, His word and visions become rare:

"The days are coming," declares the Sovereign Lord, "when I will send a famine through the land—not a famine of food or a thirst for water, but a famine of hearing the words of the Lord. Men will stagger from sea to sea and wander from north to east, searching for the word of the Lord, but they will not find it (Amos 8:11-12).

Psalm 106 details what will cause closed heavens:

◆ "Not waiting or seeking the Lord," because those who wait upon the Lord shall renew their strength.

◆ When we forget the power of our testimony: "They soon forgot His work."

◆ "They did not wait for His counsel."

The Worst of All Famines: When the Word of the Lord Becomes Rare

When God withdraws visions and His words from a people, they experience the worst of all famines. This judgment from God stands above all others. Our God is holy, and whenever the level of iniquity gets high enough, then man becomes spiritually distanced from Him. In Israel's history as a nation, the people experienced the Lord's silence on many occasions. The Bible tells of a time when the Word of God was rare in Israel under the corrupt priesthood of Eli: *"The boy Samuel ministered before the Lord under Eli. In those days the word of the Lord was rare; there were not many visions"* (1 Sam. 3:1). The prophet Isaiah reiterated this when he said:

> *Surely the arm of the Lord is not too short to save, nor His ear too dull to hear. But your iniquities have separated you from your God; your sins have hidden His face from you, so that He will not hear* (Isaiah 59:1-2).

This is also emphasized in Proverbs:

> *If you had responded to my rebuke, I would have poured out my heart to you and made my thoughts known to you. But since you rejected me when I called and no one gave heed when I stretched out my hand, since you ignored all my advice and would not accept my rebuke, I in turn will laugh at your disaster; I will mock when calamity overtakes you— when calamity overtakes you like a storm, when disaster sweeps over you like a whirlwind, when distress and trouble overwhelm you. Then they will call to me but I will not answer; they will look for me but will not find me* (Proverbs 1:23-28).

Revelations and Open Heavens

As described in the Book of Revelation, the third Heaven is the highest place of prophetic revelation. All symbols used in this passage symbolize elements of the revelatory realm.

After this I looked, and there before me was a door standing open in heaven. And the voice I had first heard speaking to me like a trumpet said, "Come up here, and I will show you what must take place after this." At once I was in the Spirit, and there before me was a throne in heaven with someone sitting on it. And the one who sat there had the appearance of jasper and carnelian. A rainbow, resembling an emerald, encircled the throne. Surrounding the throne were twenty-four other thrones, and seated on them were twenty-four elders. They were dressed in white and had crowns of gold on their heads. From the throne came flashes of lightning, rumblings and peals of thunder. Before the throne, seven lamps were blazing. These are the seven spirits of God. Also before the throne there was what looked like a sea of glass, clear as crystal. In the center, around the throne, were four living creatures, and they were covered with eyes, in front and in back (Revelation 4:1-6).

CHAPTER 5

What Do Dreams and Visions Mean?

Why We Seek Meaning

Scripture has many examples of those who sought the meaning of their dreams. Therefore, it is biblical to seek understanding of a dream or vision. Many believe that since the Holy Spirit gives dream interpretations that they do not need to search for the meaning themselves. However, the Bible says, *"It is the glory of God to conceal a matter; to search out a matter is the glory of kings"* (Prov. 25:2).

God asked Gideon to go to the enemy's camp so as to hear a dream and its interpretation. The Lord can use *other people* to give us interpretation of *our* dreams in much the same way as *we* can do interpretations for others' dreams—by giving exposition of Scripture, even though the Holy Spirit is our teacher. It's important to build up a dictionary of dream symbols that God uses to communicate with you.

Inbuilt Divine Drive

Every dream comes with an inbuilt drive to search for the true meaning. This divine drive is not easily suppressed, no matter how hard you may try to ignore it, or how much others try to dissuade you from seeking its meaning. That desire can last for years, and it only fades once true interpretation has been found. This inbuilt drive reflects the divine premium placed on such a dream; its magnitude varies from dream to dream, according to the degree of divine premium placed on it by God. For this reason, some dreams are harder to ignore than others. The inbuilt drive was so powerful with King Nebuchadnezzar that he threatened to kill all the wise men, magicians, and diviners in his kingdom:

> *The astrologers answered the king, "There is not a man on earth who can do what the king asks! No king, however great and mighty, has ever asked such a thing of any magician or enchanter or astrologer. What the king asks is too difficult. No one can reveal it to the king except the gods, and they do not live among men." This made the king so angry and furious that he ordered the execution of all the wise men of Babylon. So the decree was issued to put the wise men to death, and men were sent to look for Daniel and his friends to put them to death* (Daniel 2:10-13).

Many people ask, "Why would a loving God speak to His children in 'obscure language,' which is difficult to understand because of its symbolism?" This question is reminiscent of what the disciples asked our Lord Jesus Christ during His earthly ministry:

> *Then the disciples came to Him and said, "Why do You speak to them in parables?" And He replied to them, "To you it has been given to know the secrets and mysteries of the kingdom of heaven, but to them it has not been given. For whoever has [spiritual knowledge], to him will more be given and he will have abundance; but from him who has not, even what he has will be taken away. This is the reason that I speak to them in parables: 'because having the power of seeing, they do not see; and having the power of hearing, they do not hear, nor do they grasp and understand'"* (Matthew 13:10-13 AMP).

When we seek a dream's meaning, we gain more spiritual knowledge, and keys of wisdom of life will be given to us. What is revealed belongs to us for our benefit, but a dream's benefits do not belong to us until its meaning is revealed: *"The secret things belong to the Lord our God, but the things revealed belong to us and to our children forever, that we may follow all the words of this law"* (Deut. 29:29). However, if we do not pursue the dream's meaning, the revelation may not benefit us.

The Cupbearer and the Baker: Our dreams create in us a desire to get an understanding, no matter what circumstances we are in or where we are geographically:

60

When Joseph came to them the next morning, he saw that they were dejected. So he asked Pharaoh's officials who were in custody with him in his master's house, "Why are your faces so sad today?" "We both had dreams," they answered, "but there is no one to interpret them." Then Joseph said to them, "Do not interpretations belong to God? Tell me your dreams" (Genesis 40:6-8).

Pharaoh: God reigns supreme, be it in a palace or prison dungeon. Therefore, it's no wonder that even the king of the most powerful state on earth needed answers to questions raised by his dreams:

In the morning his mind [Pharaoh] *was troubled, so he sent for all the magicians and wise men of Egypt. Pharaoh told them his dreams, but no one could interpret them for him.... So Pharaoh sent for Joseph, and he was quickly brought from the dungeon. When he had shaved and changed his clothes, he came before Pharaoh. Pharaoh said to Joseph, "I had a dream, and no one can interpret it. But I have heard it said of you that when you hear a dream you can interpret it." "I cannot do it," Joseph replied to Pharaoh, "but God will give Pharaoh the answer he desires"* (Genesis 41:8, 14-16).

Another powerful monarch—**King Nebuchadnezzar of Babylon**— also sought meaning of his dreams on four different occasions:

In the second year of his reign, Nebuchadnezzar had dreams; his mind was troubled and he could not sleep. So the king summoned the magicians, enchanters, sorcerers and astrologers to tell him what he had dreamed. When they came in and stood before the king, he said to them, "I have had a dream that troubles me and I want to know what it means" (Daniel 2:1-3; also see Daniel 2:16 and 4:18).

King Belshazzar was another ruler of the great kingdom of Babylon, who also sought interpretation of a puzzle or a divine riddle:

Suddenly the fingers of a human hand appeared and wrote on the plaster of the wall, near the lampstand in the royal palace. The king watched the hand as it wrote. His face turned pale and he was so frightened that his knees knocked together and his legs gave way.... "Now I have heard that you [Daniel] *are able to give interpretations and to solve difficult problems. If you can read this writing and tell me what it means, you will be clothed in purple and have a gold chain placed around your neck, and you will be made the third highest ruler in the kingdom"* (Daniel 5:5-6,16).

How to Confirm the Meaning of a Dream

Confirmation can be defined as hearing further from God regarding the meaning of a particular dream. First off, there is the "inner witness," which is a covert knowledge of a dream's meaning that exists within the actual dreamer's mind. This knowledge is what confirms an interpretation as either correct or incorrect. Confirmation of a dream interpretation can occur in a variety of ways because God has made each one of us divinely unique.

Depending on circumstance, God can confirm interpretation in many different ways, including hearing further on the subject through God's audible voice or through an inner voice, other dreams and visions, and even mental pictures to inner impressions. No matter how we hear from God, we can become more receptive to His voice and more attentive to His ways through prayer, fasting, meditation, worship, and studying Scripture. Confirmation can also happen through prophets, other forms of prophecy, events (past or ongoing), and God's other revelatory means, including recurring dreams. Here's what to *avoid* in the process of confirming whether a dream interpretation is correct:

◆ The danger of over-spiritualizing matters. Be alert and wait upon the Holy Spirit: He will quicken you as to what is important.

◆ The danger of becoming too "sign dependent." Romans 1:17 (NKJV) states, *"The just shall live by faith."* To demand a sign at every stage is to doubt God or lack boldness to act on your belief. The Bible tells us that faith without works is dead (see James 2:17). Gideon was too sign-dependent:

Gideon replied, "If now I have found favor in Your eyes, give me a sign that it is really You talking to me."...Gideon said to God, "If You will save Israel by my hand as You have promised—look, I will place a wool fleece on the threshing floor. If there is dew only on the fleece and all the ground is dry, then I will know that You will save Israel by my hand, as You said." And that is what happened. Gideon rose early the next day; he squeezed the fleece and wrung out the dew—a bowlful of water. Then Gideon said to God, "Do not be angry with me. Let me make just one more request. Allow me one more test with the fleece. This time make the fleece dry and the ground covered with dew." That night God did so. Only the fleece was dry; all the ground was covered with dew (Judges 6:17, 36-40).

◆ Failing to act on your dream for lack of details. The fullness of a dream will unfold with time as you obey and let the Lord lead.

The Role of the Holy Spirit

All true dreams and visions come from God. Through the Holy Spirit's help, a dreamer is able to interact with God in a dream and to handle what is received. A true dream is the divinely coded parable language of God. Anyone without the Holy Spirit cannot understand this language, even if it appears to be simple.

…Then Pharaoh woke up; it had been a dream. In the morning his mind was troubled, so he sent for all the magicians and wise men of Egypt. Pharaoh told them his dreams, but no one could interpret them for him (Genesis 41:7-8).

This is what we speak, not in words taught us by human wisdom but in words taught by the Spirit, expressing spiritual truths in spiritual words. The man without the Spirit does not accept the things that come from the Spirit of God, for they are foolishness to him, and he cannot understand them, because they are spiritually discerned (1 Corinthians 2:13-14).

True dreams, as parables of God, require the Holy Spirit's help for understanding them. They reflect the ways of God, so, therefore, they transcend the limits of human understanding. Jesus' disciples were clearly puzzled by the extensive symbolism and parabolic language that He taught in. Like most of us, they asked Him for an explanation. Jesus explained meanings to them in private and also promised that the Holy Spirit would help them know what they might not have understood:

All this I have spoken while still with you. But the Counselor, the Holy Spirit, whom the Father will send in My name, will teach you all things and will remind you of everything I have said to you (John 14:25-26).

Therefore, it is scriptural to seek the understanding of a dream whose meaning may not immediately be clear.

How the Holy Spirit Helps Us to Interpret Dreams

In my experience, the Holy Spirit can enable us to interpret a dream in three ways:

1. *By giving a word of knowledge regarding God's mind in sending the dream*

   A majority of Christians are enabled to gain insight into their dreams by using this means. This is also how God commonly answers prayers when we ask Him for the meaning of our dreams. In the Scriptures, most angelic interpretations given in response to a dreamer's prayers came in this form.

2. *By the gift of interpretation*

   This is an offshoot of a gift of wisdom from the Holy Spirit, and it's a sovereign gift by the Lord.

3. *By acquiring the interpretative skills*

   Every dreamer needs these skills in addition to the above two gifts. Interpretation is a studied art made sharper by practice, yet few Christians consider acquiring this wonderful skill to be worthwhile. Yet it's a great resource in gaining some understanding of dreams. Whether you are gifted in interpretation or not, all of us need to be able to properly expound on the relevance of symbols to a dreamer's life.

Hidden Meaning in Dreams and Visions

The hidden things of God—which are beyond human understanding by natural reasoning—are purposely sealed by the Holy Spirit until a set time. Every dreamer will have many of these dreams. Unless the Lord reveals their meaning, they remain obscured to man.

A "Daniel-type anointing" is the ability to understand all types of dreams and visions in which God releases meaning to man. In dream interpretation, a "Daniel-type anointing" also requires a person to have the humility needed to recognize when a hidden meaning exists and to ask God for its understanding. Daniel had many personal dreams and visions with hidden meanings. This dependency helps keep the gifted interpreter in humble submission to the Holy Spirit.

In one instance, an angel revealed a hidden meaning to Daniel:

While I, Daniel, was watching the vision and trying to understand it, there before me stood one who looked like a man. And I heard a man's voice from the Ulai calling, "Gabriel, tell this man the meaning of the vision" (Daniel 8:15-16).

In other instances, Daniel acknowledged that only God knows what has been hidden in the dark:

...Then Daniel praised the God of heaven and said: "Praise be to the name of God for ever and ever; wisdom and power are His. He changes times and seasons; He sets up kings and deposes them. He gives wisdom to the wise and knowledge to the discerning. He reveals deep and hidden things; He knows what lies in darkness, and light dwells with Him" (Daniel 2:19-22).

I heard, but I did not understand. So I asked, "My lord, what will the outcome of all this be?" He replied, "Go your way, Daniel, because the words are closed up and sealed until the time of the end. Many will be purified, made spotless and refined, but the wicked will continue to be wicked. None of the wicked will understand, but those who are wise will understand" (Daniel 12:8-10).

Daniel probably had interpretations for all the dreams that people brought to him, but he was humble enough to recognize meanings hidden within his own dreams. The first step in gaining understanding of the hidden meaning of dreams is to do as Daniel did: Have a desire to gain understanding and then ask God to reveal it.

I, Daniel, was troubled in spirit, and the visions that passed through my mind disturbed me. I approached one of those standing there and asked him the true meaning of all this. So he told me and gave me the interpretation of these things (Daniel 7:15-16).

Satan's Role in Dreams and Visions

The Bible does not have any scriptural example of dreams being sent by the devil. All through the Bible, the devil and his agents could not interpret dreams of the kings of Egypt and Babylon. They were probably unable to understand because the key to understanding and interpreting dreams belongs to God. The Holy Spirit explains dreams to man, who would otherwise be unable to get the true meaning of dreams because they are divinely sealed.

Also, nightmares are not necessarily from the devil. The fact that a dream is terrifying does not mean that it is not from God. This is what the Bible says:

> For God [does reveal His will; He] speaks not only once, but more than once, even though men do not regard it [including you, Job]. [One may hear God's voice] in a dream, in a vision of the night, when deep sleep falls on men while slumbering upon the bed. Then He opens the ears of men and seals their instruction **[terrifying them with warnings]**. That He may withdraw man from his purpose and cut off pride from him [disgusting him with his own disappointing self-sufficiency]. He holds him back from the pit [of destruction], and his life from perishing by the sword [of God's destructive judgments] (Job 33:14-18 AMP).

The Book of Revelation, with all its graphic and rather terrifying imagery, is the revelation of the future of the Church, coming out from the very throne of God Himself. Ezekiel was taken in the spirit by God and shown demonic activities among the spiritual leaders of Israel. The Lord gave Ezekiel this vision, even though it was full of demonic activities.

> And He said to me, "Go in and see the wicked and detestable things they are doing here." So I went in and looked, and I saw portrayed all over the walls all kinds of crawling things and detestable animals and all the idols of the house of Israel. In front of them stood seventy elders of the house of Israel, and Jaazaniah son of Shaphan was standing among them. Each had a censer in his hand, and a fragrant cloud of incense was rising. He said to me, "Son of man, have you seen what the elders of the house of Israel are doing in the darkness, each at the shrine of his own idol?"... (Ezekiel 8:9-12)

However, evil does exist in dreams, just as it did in the Garden of Eden. The devil can cause corruption, confusion, and distortion of truths. Satan showed up in one of Zechariah's visions:

> Then he showed me Joshua the high priest standing before the angel of the Lord, **and Satan standing at his right side to accuse him.**

The Lord said to Satan, "The Lord rebuke you, Satan! The Lord, who has chosen Jerusalem, rebuke you! Is not this man a burning stick snatched from the fire?" (Zechariah 3:1-2)

Despite the fact that about one-third of the Bible deals with dreams and visions, there is no scriptural evidence of dreams or visions being sent by the devil.

In her book, *Parables in the Night Seasons*, Joy Parrott writes:

One of the greatest surprises I found during my in-depth study of the scriptures was that nowhere does it say that Satan can directly give us dreams. However, what I have found is that he can influence us in our hearts or soul area. [1]

I believe that every meaningful experience in the spirit—or any establishing doctrine on spiritual issues, for that matter—should be Bible-guided. Otherwise, we run the risk of falling into deception and hollow philosophy.

---

1. Joy Parrott, *Parables in the Night Seasons—Understanding Your Dreams* (Kent, WA: Glory Publications, 2002), 37.

CHAPTER 6

The Art of Hearing
the Voice of God

God speaks to us in many ways. And no matter how He decides to speak, it is important that we hear the voice of God for ourselves. Hearing God's voice is not an option, but a bare necessity of life. It's an indispensable survival tool to navigate the intrigues of life. Our relationship with God is, first and foremost, dependent upon our ability to hear and discern His voice. Many perish because they cannot hear God's voice, and, therefore, are unable to usher His counsel into the realities of their lives.

Job was a righteous man of outstanding reputation. Regarding him the Bible says, *"Then the Lord said to Satan, 'Have you considered My servant Job? There is no one on earth like him; he is blameless and upright, a man who fears God and shuns evil'"* (Job 1:8). Nevertheless, this great and righteous man suffered and, most notably, failed to hear the voice of God on a personal level. Job was rightly wrapped up with circumstances of his natural existence, but he suffered consequences from a lack of prophetic insight.

Our greatest asset in life is our ability to hear God's voice on a personal level. We are all called to prophetic lifestyles and to live the supernatural in our natural lives. I believe that the wishes of Moses are being fulfilled in this generation. For Moses said, *"I wish that all the Lord's people were prophets and that the Lord would put His Spirit on them"* (Num. 11:29). We must seize the momentum and be partakers in this glorious fulfillment. More than anything else, true dreams speak to the dreamer on a personal level.

We can hear God's voice in a variety of ways: through the Bible; in dreams; in visions; experiencing trances, visitations, and translations; through His audible voice or through other people. No matter how we hear His voice, we need to confirm that what we have heard is from God. Many voices exist in the spirit world, but God's voice will be recognizable if our spirit bears witness, if it lines up with Scripture, and if it speaks of His love.

True dreams are the indirect voice of God on a personal level. These are His parable language in a personalized, coded message full of symbols that are often embedded with His mysteries. In dreams and visions, He communicates with us in very individualistic forms usually taken from our life experiences and personal traits.

Other Ways of Hearing the Voice of God

The Logos and Rhema Word of God

The *logos* Word (the written Bible) is what God is saying to everyone, but what He says to an individual on a personal level is the *rhema* word of God. *"In the past God spoke to our forefathers through the prophets at many times and in various ways, but in these last days He has spoken to us by His Son"* (Heb. 1:1-2). This Son is Jesus Christ, who is the Word of God. A *rhema* word is an inspired word of God birthed within your own spirit, like the still small voice that spoke to Elijah in the cave (see 1 Kings 19). The strategy for breakthrough in any circumstance lies in discerning the *rhema* word for that particular situation.

In Luke 5:4, Peter received a breakthrough by heeding a *rhema* word for his life: *"When He [Christ] had finished speaking, He said to Simon, 'Put out into deep water, and let down the nets for a catch.'"* Note that after Jesus finished speaking generally, He spoke personally to Peter to launch out into the deep. Peter had the choice whether or not to obey. After all, Peter was a fisherman and—after having labored all night without success—he had every reason not to obey. Many questions must have passed through his mind, as they would for any of us under similar circumstances. Perhaps, he wondered, "What is the point? What does a carpenter know about fishing?" Besides, fishing was better done at night, and Jesus spoke to Peter during the daytime.

Despite all these potential reasons, Peter complied. He let down the nets and caught an incredibly large number of fish, so much so that the boat almost capsized. The principle here is that Peter's ability to discern what the Lord was saying to him on a personal level resulted in this miraculous catch of fish. That was the point at which Peter began to realize the deep things of God. From that moment onwards, he surrendered the frailty of his human mind to the sovereignty and superior wisdom of Almighty God. *"When Simon Peter saw this, he fell at Jesus' knees and said, 'Go away from me, Lord; I am a sinful man!'"* (Luke 5:8). It's little wonder that Peter was entrusted with leadership of the early Church in the Book of Acts.

Faith Is Required in Order to Hear in the Spirit

The Book of Revelation repeatedly says, *"He who has an ear, let him hear what the Spirit says to the churches"* (Rev. 2:17). The Spirit obviously has a voice, and in order to hear His voice, we must use spiritual ears (also called the ears of faith). However, this does not come to us naturally in this world of logic and reasoning. It is difficult not to place undue reliance on our perceptive senses, as they are used to navigate challenges in the physical realm. Yet I am reminded that we must *"fix our eyes not on what is seen, but on what is unseen. For what is seen is temporary, but what is unseen is eternal"* (2 Cor. 4:18). Ultimately, *faith* is intricately connected and central to hearing God's voice.

Inner Witness

The inner witness is also essential to the art of hearing from God. You must learn to pay attention to the inner witness in order to hear what the Spirit says. The voice of God comes with peace, and it's always easier to discern when we are spiritually minded and living in a godly way.

The Different Ways of Hearing From God

There are various ways of hearing from God. Some people are hearers, some are seers, some are feelers, and others are able to discern what the Spirit is saying. However, once the voice of the Spirit is heard and tested, it should prompt us to take necessary action.

The Many Voices of the Spirit World

Many voices exist in the spirit world. Therefore, whatever is heard must be tested: Does it exalt Jesus Christ? Does it comply with the Scriptures? Does it put the interest of others before self-interest? Does it encourage unity in the Body of Christ? Does it seek peace of all? Does it give hope no matter what it speaks of? Does it have respect for human life? Does it speak of the love of God? The answers to these questions will help distinguish the voice of God from other voices.

> *But solid food belongs to those who are of full age, that is, those who by reason of use have their senses exercised to discern both good and evil* (Hebrews 5:14 NKJV).

Maturity in the spirit only comes through a process of consistently using our spiritual senses. This principle applies in the natural—as explained in Hebrews 5:14—as well as in the spiritual. Mature believers are those who—through consistent exercise of their spiritual senses—can discriminate between sound and unsound doctrines and between wholesome and unwholesome conduct. The only way to grow in God is to learn to walk with God. If we are afraid of misunderstanding what God says, then we will never master the art of hearing God and walking in His obedience. We need to approach the issue with reverence and realize that no man shall prevail by strength.

Hearing from God must begin where we are, and then gradually progress forward toward maturity. Divine inspiration may occur to us as a mere impression, or perhaps a prompting, such as a flash of ideas, a picture, a birthing in the spirit, or even a knowing in our conviction. However, we require maturity to distinguish what is of God and what is not. Our only security in this process lies in walking in love and in realizing that we should come to God just as little children come to a natural father—with transparent innocence and simplicity. In other words, stepping out in faith will move us from the stage of impression into greater spiritual encounters with divinity.

The Part of Man That God Speaks To

To clearly hear what God is saying, you have to strengthen your spirit to receive correctly. A man is only as strong as his spirit is. God said, *"Let Us make man in Our image, according to*

Our likeness" (Gen. 1:26 NKJV) and also, *"And the Lord God formed man of the dust of the ground, and breathed into his nostrils the breath of life; and man became a living being"* (Gen. 2:7 NKJV). Therefore, God's breath is the center of man's life. Clearly, man is a spiritual being since God is Spirit. The breath of God lives in everyone as the human spirit—this part of man is in the likeness of God. This breath of life comes as a package to every human being and contains the seed of our destiny. This is the part of man that bears witness with the Spirit of God; He always speaks to our potentials.

However, the spirit of man lives in a *body* and has a *soul;* these two components of man sometimes interfere with the ability to hear the voice of God, who is Spirit. The body—which consists of flesh, bone, and blood—houses the soul and the spirit; ultimately, it will return to the dust of the ground upon physical death. The soul—the part of man that allows interaction between the body and spirit—consists of the mind, emotion, and will; therefore, it is not physically tangible, but instead refers to the zone immediately surrounding the human consciousness. In the Garden of Eden, the soul and the body were completely ruled by the spirit.

At the Fall, the soul of humanity became prominent when he chose to disobey God, and the Bible says, *"then the eyes of both of them were opened"* (Gen. 3:7). Mankind acquired knowledge, but also hidden in the package was the curse of separation from God. In scriptural terms, the body and soul together—without rule of the spirit—is referred to as *flesh* or *carnal nature.*

A strong human spirit enhances the art of hearing God. Prior to the fall, humanity enjoyed unbroken communion with God in the Garden of Eden. This experience was most definitely a special spiritual encounter, which led to an experiential knowledge of God. Before the Fall, humanity lived and worshiped God in a state of near spiritual purity, as they lived according to the law of the Spirit of life. Man literally lived in a state that could be described as the realm of God.

Prepare Yourself to Hear From God

The spirit is the center of man, and it consists of "communion, conscience, and wisdom":

1. **Communion**: the power derived from dwelling in His Presence (see Psalm 16, 91).

2. **Conscience**: the ability to discern; innate ability to know wrong or right; that which has been sanctified by the blood of Jesus (see Heb. 9:14).

3. **Wisdom**: life's application of the Word of God (see James 3:17), which is also called wisdom from above.

After the Fall, the reality of our Christian walk is that man's soul and spirit are pitted against each other in a conflict of warfare. *"For the flesh lusts against the Spirit, and the Spirit against the flesh; and these are contrary to one another, so that you do not do the things that you wish"* (Gal. 5:17 NKJV). The dynamics of this conflict are such that when the soul becomes prominent, the spirit gets diminished and vice versa. Therefore, when the spirit breaks through and shines, the soul becomes diminished. When your spirit is strong, then you are able to correctly hear and discern what God is saying. In order to strengthen our spirit man, we should train and exercise the spirit. The Bible says,

> *Don't waste time arguing over foolish ideas and silly myths and legends. Spend your time and energy in the exercise of keeping spiritually fit. Bodily exercise is all right, but spiritual exercise is much more important and is a tonic for all you do. So exercise yourself spiritually, and practice being a better Christian because that will help you not only now in this life, but in the next life too* (1 Timothy 4:7-8 TLB).

Whenever we spend time with God, we become less emotional; the more we apply the Word of God (which is divine wisdom), the less we depend on human will. The more we use our sanctified conscience—which means laying aside personal agendas and learning to prefer the interest of others—the less dependent we become on the human mind and the rule of head knowledge. This relationship is like a tug-of-war: communion versus emotion; conscience versus mind; and wisdom versus will. On the whole, a strong spirit enhances the art of hearing God.

Putting Off the Voice of the Mind

To truly understand what God is saying, you must be able to distinguish between voices of the mind and the voice of the spirit. The voice of the mind is one of busyness of life's routines; it echoes the triumphs, failures, sorrows, joy, worries, and contentment of daily living. To be able to hear the Spirit's voice on a consistent basis, we need to renew and continuously sanctify our mind.

Also, a strong personality will resist the voice of the Spirit and distort what God is saying. The will is humanity's decision-making venue, while emotion is the relational venue. Emotionally ruled flesh is carnality; it opposes the Spirit and prevents us from hearing and discerning God's voice. Our emotions must be controlled; otherwise our feelings will influence how we hear or see spiritually.

It is the birthright of every born-again Christian to hear God on a personal level, whether through His audible voice, dreams and visions, or the eternal Word of God.

CHAPTER 7

Time to Return to Biblical Perspectives of Dreams and Visions

Now is the time to return to scriptural perspectives of dreams and visions. But remember that *what is personally descriptive should not be taken as generally prescriptive*. God deals with each of us in unique, diverse ways. As we know, God's ways are anchored on His Word.

Paul warns us:

I tell you this so that no one may deceive you by fine-sounding arguments... See to it that no one takes you captive through hollow and deceptive philosophy, which depends on human tradition and the basic principles of this world rather than on Christ. For in Christ all the fullness of the Deity lives in bodily form... (Colossians 2:4, 8-9).

Extra-Biblical Spiritual Experiences

To redeem dreams and visions to their proper place in God's purposes, we must realize that extra-biblical experiences may be true spiritual experiences. Therefore, we should regard them as valuable, but not generally prescriptive; otherwise, some people will chase after what are uniquely personalized dealings of God in other people's lives. Therefore, every experience in one's dreams and visions should be Bible-guided, with a realization that God can move in a new way, but only for experiential knowledge—it's not to be taken as doctrine.

Dreams and visions are valuable tools in the next stage of divine advancement in God's kingdom. Evil has multiplied exponentially, and worldly wisdom has grown astronomically. Consequently, there's an emerging need for us to have accuracy in spiritual matters so we can match any challenges in this perilous time. These days are like when God heralded Jesus Christ's birth and ministry with a series of short, clear, and directional dreams, visions, and angelic interactions. More than ever before, we cannot afford to face today's challenges with yesterday's mandate. On a daily basis, we need a fresh mandate. If God so desires, dreams and visions are particularly unique in keeping us in tune with the Father's heart, particularly when most other methods have failed.

For those in the secular world, audio-visual aides are indispensable tools for effective communication. In like manner, we can equate dreams and visions as divine, audio-visual, strategic dialogues; these have lingering impact on dreamers in a way that words alone cannot. More than that, the visual impact brings a dreamer into a degree of faith, which leads to conviction and commitment that's hard to ignore.

The Dispensational Patterns and Future Shapes of Dreams

The evolving history of dreams over periods recorded in the Bible need a proper understanding, especially if we are to appreciate changing patterns of dreams that will occur as God pours out His Spirit on all flesh. In my mind, we can liken this to a "dispensational pattern" of dreams and visions; this refers to historical periods of dream-communication, when God communicated with man according to a particular spiritual closeness, with clarity, interaction, and angelic involvement. Also, during each period, God gave a variable degree of wisdom, grace, and special attributes to the dreamers. I have arbitrarily chosen these periods in Bible history to help me illustrate my points in this discourse.

Garden of Eden Era

In this age of innocence, mankind enjoyed an immortal life in God's realm. Man was also capable of direct and unbroken communion and fellowship with God. Natural senses had not been "opened." *"The man and his wife were both naked, and they felt no shame"* (Gen. 2:25). Spiritual senses were more active than the natural senses. In this state of near spiritual purity, man could also communicate with the devil without fear. Evil existed on earth, but man had no knowledge of it. Because of unbroken communion with God, there was no need for dreams or visions; man experienced life in a direct fellowship with God.

Following the Fall, man lost that heightened level of spirituality and unbroken intimacy with God. Eventually, dreams and visions emerged to allow us opportunity once again to experience life in God's realm. During unbroken fellowship with God, emotions, mind-sets, and the human will (with its ambitions, goals, and expectations) all get bypassed. These factors of an "activated soul" are what hinder and corrupt reception and understanding of God's mysteries in the natural world.

From the Fall of Man to the Time of Abraham

During this period death became inevitable as a consequence of disobedience to God. As man fell, his spiritual senses became dampened and the activated soul assumed pre-eminence. The Fall opened a door to the knowledge of good and evil, which started a thought process of logic that has continued to grow ever since. Direct fellowship with God was no longer possible in an unbroken manner. Humanity also became more limited in relationship to time. Lucid, interactive dreams and visions emerged and were frequent. God also spoke audibly and sent messages through angelic interaction. In Genesis 15, Abraham had an interactive dream in which he dialogued with God about his covenant.

After the Death of Abraham to Present Age

Progressively, sin and wickedness multiplied. Mankind's soul grew astronomically as humanity ran after the wisdom of this world. In the Book of Daniel, the Bible says, *"But you, Daniel, close up and seal the words of the scroll until the time of the end. Many will go here and there to increase knowledge"* (Dan. 12:4).

Lucid dreaming and interaction in dreams became rare occurrences. As modern lies about dreams escalated, many people treated them as omens. Dreams began being used in ungodly ways, such as with the sin of divination. (Consequently, there emerged a corresponding lack of appreciation and awareness for dreams/visions and the Joseph- and Daniel-type anointing). God began speaking to humanity more in symbolic language and parables. God coded dream messages to hide them from worldly people and the devil. (This is also why Jesus Christ said in Matthew 13:11, *"The knowledge of the secrets of the kingdom of heaven has been given to you, but not to them* [the heathen].*"*) Instead, He revealed their meaning by the Holy Spirit only to His children, who are those with receptive hearts. One example of a message concealed in extensive symbolism occurs when an angel spoke to the prophet Zechariah (see Zech. 4).

The Days Ahead

I believe that the coming days will see a return to interactive dreams, dialoguing in dreams, and more trances, translations, and angelic encounters. This will be the time for a fulfillment of the prophecy given by the prophet Joel, which was again reiterated by the apostle Peter:

> *In the last days, God says, I will pour out My Spirit on all people. Your sons and daughters will prophesy, your young men will see visions, your old men will dream dreams. Even on My servants, both men and women, I will pour out My Spirit in those days, and they will prophesy* (Acts 2:17-18).

It is my opinion that knowledge of God's glory permeating the air will multiply the number and clarity of dreams and visions. This time will also see a marked increase in an awareness of angelic ministry. Habakkuk 2:14 states, *"For the earth will be filled with the knowledge of the glory of the Lord, as the waters cover the sea."* The Spirit of God poured out upon all flesh will result in an increase of experiential knowledge of God. There will be an increase in dreams, with lucidity and interaction in an atmosphere of more awareness of the supernatural. At the same time, God will reawaken the Joseph- and Daniel-type anointing. Speaking of Daniel, the Bible says, *"And Daniel could understand visions and dreams of all kinds"* (Dan. 1:17). God will once again bring men and women to this level of great insightful knowledge through the Holy Spirit's help.

DEVELOPING DREAM LIFE AND INTERPRETATION

PART II

CHAPTER 8

Advanced Understanding of Dreams and Visions

Before the Fall, man had perpetual, direct communication with God. God came down in the cool of the evening to fellowship with Adam and Eve: *"Then the man and his wife heard the sound of the Lord God as He was walking in the garden in the cool of the day"* (Gen. 3:8).

After the Fall, however, man was separated from that heightened level of intimacy with God. Thus, it became necessary to somehow reach out to God. What resulted was a gradual emergence of indirect means of communication such as dreams and visions. Soon, it became evident also that men ought to pray. The need to call on God's name became obvious; as we read in Genesis 4:26, the time came when *"men began to call on the name of the Lord."*

Dreams and visions gained relevance as man became spiritually distant from his perpetual stay in God's experiential presence. Over the years, this spiritual distance from a state of unbroken communion with God has grown larger. Immediately after the Fall, for instance, man was still spiritually close enough to God to intermittently experience His realm in a direct manner.

That relationship is evident with the frequent occurrences of lucid and interactive dreams and great supernatural awareness that existed immediately after the Fall. But, sadly, the reality and likelihood of experiencing such life in God's realm continues to decrease as evil increases in the world. As a result, direct communication with God has progressively become more restricted, while lucid and interactive dreaming has become even more rare.

The prevalence of lucid dreams and interactive dreams reflects the amount of God's glory available in an environment, as well as the dreamer's giftedness and quality of lifestyle. In the days to come, the full extent of Joel's prophecy will only be truly appreciated on the basis of this understanding. When God pours His Spirit on all flesh, His glory will permeate the atmosphere. Not only will dreams and visions increase in number, but so will the clarity and ability to interact with God in dreams. The prophet Habakkuk spoke of these days when he said, *"For the earth will be filled with the knowledge of the glory of the Lord, as the waters cover the sea"* (Hab. 2:14).

Modern Lies About Dreams

The superstitious attitude regarding dreams stems from the fact that they are available to all of humanity, including those heathen without the Holy Spirit. Some non-believers treat dreams as omens and seek to utilize them outside God's purposes. Using spiritual principles in an ungodly way is called divination. In *The Parables of Jesus*, Dr. R.T. Kendall writes:

> *A parable may be defined as a simple story that illustrates a profound truth. Telling parables was Jesus' main way of helping His followers grasp spiritual truths. He was building a bridge from the natural to the spiritual. It was Jesus' way of helping people to make the transition that each of us must make every day of our life—to move from the natural level of life to the spiritual level of life. Jesus revealed these insights through parables so that those for whom the truth was intended might know the meaning, but those for whom it was not intended would not understand.* [1]

> *The disciples came to Him and asked, "Why do You speak to the people in parables?" He replied, "The knowledge of the secrets of the kingdom of heaven has been given to you, but not to them* [heathen]*"* (Matthew 13:10-11).

The abuse and resultant misconception of the nature of dreams—which is due to a lack of understanding—should not diminish the value of this awesome means of communicating with God.

"Seals Their Instruction"

*[One may hear God's voice] in a dream, in a vision of the night, when deep sleep falls on men while slumbering upon the bed. Then He opens the ears of men and **seals their instruction** [terrifying them with warnings]* (Job 33:15-16 AMP).

Every dream comes with meaning to man's spirit, but this meaning remains hidden to the dreamer's mind until unfolded by the Spirit of God. This is why the dreamer is the only one who can tell when an interpretation is correct; in tales of Pharaoh and Nebuchadnezzar's dreams, interpretations were given by other people, but these kings could recognize a true interpretation when presented with one. The Lord seals dream instruction and only the Spirit of God can unfold it, no matter how simple the dream might seem. As the Bible says, interpretation belongs to God.

The Indirect Voice of God

A dream is the indirect voice of God in a world spiritually distant from experiencing the reality of the Almighty God's presence. In *The Coming Prophetic Revolution,* Jim Goll defines dreams as: "The inspired pictures and impressions given to the heart, while one is sleeping. These are given by the Holy Spirit in order to teach, exhort, reveal, warm, cleanse or heal."[2]

I believe that this understanding helps set dreams in a correct perspective.

The Dreamer's Immediate Setting

Elements and symbolic actions in dreams come out of settings in the dreamer's life, especially immediate circumstances. At times, a dream reaches far beyond the dreamer's conscious experience, perhaps even far into the future. Therefore, truly grasping the message in a dream means examining it from the prevailing setting of a dreamer's life. This is the framework by which God gives a crucial message that may reach far beyond the dreamer's immediate consciousness.

In my experience, a great majority of dream messages are allegorized within a dreamer's immediate circumstance. In a similar vein, most biblical dreams also featured similar allegories. Perhaps that is why the Bible says, *"As a dream comes when there are many cares…"* (Eccles. 5:3). To my mind, this is the most appropriate translation of this verse. Nowhere is it truer than in dream life—if you pay attention to something, you will make room for it. This may also explain why a great percentage of our dreams are on personal issues. But you can widen the scope of your dream-coverage by making room for other people in your prayer life.

Issues that preoccupy our minds can play out in our dreams, but they do not cause dreams to happen. God uses what is prominent in a dreamer's mind to allegorize circumstances, events, and personalities of the dream's message. God revealed to King Nebuchadnezzar what was yet to happen because of thoughts in his heart: *"As you were lying there, O king, your mind turned to things to come, and the revealer of mysteries showed you what is going to happen"* (Dan. 2:29). Peter's groundbreaking vision about global expansion of God's kingdom to include Gentiles was predicated on his hunger at the time. Hunger did not cause the vision, but it did allegorize the vision's message while the heavens opened over him.

> *He saw heaven opened and something like a large sheet being let down to earth by its four corners. It contained all kinds of four-footed animals, as well as reptiles of the earth and birds of the air. Then a voice told him, "Get up, Peter. Kill and eat." "Surely not, Lord!" Peter replied. "I have never eaten anything impure or unclean." The voice spoke to him a second time, "Do not call anything impure that God has made clean." This happened three times, and immediately the sheet was taken back to heaven* (Acts 10:11-16).

Daniel was praying about the prophecy of Jeremiah when God sent an angel to reveal its fulfillment in a vision.

> *In the first year of Darius son of Xerxes (a Mede by descent), who was made ruler over the Babylonian kingdom—in the first year of his reign, I, Daniel, understood from the Scriptures, according to the word of the Lord given to Jeremiah the prophet, that the desolation of Jerusalem would last seventy years. So I turned to the Lord God and pleaded with Him in prayer and petition, in fasting, and in sackcloth and ashes. I prayed to the Lord my God and confessed: "O Lord, the great and awesome God, who keeps His covenant of love with all who love Him and obey His commands".… While I was speaking and praying, confessing my sin and the sin of my people Israel and making my request to the Lord my God for His holy hill—while I was still in prayer,*

Gabriel, the man I had seen in the earlier vision, came to me in swift flight about the time of the evening sacrifice. He instructed me and said to me, "Daniel, I have now come to give you insight and understanding. As soon as you began to pray, an answer was given, which I have come to tell you, for you are highly esteemed. Therefore, consider the message and understand the vision..."(Daniel 9:1-4, 20-23).

Every True Dream Has Value

Although some dreams may bear more immediate significance than others, I do not believe that a throwaway true dream exists. We tend to judge the value of a dream sent by God within limits of our reasoning or knowledge. But that means using our limited, natural wisdom to judge revelation of divine origin and superior wisdom. Some dreams do not immediately mean much to us because we lack understanding. For instance, a dream's significance may only become apparent after we experience events that God revealed to us ahead of time in the dream. Also, the value of a soul dream is that it reveals hidden intents of our hearts. One value of demonic dreams is that they give revelation about activities and plans of satan.

The Heart Condition of the Dreamer

The influence of a dreamer's heart condition is profound and can radically color what is received in a dream. Sometimes what we dream about reflects the intents of our hearts, especially as God exposes whether it hinders or lines up His will in our lives. The Bible says, *"A person who is pure of heart sees goodness and purity in everything; but a person whose own heart is evil and untrusting finds evil in everything, for his dirty mind and rebellious heart color all he sees and hears"* (Titus 1:15 TLB).

Blind Spots

Dreams may reveal blind spots in our thinking. In dreams, God bypasses our logic—our preconceived notions and other obstacles of our conscious mind—to connect with our spirit, which is the center of man. Like a mirror, perhaps, a dream may have most relevance when it reflects what is wrong with us. Yet, this is often where we misunderstand our dreams. Most people struggle when dreams expose and address blind spots in their thinking.

The danger in deciding that some dreams are valid and others are not comes when we choose dreams that we like and discard ones we dislike. This is a dangerous practice because we are bound to lose valuable instructions from God. A true dream is a message from God specifically designed and coded in personal symbolism. God uses dreams to get through to us when other avenues may have failed.

How Dreams Eventually Fade

When a dream has fulfilled its purpose, it fades from our consciousness. Until that time, it can last for years while waiting for its divine timing. However, if we neglect the dreams, the divine premium placed on them—which drives us to look for its meaning and attain its fulfillment—can be withdrawn; therefore, it gradually fades from the mind. While the divine premium placed on a revelation may fade if neglected, the substance of that revelation remains valid. *"Through your own fault you will lose the inheritance I gave you"* (Jer. 17:4).

> *If at any time I announce that a nation or kingdom is to be uprooted, torn down and destroyed, and if that nation I warned repents of its evil, then I will relent and not inflict on it the disaster I had planned. And if at another time I announce that a nation or kingdom is to be built up and planted, and if it does evil in My sight and does not obey Me, then I will reconsider the good I had intended to do for it* (Jeremiah 18:7-10).

In my experience, warning dreams have short-lived premium and are meant to guide us through certain events in life. Once this has passed, we should know that the warning is no longer relevant and should not live in perpetual fear. However, wisdom derived from such an experience may apply to other situations in life.

---

1. R.T. Kendall, *The Parables of Jesus: A Guide to Understanding and Applying the Stories of Jesus* (Sovereign World, 2004), 12.

2. Jim Goll, *The Coming Prophetic Revolution* (Grand Rapids, MI: Chosen Books, 2001), 292.

CHAPTER 9

How to Respond to
Your Dreams and Visions

God's major purpose in giving dreams is for us to respond appropriately on earth to what He is doing in Heaven. You should pray for all the elements, events, and persons within a dream, even before you gain understanding of its meaning. The next useful step is to record the dream and pay attention to whether God is warning, encouraging, or correcting.

The following are the steps that I normally take in responding to my dreams.

Steps to Take

◆ Allow peace to reign in your mind immediately upon waking up. Avoid emotional backlash. Then ask God what you have seen in the night, while also maintaining stillness in your inner man to allow the dream to flow into your mind.

◆ Try to rerun events as they played out in the dream. This helps to transcribe the message into more permanent memory ink.

◆ Write out the dream and study it.

◆ Pray about all elements, events, and circumstances of the dream.

◆ It's sometimes helpful to share the dream with responsible trusted people, particularly your spouse or those in spiritual authority over you—if the Holy Spirit allows. Seek interpretation from the Holy Spirit and ask for clarification from those with the gift of interpretation who have a track record of true and trustworthy interpretation. A dreamer must try interpreting a dream before asking others for help.

♦ Do not act on the dream before its interpretation is confirmed.

♦ When the dream's meaning has been confirmed, first begin by making only minor adjustments toward the dream's fulfillment. Start with what will not drastically alter your personal circumstance. Remember, obedience is better than sacrifice. For example, many people want to quit a secular job for full-time ministry when they have yet to master faithfulness in paying tithes. As you obey in the little, God will unfold greater responsibility. Allow your faith to gradually build up before you take the stake to a higher level.

♦ Always remember that dreams are possibilities and not inevitabilities.

♦ A dream may not always sound logical, but hang on to it and treasure it until the appointed time:

But Mary treasured up all these things and pondered them in her heart (Luke 2:19).

When he told his father as well as his brothers, his father rebuked him and said, "What is this dream you had? Will your mother and I and your brothers actually come and bow down to the ground before you?" His brothers were jealous of him, but his father kept the matter in mind (Genesis 37:10-11).

♦ Dreams will always lead to a process. Identify the direction you are drawn to. An appropriate interpretation should bring you closer to God. The journey is as important as the destination to God. He measures maturity and character, but the dreamer may be more time conscious of progress as a measure of time. The process took Joseph 17 years to fulfill, but it was worth all the waiting.

♦ Plant dreams in your spirit and wage war with the promise when circumstances seem to run contrary to the dream.

◆ Respond truthfully to corrective dreams; it is between you and God.

When I kept silent, my bones wasted away through my groaning all day long. For day and night Your hand was heavy on me; my strength was sapped as in the heat of summer. Then I acknowledged my sin to You and did not cover up my iniquity. I said, "I will confess my transgressions to the Lord"—and You forgave the guilt of my sin (Psalm 32:3-5).

Responding to Warning Dreams

We all receive dreams that warn against an impending danger, errors in judgment, misplaced priorities, and life-changing situations. With all of these, we must seek understanding of why God has given the warning. Usually, it is so that prayers may be offered and calamity averted. Therefore, it's a privilege that God has considered it worthwhile to give you a revelatory warning.

Is that the right reply for you to make, O House of Jacob? Do you think the spirit of the Lord likes to talk to you so roughly? No! His threats are for your good, to get on the path again (Micah 2:7 TLB).

It is important to remain calm and not jump to hasty conclusions. Quiet your soul before the Lord, and ask Him to bring His peace and further divine revelation on the subject. The purpose of the warning is to make intercession and avert judgment. Nebuchadnezzar did not heed the advice that Daniel had given him, so calamity eventually overtook him.

"Therefore, O king, be pleased to accept my advice: Renounce your sins by doing what is right, and your wickedness by being kind to the oppressed. It may be that then your prosperity will continue." All this happened to King Nebuchadnezzar. Twelve months later, as the king was walking on the roof of the royal palace of Babylon, he said, "Is not this the great Babylon I have built as the royal residence, by my mighty power and for the glory of my majesty?" The words were still on his lips when a voice came from heaven, "This is what is decreed for you, King Nebuchadnezzar: Your royal authority has been taken from you..." (Daniel 4:27-31).

With warning dreams, many people become terrified instead of being thankful for advance notice and a chance to alter the course of future events. Seek healing for any areas of fear that the dream might have stirred up. Ask God to eliminate any stronghold of fear from your life and to remove any emotional backlash from your soul. Always remember that it's only a warning!

My Personal Experience

I had a warning dream during a personal time of retreat to seek the Lord's face. At times like that, I thought I should have victory dreams; after all, I was in a sacrifice of intense prayer and fasting.

In this dream, I was in prayer in my living room. Then, I noticed that one of the windows was slightly open and also that fans had not been put on—even though the room was getting quite hot. I also noticed an ugly animal trying to force its way into the room. My first inclination was to ignore it and continue with my prayer, but it continued relentlessly to force itself into the room. Realizing that my children were at home, I thought it might be better to completely shut the window to prevent the creature from gaining entrance into the room. As I try to do this, the animal gets hold of my hand—at this point, I woke up.

My first reaction came from the realm of my soul; I was upset that an animal could get hold of my hand, even during a time of such prayer and sacrifice. A week following the experience, God spoke to me clearly on this issue and asked if it would have been better if I had not been warned. This brought the dream's true significance to me. Furthermore, God reminded me that it has not happened; rather, in response to my prayers and fasting, He sent me a warning. At this point in time, there was a family issue that I had not taken seriously enough; God was telling me that I needed to pay more attention to it, otherwise the enemy could use this weakness or negligence as a loophole for entry.

Responding to Warning Dreams

◆ Pray about it:

Hezekiah became ill and was at the point of death. The prophet Isaiah son of Amoz went to him and said, "This is what the Lord says: Put your house in order, because you are going to die; you will not recover." Hezekiah turned his face to the wall and prayed to the Lord...and Hezekiah wept bitterly. Before Isaiah had left the middle court, the word of Lord came to him. "Go back and tell

Hezekiah, the leader of My people, this is what the Lord, the God of your father David, says: 'I have heard your prayer and seen your tears; I will heal you...and this city from the hand of the king of Assyria'" (2 Kings 20:1-6).

♦ Seek help in understanding it. Pharaoh and Nebuchadnezzar sought help from the God of the Hebrews (through Joseph and Daniel) about warning dreams they received.

♦ Realize that not every vision is ready for public pronouncement. This is particularly relevant when the warning concerns other people, an organization, or church. Ask God for the opportune time for pronouncement. Know that as the stakes get higher, a certain level of authority is required to announce the revelation, particularly in the area of warning or a word of direction for people groups.

♦ Know when a warning revelation has outlived its immediate relevance; do not live in perpetual fear or bondage of a warning. A principle inherent in a spiritual warning can be applicable for life, but the specific danger it warns of is often for a time and a season.

What to Do With a Dream or Vision You Do Not Immediately Understand

♦ Pray about it.

♦ Seek help to understand it.

♦ Receive and keep it in your heart.

♦ Ponder it in your mind.

♦ Remain obedient to God in what you do understand.

♦ Remain spiritually sensitive, but don't over-spiritualize matters in the process; wait on the Holy Spirit.

♦ Wait for matters to unfold with time.

The process of waiting for circumstances to unfold in time requires certain critical steps. These steps are enunciated in a vision of the apostle Peter, and the unfolding of its revelation that he was to go to the Gentiles and preach the gospel (see Acts 10:11-20). How did Peter unravel the truth of the vision? He waited, stayed spiritually sensitive, and remained obedient to God in what he understood. Then, he approached the situation with an open, teachable spirit. The vision's understanding unfolded to Peter in stages:

1. "But God has shown me that I should not call any man impure or unclean":

   Talking with him, Peter went inside and found a large gathering of people. He said to them: "You are well aware that it is against our law for a Jew to associate with a Gentile or visit him. But God has shown me that I should not call any man impure or unclean. So when I was sent for, I came without raising any objection. May I ask why you sent for me?" (Acts 10:27-29)

2. God shows no favoritism:

   Then Peter began to speak: "I now realize how true it is that God does not show favoritism but accepts men from every nation who fear Him and do what is right..." (Acts 10:34-35).

3. The gift of the Holy Spirit was poured out on Gentiles:

   While Peter was still speaking these words, the Holy Spirit came on all who heard the message. The circumcised believers who had come with Peter were astonished that the gift of the Holy Spirit had been poured out even on the Gentiles. For they heard them speaking in tongues and praising God (Acts 10:44-46).

4. No man can stand in the way of God:

   Can anyone keep these people from being baptized with water? They have received the Holy Spirit just as we have (Acts 10:47-48).

5. "Who was I to oppose God?" It is futile to oppose God:

   "As I began to speak, the Holy Spirit came on them as He had come on us at the beginning. Then I remembered what the Lord had said: 'John baptized with water, but you will be baptized with the Holy Spirit.' So if God gave them the same gift as He gave us, who believed in the Lord Jesus Christ, who was I to think that I could oppose God?" When they heard this, they had no further objections and praised God, saying, "So then, God has granted even the Gentiles repentance unto life" (Acts 11:15-18).

Waiting for the Fulfillment of a Dream or Vision

The Principles of Active Waiting

Waiting does not imply not doing something about the revelation. Rather, it means actively waiting with expectation, while pondering and remaining sensitive in spirit. The principles of active waiting are well enunciated by the prophet Habakkuk regarding what God told him concerning his complaints:

> *I will climb my watchtower now and wait to see what answer God will give to my complaint. And the Lord said to me: "Write My answer on a billboard, large and clear, so that anyone can read it at a glance and rush to tell the others. But these things I plan won't happen right away. Slowly, steadily, surely the time approaches when the vision will be fulfilled. If it seems slow, do not despair, for these things will surely come to pass. Just be patient! They will not be overdue a single day!"* (Habakkuk 2:1-3 TLB)

The following points stand out from the passage:

◆ The need for prayers: *"climb my watchtower."*

◆ It is your responsibility to take some form of action on your revelation: Write it *"on a billboard."*

◆ Seek clear understandings of your dream/vision in order to understand and prioritize your response: *"large and clear."*

◆ Wait for it; the vision is for an appointed time: *"just be patient."*

◆ Hold on to your promise: *"Do not despair, for these things will surely come to pass."*

◆ Dream or vision speaks of the end—it doesn't lie.

Here are five things to remember while waiting for a dream's fulfillment:

1. Do not force the situation.

2. Fulfillment belongs to God. He is more than able to fulfill what He has promised.

3. Do not be weary in doing what is right.

4. Do not neglect fellowship with God. Human counseling is essential, but divine guidance in the form of direct witness from God is even more important.

5. Do not use your personal circumstance to determine the feasibility of the promise.

Life Application and Appropriation of Dreams

1. Only confirmed, correctly interpreted dreams should be applied.

2. First, simply apply the dream and its symbols to yourself.

3. Start with simple changes that do not entail major shifts in your circumstances, unless the dream specifically says to do so.

4. Always move according to the proportion of your faith, because without faith it is impossible to please God.

5. Appropriate the dream.

Appropriation is the process by which the dreamer in faith assumes or adopts the promise of the dream. Appropriation consists of:

◆ Faith.

◆ Diligent seeking, such as studying relevant Bible passages.

◆ Preparing the soil of your heart by encouraging yourself in the Lord.

◆ Paying attention to fine details.

CHAPTER 10

The Dreamland and the Image Center

The Dreamland

Dreaming is like experiencing the spiritual atmosphere of the Garden of Eden—back when a person had capabilities of operating in the realm of God. The spiritual atmosphere and abilities in dreams are distinct from our experience in the natural realm. In this spiritual atmosphere, a dreamer can often do what is humanly impossible or beyond the scope of human imagination, such as flying like Superman. Therefore, I will refer to this atmosphere as "dreamland."

Conceptually, "dreamland" is the land of the spirit, so the man's mind is almost completely closed and not limited in time; therefore, God can take us backward or forwards in time. God is supreme in dreamland, and this supremacy is affirmed in Scripture: *"For by Him all things were created: things in heaven and on earth, visible and invisible, whether thrones or powers or rulers or authorities; all things were created by Him and for Him"* (Col. 1:16). Other characteristics of dreamland are as follows:

♦ Evil exists in dreamland just as it did in the Garden of Eden, in spite of the spiritual atmosphere that prevailed in Eden.

♦ In dreamland, man's understanding transcends the limits of physical intellect.

◆ In dreamland, man can be imparted to or receive impartation from God.

◆ A false dream is a made-up story, so it does not involve dreamland. Such dreams are a product of the dreamer's delusion. Scripture calls any dream not sent by God as false, a made-up story, and a delusion of the human mind.

◆ In dreamland, much is laid bare before the dreamer more openly than in the natural realm. Therefore, if God allows you the privilege of seeing activities of the evil ones, it is often called a "demonic dream." If God allows a dreamer to see the intent and depths of the soul, it is often referred to as a "soul dream." Other dreams can be classified according to God's purpose for giving them, or by what God allowed to dominate in the dream's dramatization.

◆ The language of dreamland is the parable language of the Spirit. Parable language is the use of symbols to dramatize revelation.

Image Center

Spiritual revelation is fed into the mind from the human spirit. Functionally, the mind consists of:

◆ **Memory**, which is a word depository that deals with issues of the past.

◆ **Contemplation**, which deals with current issues as well as being the arena for conceptualization.

◆ **Imagination**, which contains the pictorial depository and handles issues of the future, such as planning and conceptualization.

This pictorial depository of our imagination can also be referred to as our mind's image center. As a pictorial language, dreaming must undergo necessary processing. Our image center should be made conducive to receive pictorial revelations from the spirit, and be made capable of resisting pollution from unholy, worldly images.

Research has found that the human brain has two sides, which function and respond differently to specific types of stimuli:

◆ The left hemisphere's forte is analysis, reason, and logic.

- ◆ The right hemisphere is dominant in visual and other sensory processes, as well as in exercising emotion and recognizing humor and metaphor.

- ◆ Conceptual and emotionally neutral words activate the left hemisphere.

- ◆ Words that name images and are emotionally laden activate the right hemisphere.[1]

The Dynamics of the Image Center

Our image center needs sanctification on a regular and continuous basis. Sanctifying the image center begins with not using it for evil, unclean images and thoughts. Protecting the image center in this way allows the Holy Spirit to prepare it to more easily receive divine spiritual inspirations. This will open up the dreamer for more spiritual encounters. The dreamer's level of faith and the busyness of his mind influence translation from the spirit of man to his image center.

Dreams translate to our image center more successfully when the mind is still. Spend some quiet time after waking up so that dreams can drift from the spirit into the image center before the day's demands set in. In her book, *Third Heaven, Angels, and Other Stuff,* Patricia King said, "Much of spiritual revelation is fed into our image center (imagination) or our mind."[2]

Most human minds process information in pictures. Images in the pictorial depository have a gripping effect on a person and are often hard to erase. No wonder we struggle for days, weeks, or even months with persistent recurrences of a single flash of a picture accidentally seen— even if for only a few seconds—on television or in a newspaper. Such is the power that images have in the image center; impressions there are long lasting. As a consequence, addictions such as pornography, or phobias such as the fear of heights, are the most difficult to overcome.

Sanctification of Your Image Center

We must make a conscious effort to prepare our image center to receive divine revelations, for God expresses "spiritual truth in spiritual words." Practicing holy imagination through meditation on Bible images sanctifies the image center. The Bible states in Psalm 119:27,

"Let me understand the teaching of Your precepts; then I will meditate on Your wonders." A conscious effort should be made to override constant bombardment of worldly imagery that pollutes our image center. Sanctify the image center by filling your imagination with images from God's Word and by reading and visualizing the Scriptures. The power of the Word will transform the soil of your mind. Then, most of our spiritual encounters will begin to become relevant in the realm of our sanctified image center.

Sanctification leads to the spirit of sound mind, *"For God has not given us a spirit of fear, but of power and of love and of a sound mind"* (2 Tim. 1:7 NKJ). A sound mind is one balanced and anchored in God. We use the mind to appreciate and translate divine knowledge into everyday routines of life. Often, God uses routines of life to speak to us. The spirit of a sound mind also enables us to enter into godly liberty. *"Now the Lord is the Spirit; and where the spirit of the Lord is, there is liberty"* (2 Cor. 3:17 NKJV). If you do not feel liberty in your spirit, then you are not released to minister in the Spirit, and, therefore, you cannot operate in the supernatural. The spirit of a sound mind is a divine insurance that guards against the error of presumption; it helps the delicate balancing of human thought processes so that we may see from God's perspective; and it's also the security that enables us to differentiate between what is of God and what is not.

Revelation can be distorted in an image center that is polluted with unclean and ungodly images. That is why the Bible describes the pure in heart as follows:

> *To the pure, all things are pure, but to those who are corrupted and do not believe, nothing is pure. In fact, both their minds and consciences are corrupted* (Titus 1:15).

Purifying our imagination comes from constant practice of visualizing holy imagery in the Scriptures. Worshiping and listening to anointed Christian teaching can also help to sanctify our minds.

Translation of Dreams to the Image Center

One place that dreams can be lost, corrupted, or fragmented is in the process of translation to the image center. Factors that adversely affect reception and processing of dreams at the image center are:

- Pollution through constant bombardment by worldly images.

- Busyness with matters of this world, which tends to choke the flourishing of God's Word.

- A mind-set with a product of life experiences, worldly knowledge, and/or prejudice.

- Sins, unforgiveness, and bitterness.

Covert Knowledge

A dreamer may not have immediate fruitfulness in understanding a dream at the level of human consciousness—as in the case of Nebuchadnezzar. A dream can remain dormant in the spirit without being fruitful to the mind; that is, until the Holy Spirit releases human understanding through correct interpretation. King Nebuchadnezzar could not remember his dream. The Living Bible rendition of Daniel 2:1-3 says, *"One night in the second year of his reign, Nebuchadnezzar had a terrifying nightmare, and awoke trembling with fear. And to make matters worse, he could not remember his dream!"* However, his spirit bore witness to the correct interpretation when it was given to him by Daniel. In the same manner, our spirit knows the meaning of a dream we receive, even though it may be unfruitful to our immediate understanding.

In another instance, King Nebuchadnezzar did not accept the magicians' interpretation of his dream, but he did acknowledge trustworthiness in Daniel's interpretation:

> *This is the meaning of the vision of the rock cut out of a mountain, but not by human hands—a rock that broke the iron, the bronze, the clay, the silver and the gold to pieces. "The great God has shown the king what will take place in the future. The dream is true and the* **interpretation is trustworthy."** *Then King Nebuchadnezzar fell prostrate before Daniel and paid him honor and ordered that an offering and incense be presented to him* (Daniel 2:45-46).

This occurred because Nebuchadnezzar's spirit recognized the correct interpretation, as given by Daniel. Another example is when Joseph's spirit was quickened to remember his dream, *"Although Joseph recognized his brothers, they did not recognize him. Then he remembered his dreams about them and said to them..."* (Gen. 42:8-9). The covert knowledge of a dream's meaning in the dreamer's spirit gets quickened upon hearing its correct interpretation. This quickening releases life from the Spirit to the dreamer's mind and brings confirmation as to the trustworthiness of such an interpretation.

How to Plant Your Dreams Successfully

If you sow in the spirit, then you will reap in the spirit; if you sow in the soul, then you will reap in the soul. If you plant a good dream promise in the spirit realm, then you will reap the fruit of the spirit. On the other hand, the outcome of planting a dream in the soul realm can include anxiety, worry, anger, bitterness, vengeance, unholy fear, hopelessness, condemnations, and insecurity. Planting your dream in the soul realm happens when your emotions and mind-sets cloud your understanding; so then you become blind as to a dream's real spiritual connotations, which is a problem since some dreams may address blind spots in a dreamer's thinking pattern.

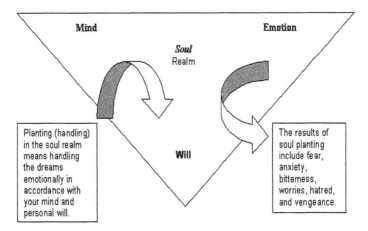

The outcome of planting a dream in the spirit includes peace, love, self-control, faith in God, drawing closer to God, and trusting that all is well. Planting a dream in the spirit realm means seeing all its elements with an open, sensitive spirit; you truthfully accept when God guides you over its circumstance—even if it runs contrary to your thinking. This also affords you a chance to see the whole picture from God's perspective.

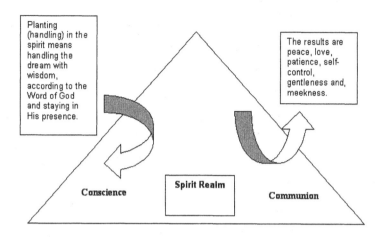

Planting (handling) in the spirit means handling the dream with wisdom, according to the Word of God and staying in His presence.

The results are peace, love, patience, self-control, gentleness and, meekness.

Conscience

Spirit Realm

Communion

A properly planted dream enables the dreamer to dialogue with God.

My Personal Experience

I remember a series of dreams that I had many years ago. At the time, I had been voted (in absentia) into the leadership of an interdenominational Christian fellowship in the city. However, I didn't want this role for many reasons and had decided to decline the position.

In the first dream, I was walking along a pathway in the company of another gentleman. As we were walking along, a third person (unknown) came on the scene and announced that one of us had failed an examination. On waking up, I prayed about this. At that time, I was not about to make any major decision. After the prayers, I drifted back into sleep. I had another dream in which the same unknown person handed me a letter and said that I was the one out of the two of us who had failed the examination. I was awakened from sleep once again. This time, my wife joined me in prayers. After praying, I drifted back to sleep. I had another dream in which the same gentleman announced to me that I had failed the same test three times in the past.

Over the next few days, I continued to ponder these dreams and seek further understanding. In the second week, I realized that just before I had the first dream, my wife and I had decided that I should not accept the leadership role in the seemingly small fellowship. Immediately, I knew that the dreams referred to this decision. I was quite excited about coming to this understanding. That night I had another dream in which the same gentleman from my previous dreams reappeared to announce that I had scored 105 percent. I believe that the extra mark of five percent was for the diligent search to gain understanding of it.

So, I accepted the leadership role, and God expanded the fellowship in many areas, including an increase in numbers from under 20 families to well over 100 families within two years.

---

1. *Dictionary of Biblical Imagery*; (Downers Grove, IL: IterVarsity Press, 1998), xiii.
2. Pat King, *Third Heaven, Angels and Other Stuff*; (Belleville, Ontario: Essence Publishing, 2002), 97.

CHAPTER 11

Deeper Dynamics
of Dreams

Most people regard dreaming as a passive aspect of their spiritual life. This has not been my experience, as I have found that dreaming can become active as I cooperate and allow God to further His communication with me. No one can initiate a dream discussion with God, but once He begins a conversation in dreams, I believe that you can take it further with Him. Everyone should aim to further his dream communication ability with God, as He rewards every effort we make to get closer to Him.

> *In fact, though by this time you ought to be teachers, you need some-one to teach you the elementary truths of God's word all over again. You need milk, not solid food! Anyone who lives on milk, being still an infant, is not acquainted with the teaching about righteousness. But solid food is for the mature, who by constant use have trained themselves to distinguish good from evil* (Hebrews 5:12-14).

> *And without faith it is impossible to please God, because anyone who comes to Him must believe that He exists and that He rewards those who earnestly seek Him* (Hebrews 11:6).

> *God did this so that men would seek Him and perhaps reach out for Him and find Him, though He is not far from each one of us. "For in Him we live and move and have our being"* (Acts 17:27-28).

If we pay attention to our dreams, respond appropriately, and diligently seek God's face, then our dreams will increase—with greater detail, more explained mysteries, more impartation of divine power, and greater understanding of our nightly encounters.

The Heart Connection in Dreams

From the beginning of time, God's desire has been to enter into the most profound, intimate relationship with us. One of God's primary objectives in communicating in dreams and visions is to establish a heart-to-heart connection. Another aspect of God's desire is for us to experience the realities of who He is, even on our worst day. God also wants us to have a living encounter with His character in an atmosphere uninfluenced by mind-set, so we can imbibe His true attributes.

Dreams are valuable because their visual impact allows a message to linger in our spirit until we are brought to meditate on the dreams and allow thoughts of them to flow into our memory. God may also dramatize His Word in dreams, making certain portions of Scripture come alive to us as real and living. The first step in advancing your dream-life is to ask for more dreams.

The Word of God and Dream Communication

The parable language of dreams is similar to the Bible's pattern of speech. Visualizing imagery in the Bible trains our mind to understand the Word of God. On the other hand, the Word of God comes with enough spiritual power to transform our minds for better understanding of His ways. Dreams increase our knowledge of God and His heart, and connect us to His ways. As a dreamer spends more time studying the Word of God, his dreamlife will become more clear and rich. The Word of God's lordship over your life reflects the lordship of Jesus Christ over your life, and this relationship determines the height of your dream-life.

Dream Phrases

Insightful statements are made in dreams. Dream phrases should be recorded exactly as the dreamer has heard them because their divine insights may run far beyond the limits of human reasoning. Dream phrases that run contrary to Scripture are not from God, no matter how smooth, appropriate, alluring, and wise they may sound.

Dream phrases from God have the following characteristics: They are often clear, short, and sharp; they may require prompt attention and action; and they usually come with little ambiguity.

Angels are commonly associated with the majority of dream phrases. Sometimes, a spiritual leader or a respected Christian in a dreamer's life can pronounce dream phrases. However, voices in our dreams should be carefully discerned. The voice of God will bear witness with the dreamer's spirit, like a knowing in the inner being that God is stirring something within. The Bible says, *"his sheep follow him because they know his voice. But they will never follow a stranger..."* (John 10:4-5) and *"But you have an anointing from the Holy One, and all of you know the truth"* (1 John 2:20). We have the Holy Spirit anointing and the seal of God within to tell us the truth. Even statements from angels need to be judged as Galatians 1:8 warns, *"But even if we or an angel from heaven should preach a gospel other than the one we preached to you, let him be eternally condemned!"*

Sometimes, phrases from the second heaven—the domain of the devil and his agents—will appear in the dreamer's subconscious. So, what was said will not sit well with the dreamer, or he will have a deep reservation about the information. Every dream phrase needs to be subjected to the following tests. First, does it line up with Scripture? Second, does it pass the love test? And finally, does it pass the wisdom test? The ultimate test for wisdom from God is if the revelation has respect for human lives, no matter whose life is involved.

Exaggeration in Dreams

In dreams, God allows us to see the intent of our mind in its truest forms, which means without moderation of earthly precautions. One reason why situations appear exaggerated in dreams is because normal restraints are absent. This is also why most dreamers find themselves doing activities in dreams that they normally would not do in real life. Perhaps what remains hidden is the fact that only societal norms restrain us from such action. When societal influence holds us back long enough from unacceptable behavior, overindulgence, or sinful action, we sometimes assume that the issue is dealt with.

However, desires that could be resurrected when no one else is looking can surface in our dreams; God does this to warn us against such presumption.

Another reason for exaggeration in dreams is that God wants to draw our attention to the severity of an issue that might otherwise look innocuous. Also, God uses exaggeration in dreams to help prioritize our response to a dream's different issues.

Expanding the Scope of Our Dreams

The "scope of our dreams" could be regarded as the overall coverage that gives revelation on other people and does so without any direct relevance to our personal circumstance. The scope of our dreams also includes sensitivity of the information and security of its content. Determine the percentage of your dreams that relate to you, those that relate to others without direct bearing to yourself, and those that jointly relate to you and others. Some estimates state that about 95 percent of a person's dreams relate to his life.

However, people with a watchman anointing have a widened scope that includes their area of calling; if that is the case, then a good percentage of their dreams would normally relate to other people. This point is crucial in accepting the value of the watchman ministry in our churches. The watchman may need help in managing personal issues, while also dreaming of strategic insights into the enemy's plans and the path lying ahead for the Church. Dreamers who pay attention to others and then intercede for them will naturally have their dream scope widened. When God begins speaking to you in dreams regarding others, it's usually a result of your increasing concern for their welfare. Perhaps this explains why our immediate family members frequently turn up in our dreams.

Managing Sensitive and Secure Information

The sensitivity and security content of a dream reflects the trust that God has in the dreamer. First off, God will trust the dreamer with sensitive information concerning his life in the following order:

1. **Potential events**: what is likely to happen, but is not inevitable in the dreamer's life.

2. **Decreed events:** what God has ordained to happen, no matter what, in the dreamer's life.

3. **God's sovereign plan for the dreamer:** which is the very reason for his or her life experiences.

Handling sensitive revelation concerning a dreamer's life may seem quite obvious. But many dreamers misuse such privileged revelation and become arrogant about the good promises given by God. Doing so compromises and delays fulfillment of a promise. Public pronouncement of a personal promise must only be for building up the lives of other people. In this regard, we must know that not all revelations are ready for public pronouncement. Timing is a key factor. God Himself told Daniel, *"But you, Daniel, close up and seal the words of the scroll until the time of the end. Many will go here and there to increase knowledge"* (Dan. 12:4). Also, Nehemiah stated,

> I set out during the night with a few men. I had not told anyone what my God had put in my heart to do for Jerusalem. There were no mounts with me except the one I was riding on. By night I went out through the Valley Gate toward the Jackal Well and the Dung Gate, examining the walls of Jerusalem, which had been broken down, and its gates, which had been destroyed by fire (Nehemiah 2:12-13).

If God can trust you with sensitive information concerning your ministry, then He will progress to trust you with information about other people. He will first begin with potential events; follow with decreed events, and then conclude with His sovereign plans for them. If these levels are well-managed, then God will entrust you with knowledge about other people's weaknesses for the purpose of intercession.

Responding to Other People's Dreams

Divine principles revealed in any true dream—once carefully and prayerfully applied—can become quite helpful. Dreams received by members of the dreamer's family are nearly as valid as if the dreamer had received them personally. Many people have lost valuable wisdom keys by disregarding such true dreams.

> Gideon arrived just as a man was telling a friend his dream. "I had a dream," he was saying. "A round loaf of barley bread came tumbling into the Midianite camp. It struck the tent with such force that the tent

overturned and collapsed." His friend responded, "This can be nothing other than the sword of Gideon son of Joash, the Israelite. God has given the Midianites and the whole camp into his hands." When Gideon heard the dream and its interpretation, he worshiped God. He returned to the camp of Israel and called out, "Get up! The Lord has given the Midianite camp into your hands (Judges 7:13-15).

On this occasion, Gideon won the battle with encouragement he received from a dream of the enemy.

Can a Gifted Person Cross Over to Power From the Dark Side?

The answer is undoubtedly, "Yes!" Sin, disobedience, and wrong motivation have a profound impact on our gifts. For instance, disobedience leads to rebellion; in such a place of darkness, a gifted person can draw power from the satanic network. If giftedness is corrupted, then a gifted person can imperceptibly cross over from operating in divine power to the power of darkness. The dividing line can often be quite fine, both for weary and seasoned believers. Many biblical examples exist of this crossover phenomenon. A classic example is the life of King Saul. Since the gifts of God are irrevocable, it is not uncommon for gifted people to stray into the domain of evil power and still show evidence of giftedness. Saul was once anointed of God:

As Saul turned to leave Samuel, God changed Saul's heart, and all these signs were fulfilled that day. When they arrived at Gibeah, a procession of prophets met him; the Spirit of God came upon him in power, and he joined in their prophesying. When all those who had formerly known him saw him prophesying with the prophets, they asked each other, "What is this that has happened to the son of Kish? Is Saul also among the prophets?" (1 Samuel 10:9-11).

However, due to disobedience and rebellion, Saul allowed himself to be dragged into a life of bitterness, jealousy, unforgiveness, and vengeance. As a result, God sent into him an evil spirit, which affected his physical life and permeated his spiritual walk with God. Later, God further distanced Himself from Saul, who, in desperation, sought revelation and power from the dark world.

When Saul saw the Philistine army, he was afraid; terror filled his heart. He inquired of the Lord, but the Lord did not answer him by dreams or Urim or prophets. Saul then said to his attendants, "Find

me a woman who is a medium, so that I may go and inquire of her."
"There is one in Endor," they said. So Saul disguised himself, putting
on other clothes, and at night he and two men went to the woman.
"Consult a spirit for me," he said, "and bring up for me the one I
name"(1 Samuel 28:5-8).

Balaam was gifted by God in prophecy, but his lust for money and
things of the world caused him to crossover into divination. He then
received a rebuke by a mere donkey.

> They have left the straight way and wandered off to follow the
> way of Balaam son of Beor, who loved the wages of wickedness.
> But he was rebuked for his wrongdoing by a donkey—a beast
> without speech—who spoke with a man's voice and restrained the
> prophet's madness. These men are springs without water and mists
> driven by a storm. Blackest darkness is reserved for them (2 Peter
> 2:15-17).

Even though gifted to hear from God, Balaam operated in mixture
and dabbled in divination and sorcery. To operate in mixture is to use
God's gifts both in a godly and ungodly manner.

> Now when Balaam saw that it pleased the Lord to bless Israel, **he
> did not resort to sorcery** as at other times, but turned his face
> toward the desert. When Balaam looked out and saw Israel
> encamped tribe by tribe, the Spirit of God came upon him and he
> uttered his oracle: "The oracle of Balaam son of Beor, the oracle of
> one whose eye sees clearly, the oracle of one **who hears the words of
> God, who sees a vision from the Almighty**, who falls prostrate, and
> whose eyes are opened..."(Numbers 24:1-4).

Many people gifted to receive revelation and dreams have unknow-
ingly become corrupted. Rather than receiving revelation from God,
they become prone to operating in satanic evil. Many New Age people
actually have God's gifts, but then they crossed over to power from the
dark side.

All True Dreams, Visions, and Prophecies Seem to Correlate

Over the years, I have noticed that true dreams, visions, and
prophecies on the same subject do not contradict one another. Could
they, therefore, originate from one single source? Dreams and visions

in the Bible follow this pattern, regardless of the time, place, or people group involved. The Bible is clear: All true prophecies correlate and are inspired by the Holy Spirit.

> *For He [Who is the source of their prophesying] is not a God of confusion and disorder but of peace and order* (1 Corinthians 14:33 AMP).

> *The purpose of all prophecy and all that I have shown you is to tell about Jesus* (Revelation 19:10b TLB).

> *This will be my third visit to you. "Every matter must be established by this testimony of two or three witnesses"* (2 Corinthians 13:1).

> *And we have the word of the prophets made more certain, and you will do well to pay attention to it, as to a light shining in a dark place, until the day dawns and the morning star rises in your hearts* (2 Peter 1:19).

Revelations from the Holy Spirit—whether by means of dreams, visions, or prophecies—do not contradict one another. Below are scriptural examples that lay credence to this observation.

CORNELIUS' VISION	PETER'S VISION	KINGDOM PURPOSE
The angel answered, "Your prayers and gifts to the poor have come up as a memorial offering before God. Now send men to Joppa to bring back a man named Simon who is called Peter. He is staying with Simon the tanner, whose house is by the sea" (Acts 10:4-6).	*He saw heaven opened and something like a large sheet being let down to earth by its four corners. It contained all kinds of four-footed animals, as well as reptiles of the earth and birds of the air. Then a voice told him, "Get up, Peter. Kill and eat." "Surely not, Lord!" Peter replied. "I have never eaten anything impure or unclean"* (Acts 10:11-14).	To take the gospel to non-Jewish people.

SAUL OF TARSUS' VISION AND CONVERSION	ANANIAS' VISION	KINGDOM PURPOSE
As he neared Damascus on his journey, suddenly a light from heaven flashed around him. He fell to the ground and heard a voice say to him, "Saul, Saul, why do you persecute Me?" (Acts 9:3-4)	*The Lord called to him in a vision, "Ananias!" "Yes, Lord," he answered. The Lord told him, "Go to the house of Judas on Straight Street and ask for a man from Tarsus named Saul, for he is praying. In a vision he has seen a man named Ananias come and place his hands on him to restore his sight"* (Acts 9:10-12).	Conversion of Saul of Tarsus as God's chosen instrument to take the gospel to the Gentiles.

DREAM/EVENT	DREAM/EVENT	DREAM/EVENT	KINGDOM PURPOSE
Joseph's dreams. (Genesis 37)	Butler's dream. (Genesis 40)	Pharaoh's dreams. (Genesis 41)	For Joseph to become prime minister of Egypt and save the Jews.
Gideon's lack of faith to obey God's instruction. (Judges 6)	Midianite dream at the enemy's camp. (Judges 7)	Interpretation by another Midianite. (Judges 7)	To encourage Gideon to lead the Jews to victory.
Prophecy of large tree. (Ezekiel 31)	Nebuchadnezzar's dream of large tree. (Daniel 4)	Punishment for disobedience. (Leviticus 26 fulfillment).	That God's Word must be fulfilled.

SUBJECT	EZEKIEL'S VISION	JOHN'S VISION
The gates to the city: these twelve gates, named after the twelve tribes of Israel, are also described in the new Jerusalem.	Ezekiel 48:30	Revelation 21:21
The view from a high mountain.	Ezekiel 40:2	Revelation 21:10
The guide angel.	Ezekiel 40:3	Revelation 21:9-10
The river for the healing of the nations.	Ezekiel 47:12	Revelation 22:1-3
The name of the city.	Ezekiel 48:35: *"The Lord is there."*	Revelation 21:3: *"Now the dwelling of God is with men, and He will live with them."*
The Gog and Magog: battle with God's people.	Ezekiel 39:1	Revelation 20:8

In many instances, Ezekiel and John's visions also spoke of the same subject—despite the disparity in geography, generations, dispensations, and people groups involved. These revelations could only have come from God's mind, and only the Spirit of God can tell what is on His mind.

Dream Clustering

There are periods when people connected in some way receive the same message, although dramatized with individual characteristics. For instance, a river bursting its banks may play up in dreams of many people living within a specific geographical location. This could reflect a divine message in the people's spiritual atmosphere. Scriptural examples include:

◆ The cupbearer and baker's dreams (see Gen. 40:2-23).

◆ Nebuchadnezzar and Daniel's dreams (see Dan. 2 and Dan. 7).

CHAPTER 12

The Gift of Interpretation

The gift of interpreting dreams is an offshoot of the spirit of wisdom. This special type of divine wisdom is given to understand God's mind in sending a true dream by the Holy Spirit. The gift of interpretation is often associated with the spirit of counsel and administrative ability. The "power of proclamation" can also be given to a gifted interpreter:

Now to each one the manifestation of the Spirit is given for the common good. To one there is given through the Spirit the message of wisdom, to another the message of knowledge by means of the same Spirit (1 Corinthians 12:7-8).

"We both had dreams," they answered, "but there is no one to interpret them." Then Joseph said to them, "Do not interpretations belong to God? Tell me your dreams" (Genesis 40:8).

The Gift of Interpretation and the Spirit of Wisdom

The connection between the gift of interpretation and the spirit of wisdom is evident in the following passages:

In every matter of wisdom and understanding about which the king questioned them, he found them ten times better than all the magicians and enchanters in his whole kingdom (Daniel 1:20).

There is a man in your kingdom who has the spirit of the holy gods in him. In the time of your father he was found to have insight and intelligence and wisdom like that of the gods. King Nebuchadnezzar your father—your father the king, I say—appointed him chief of the magicians, enchanters, astrologers and diviners. This man Daniel, whom the king called Belteshazzar, was found to have a keen mind and knowledge and understanding, and also the ability to interpret dreams, explain riddles and solve difficult problems. Call for Daniel, and he will tell you what the writing means (Daniel 5:11-12).

The wise men and enchanters were brought before me to read this writing and tell me what it means, but they could not explain it. Now I have heard that you are able to give interpretations and to solve difficult problems... (Daniel 5:15-16).

When speaking of Joseph's wisdom and his associated ability to interpret dreams, Pharaoh spoke the following words:

Then Pharaoh said to Joseph, "Since God has made all this known to you, there is no one so discerning and wise as you. You shall be in charge of my palace, and all my people are to submit to your orders. Only with respect to the throne will I be greater than you" (Genesis 41:39-40).

The Gift of Interpretation and the Spirit of Counsel

The gift of interpretation is often connected with the spirit of counsel:

"And now let Pharaoh look for a discerning and wise man and put him in charge of the land of Egypt. Let Pharaoh appoint commissioners over the land to take a fifth of the harvest of Egypt during the seven years of abundance. They should collect all the food of these good years that are coming and store up the grain under the authority of Pharaoh, to be kept in the cities for food. This food should be held in reserve for the country, to be used during the seven years of famine that will come upon Egypt, so that the country may not be ruined by the famine." The plan seemed good to Pharaoh and to all his officials. So Pharaoh asked them, "Can we find anyone like this man, one in whom is the spirit of God?" (Genesis 41:33-38)

Therefore, O king, be pleased to accept my advice: Renounce your sins by doing what is right, and your wickedness by being kind to the oppressed. It may be that then your prosperity will continue (Daniel 4:27).

Maintaining and Developing the Gift of Interpretation

The gift of interpretation is given by the Holy Spirit. It can be enhanced and intensified in a person's life by studying the Word of God; keeping a pure conscience; laying aside personal agendas; surrendering one's will; and living in constant communion with God. Bearing this in mind, one can say that eventual proficiency at dream interpretation is a studied art. The more you practice interpreting dreams, the better you become.

Every dreamer can develop and improve skills of interpretation. Joseph took 17 years to become proficient in the interpretation of dreams; he did not handle pronouncement of his first two dreams with much wisdom. However, Joseph's interpretation of Pharaoh's dreams many years later showed evidence of wisdom. We should all continue to improve our skills.

Gaining Proficiency in Interpreting Dreams

Over the years, I have noticed that only those people who remember dreams on a consistent basis can become proficient at skillfully interpreting dreams. Therefore, the gift of interpretation can be regarded as an offshoot of a prophetic anointing; those individuals who receive dreams and remember them consistently can be called "prophetic." A dream's covert meaning actually exists in the dreamer's spirit, but it may be unfruitful to the dreamer's mind until a true interpretation is given. When correct interpretation comes, the dreamer will usually acknowledge trustworthiness of that interpretation.

The Power of Proclamation and the Gift of Interpretation

Some gifted interpreters have the power of proclamation, which is the divine inspiration to declare an option. This power of proclamation becomes valuable when the dreamer wakes up prior to, or at a moment of decision in a dream. Under such conditions, God is usually leaving room for the dreamer to intercede and help influence a situation's eventual outcome. A person with the power of proclamation can add his agreement in faith to help a dreamer tilt the balance in the desired direction.

Interpretation by Word of Knowledge

All true interpretation comes with the Holy Spirit's help, although its actual outworking is either through a word of knowledge, a gift of interpretation, or a process of acquired interpretative skills. A word of knowledge is the spiritual gift of knowing information beyond natural means, as through God's revelation: *"To one there is given through the Spirit the message of wisdom, to another the message of knowledge by means of the same Spirit..."* (1 Cor. 12:8).

Many prophetic people interpret dreams by a word of knowledge rather than through acquired interpretative skills. Such people often cannot explain how they arrived at an interpretation on the basis of a dream's elements. When God gives interpretation by word of knowledge, He sows its meaning into a person's mind without necessarily expounding on relevance of the dream's elements.

This is also why some people awaken from dreams with a prompting to a specific Bible passage. It's the result of God's sowing the relevant Scripture in the dreamer's mind. Word of knowledge interpretation, however, will usually not explain the relevance of a dream's elements to the life circumstances of the dreamer; so, in that sense, it is restricted in details. There's enough detail to keep the dreamer from falling into a disastrous mistake, but every word of knowledge interpretation should be complemented with an acquired skill of interpretation.

Word of knowledge interpretation gives only a certain percentage of a dream's full meaning; therefore, it's short on intended keys of wisdom inherent in dreams. However, such interpretation is nearly always the correct essence of its message. Most angelic interpretations in the Bible appear to be word of knowledge interpretations; yet, if asked, the angels usually also gave further exposition on elements of the dreams or visions. Having a word of knowledge is the most common way that dreamers with undeveloped interpretative skills can gain understanding of dreams.

Biblical Example for Word of Knowledge Interpretation

♦ **The Dream**

Then the angel who talked with me returned and wakened me, as a man is wakened from his sleep. He asked me, "What do you see?" I answered, "I see a solid gold lampstand with a bowl at the top and seven lights on it, with seven channels to the lights. Also there are two olive trees by it, one on the right of the bowl and the other on its left." I asked the angel who talked with me, "What are these, my lord?" (Zechariah 4:1-4)

♦ **The Interpretation**

He answered, "Do you not know what these are?" "No, my lord," I replied. So he said to me, "This is the word of the Lord to Zerubbabel: 'Not by might nor by power, but by My Spirit,' says the Lord Almighty..." (Zechariah 4:5-6).

♦ **My Personal Exposition of Elements in Zechariah's Dream**

I believe this probably means that as long as Zerubbabel remains connected to the source of anointing—as symbolized by the two channels connecting the bowl and the two olive trees—then the light (the Spirit) will continue to burn in him. It will not be by might nor by power, but by the Spirit of the Almighty that Zerubbabel will succeed.

Compare this with the interpretation by skills, as given by Daniel when he reveals the king's dream (in Dan. 2:31-35) and then gives its interpretation (in Dan. 2:36-45). A complementing interpretation by word of knowledge with acquired skill is also demonstrated by Daniel. Review his dream of the four great beasts and the Ancient of Days (see Dan. 7:1-14), his resultant interpretation (see Dan. 7:15-18), and when an angel expounds on the symbol in response to Daniel's request.

Acquired Skills of Interpretation

With acquired skills of interpretation, a dreamer applies a correctly derived "personal dictionary" of dream symbols in the interpretative process.

How Much of the Dream Message Is Revealed?

A true interpretation will give approximately more than half of a dream message and will also cover the intended reason for its divine selection of elements (such as people, places, and symbolic actions). A truly interpreted dream can be added to by way of further revelation from dream elements. But such interpretations should not be contradicted by further revelation from the dream. As a result of further Holy Spirit prompting, such additions may come from the same (or another) interpreter. A dream should only have one true interpretation. A correctly interpreted dream, however, can have multiple applications and may unfold its relevance in stages.

How God Interprets Dreams to Unbelievers

God gives dreams to unbelievers. When He wishes to give them some understanding, He sows the dream's essence as a thought in the unbeliever's mind. This thought as to what God is saying may come as an impression, a flash of idea, or a knowing in the dreamer's mind. In this way, Pilate's wife had some understanding of her dream, and the Magi understood not to return via their arrival route because of Herod's evil intentions.

Summary

Here is a recap of the three main ways that God helps us to interpret our dreams:

1. By giving word of knowledge regarding His mind in sending the dream.

2. By the gift of interpretation.

3. By acquiring the interpretative skills.

There are also various combinations of these three:

♦ Word of knowledge plus acquired skills is the most common combination. Most people in some form of prophetic ministry will use this mode.

♦ Gift of interpretation and acquired skills comprises people with a gift of interpretation who have made the effort to develop that gifting. These are people with a Daniel-type anointing. Remember, Daniel was not only gifted, but was also skilled at learning and gaining knowledge (see Dan. 1:17).

♦ Gift of interpretation without acquiring skills of interpretation applies to people who make no effort to acquire more skills at interpreting dreams.

CHAPTER 13

The Interpretative Process

"For God speaketh once, yea twice, yet man perceiveth it not" (Job 33:14 KJV). The word *perceive* means to achieve understanding of, or to apprehend. Correctly perceiving what God is saying in dreams and visions is not only for prophets, but for all the saints of God. To understand what God is saying in dreams, we need to interpret what we receive from God. Interpretation is a by-product of our relationship with God because it's achieved through the Holy Spirit's help. In this regard, the Holy Spirit helps us to draw from the reservoir of God's Word, which is an incredible revelatory wellspring. Together with biblical imagery, Scripture equips us to understand many forms of spiritual communication from God.

All revelation needs some form of interpretation—whether symbolic or literal, or perhaps a combination of the two. All these forms of interpretation may be applied to a single revelation. However, one must avoid assumption, and only allow logical deduction from what has been revealed. Adding assumption to what has been revealed may confuse the picture.

We should not get bogged down with rigid application of types and symbols, but, instead, practice a broad principle of interpretation. The fact that you have received a revelation does not automatically entitle you to its interpretation, which always comes from the Holy Spirit. One crucial point worth remembering is that interpretation

121

should come into our mind by a gradual inflow of the Holy Spirit; true interpretation does not come by intensive or rigorous reasoning. After receiving prompting from the Holy Spirit, the interpreter should apply minimal reasoning to elaborate.

Interpretation

Interpretation is the deciphering of a parable language. A symbol is an element used to represent another element. After receiving prompting from the Holy Spirit, my first move when interpreting a dream is to bring meaning to its symbols. Deriving meaning for symbols should be predominantly centered on the Word of God. Then, I expound upon the relevance of the symbols to a dreamer's life circumstance.

Exposition brings understanding to these symbols and events as they relate to the dreamer's personal experience. Deriving meaning for symbols must go along with exposition to truly interpret a dream or vision. True and complete interpretation must take the following into consideration:

1. Scripture.

2. The inherent meaning of the symbol.

3. The dreamer's personal experience.

4. The social influences of the dreamer (such as the culture and colloquial expressions that he is used to).

Steps to Correct Interpretation

One should not advocate a formula-based approach to dream interpretation. Reliance on the Holy Spirit is an absolute necessity. However, I have found the following to be helpful in my teaching program.

◆ Wait for the prompting of the Holy Spirit. Correct interpretation does not come by human reasoning, but by an inflow into our hearts or subconscious from God.

◆ Understand the meaning of the symbols and actions.

◆ Explain the relevance of events and symbols to the dreamer's circumstance.

Always be sure to always put together a possible storyline for the dream. The plot should assemble the dream's elements and events without any contradiction. What follows is helpful in determining whether the storyline is correct:

* All elements will agree with or fit into the plot.

* All actions will fit into the context of the plot.

* If only one or two elements do not fit with the plot while the majority of others are in agreement, then the derived "meaning" of the symbol is not the appropriate one. Therefore, check other meanings of the symbol. If more than two elements don't fit into the plot, then be sure to review it.

◆ Proclamation: declaring God's sovereign message in the dream with the Holy Spirit's help. The proclamation must be based on why the interpreter perceives that God sent the message. Therefore, proclamation is more than mere compilation of a correctly derived meaning of symbols; it includes the interpreter's attempt to declare God's mind in sending a vision. Unfortunately, most dreamers are satisfied with just seeing dreams come to pass. But some dreams and visions may be given for the purpose of influencing future events; intercession can avert judgment or bring promises into reality.

◆ Application: bringing the message and the dream's wisdom to practical usefulness in the dreamer's life.

Symbols

To interpret a dream, we must think symbolically. A symbol's meaning must be revealed to the dreamer for each dream. The same symbol may be different for distinct dreams, even though certain symbols may be used more commonly for some people. One meaning of a symbol is not necessarily its meaning for all dreams. Also, do not get fixed on a symbol's single meaning because it may change as you grow in your walk with God. As you study the Word of God, you will draw less on your own life experience and more from a biblical reservoir of examples.

We must interpret symbols from a life with which a dreamer is familiar. Each symbol may have a unique association, as drawn from the dreamer's own experience. Symbols are not used haphazardly—they are specific and purposeful. In addition, there are particular symbols that cannot represent certain elements; for instance, being enticed by a prostitute could not represent the move of God, as we are *tempted* by the desire of our flesh.

If a symbol's inherent meaning conflicts with a meaning derived from God's Word, then a biblical understanding of symbols takes precedence over any other possible meaning. The scriptural meaning always supersedes. The meaning of symbolic actions is drawn primarily from the dreamer's background, but it should never contradict spiritual principles. Since symbols in dreams are chosen for very specific purposes, you must first identify God's purpose for using a particular symbol.

Understanding the Components of a Dream

A dream's elements are symbolic in most cases, but some of them can be literal. By and large, there is a higher percentage of symbolic dreams than literal dreams. Actions in dreams are typically symbolic as well. *The context of the dream* is the circumstance in which the events occur, or its sequence of events. *The background* is the setting or place in which the dream occurs.

The Internal Component of Dreams

Every dream has an internal component, which is when the dreamer's emotional composure factors into its dramatization. Such depictions usually find expression as excessive anger, excessive insecurity, unwarranted distrustfulness, superstition, excessive crave for worldly pleasures, unfounded fear, or overbearing reactions. God will highlight such reactions amidst a dream message so that it can be addressed. A woman once presented me with this dream:

While she was in the ladies changing room about to go into a public swimming pool, a certain man came to interrupt her preparation on three occasions. The first time he interrupted her, she was just upset about it. On the second occasion, she was really angry. But on the third occasion, she went into a rage and ended up not going for the swimming exercise.

In this dream, God highlighted the lady's inner struggle with temperament, which should be addressed before it hinders her in the future. However, the dream's main message is that some unfair circumstances of life may interfere with her desire to flow in the Holy Spirit. This dream calls for two prayer points: first, her struggle with temperament; and second, to avoid unfair circumstances that could rob her desire to move with God.

The Three Levels of Skill in Dream Interpretation

Over the years, I have found that human attempts to interpret dreams will fall into one of three categories: Level 0, 1, or 2.

♦ *Level 0* is the attempt by non-believers to interpret dreams.

♦ *Level 1* is a believer's compilation of dictionary-derived meanings of symbols, without any prompting of the Holy Spirit.

♦ *Level 2* is the true interpretation, as prompted by the Holy Spirit.

Here are some key Bible texts relevant for this categorization:

...but God has revealed it to us by His Spirit. The Spirit searches all things, even the deep things of God. For who among men knows the thoughts of a man except the man's spirit within him? In the same way no one knows the thoughts of God except the Spirit of God. We have not received the spirit of the world but the Spirit who is from God, that we may understand what God has freely given us (1 Corinthians 2:10-12).

He told them, "The secret of the kingdom of God has been given to you. But to those on the outside everything is said in parables so that, 'they may be ever seeing but never perceiving, and ever hearing but never understanding...'" (Mark 4:11-12).

The key point in true interpretation is being able to reveal God's mind in sending the dream. So a true and complete interpretation will always answer this question: "Why did God send the dream?"

NON-BELIEVERS	BELIEVERS	
LEVEL 0	LEVEL 1	LEVEL 2
"Soulish" emotion based on emotion, sentiment, and feelings.	The mind of God is not usually reflected.	The mind of God is revealed by the Holy Spirit.
Causes strife, always emphasizes the negative and takes away hope.	Misplaced priorities—does not have the wisdom of the Holy Spirit.	The dreamer acknowledges the true worthiness of the interpretation and speaks God's wisdom into the situation.
Seeks self-interest—no respect for human life, especially the life of an enemy.	Does not lead to a closer walk with God—it may cause confusion.	Speaks God's mind into the situation and gives clear, unambiguous instruction for the way forward.
Does not speak of love—drives the dreamer from God and seeks vengeance.	The dreamer's yearning is not satisfied.	Bears relevance to the dreamer's circumstances.
Leads to bondage.	Creates fear and lack of faith.	Always speaks of love. Leaves the dreamer with hope and builds up faith.
Interpretative attempts are not based on principles, and therefore, are unable to link a series of dreams on the same subject.	May be correct symbol-derived meaning, but relevance to the dreamer's life situation and proclamation are wrong.	It is truthful—even if it's a warning. Correctly links related series of dreams and brings appropriate exposition and proclamation.

Joseph's Track Record of Interpretation

In the later part of life, Joseph operated at the Level 2 category. But in his younger days, he remained ignorant of the spiritual principle that public pronouncement of divine revelations should only be to bring about change in a positive way; it should never be done for self-aggrandizement. Joseph took 17 years to reach the Level 2 grade.

Joseph Interprets the Cupbearer's and the Baker's Dreams

THE CUPBEARER'S DREAM Genesis 40:9-11	Within three days, Pharaoh will lift your head and restore you to your position.
"I saw a vine in front of me..."	A "vine" is life, for Jesus said, "I am the vine, the source of life.""Front of me" means ahead of the dreamer.
"On the vine were three branches..."	Three branches indicate three days. Perhaps the vine tree sprouts one branch per day.
"It budded, it blossomed, and its clusters ripened into grapes..."	A miraculous and speedy progression of future life events that result in fruitfulness.
"Pharaoh's cup was in my hand, and I took the grapes, squeezed them into Pharaoh's cup..."	"Pharaoh's cup": responsibility in high places. "In my hand": hand is the symbol for service and "my" indicates the dreamer's service.
"Put the cup in his hand..."	A restoration to former position and service.

THE BAKER'S DREAM Genesis 40:16-17	To be held responsible for, or to bear consequences for one's actions.
"On my head were three baskets of bread..."	The baskets indicate judgment. Bread is also a symbol for life, or a source of nourishment for life. Putting the two symbols together refers to judgment.
"Three baskets..."	Indicates three days of baking because there were no means of preservation, thus there was a need for daily baking.
"...basket were all kinds of baked goods for Pharaoh, but the birds were eating them out of the basket on my head."	The birds: agents representing leadership. Eating the substance of life from his head: death.

Jacob's Track Record of Interpretation

Jacob was a dreamer, who, most of the time, operated in the Level 1 category of interpretation. He interpreted "the moon and the sun" of Joseph's dream (see Gen. 37:9-10) to mean himself and Joseph's mother, but we know that neither of them ever bowed down to Joseph. Jacob also took on surface value his dream of the *"stairway resting on the earth, with its top reaching to heaven, and angels of God were ascending and descending on it"* (Gen. 28:12). Yet, it affirmed God's promises to him by election and the grace of God. This dream also conveyed that he did not need to continue striving or relying solely on human effort. This dream was given within a context of his fleeing from deception, manipulation, family intrigue, and struggles for Esau's birthright.

THE LADDER TO HEAVEN DREAM Genesis 28:11-13	For Jacob to know that it was all by grace and by election
"A ladder resting on the earth, with its top reaching to heaven."	God assured Jacob that he was the carrier of both the seed and the covenant of Abraham and also assured him of personal safety and blessing. But man must reach out to God in Heaven, hence the ladder was from earth reaching to Heaven.
"Angels of God were ascending and descending."	Two-way relationship between God and man. Angels bringing provisions from God.
"There above it stood the Lord."	God oversees the plans of men on earth.
Confers the Abrahamic Covenant on Jacob.	Induced Jacob with anointing for the call on his life.
God's mind in sending the dream.	For Jacob to know that it was all by grace and by election hence he should stop scheming and trust God for the future. Also to establish a personal relationship with Jacob. From this point on God became known as God of Abraham, Isaac, and Jacob.

Transitioning Between Levels

NON-BELIEVERS	BELIEVERS	
LEVEL 0	LEVEL 1	LEVEL 2
Transition required:	*Transition required:*	*Transition required:*
Salvation.	Waiting upon the Lord and allowing the Holy Spirit to take control.	Nothing, except to continuously dwell in God's presence and allow the prompting of the Holy Spirit to flow into the mind.
Making Jesus Christ the Lord over everything.	Constant study of the Word of God, regular fasting, praise and worship, and obedience to the things of God. Hebrew 5:14 principle *"But solid food is for the mature, who by constant use have trained themselves to distinguish good from evil."* Experience counts.	Constant sanctification of the mind with the Word of God, for it has divine substance to continuously transform the soil of the mind to receive from God. At this level there is also divine wisdom to handle and deliver the meaning of the dream or vision to people.

Most believers will recognize when their interpretation is only on a Level 1 because it will not sit well with their consciousness; just as Jacob knew his understanding of Joseph's dream was incomplete: *"His brothers were jealous of him, but his father kept the matter in mind"* (Gen. 37:11). Our goal should be to increase percentages of interpretations that fall into a Level 2 category and to possess the grace to know when interpretations only reach a Level 1 category.

How to Improve Your Interpretative Skills

General Points

This is not a *carte blanche* for dream interpretation.

◆ Interpretation comes from God.

◆ Commit everything to God in prayer.

◆ You can receive interpretation instantaneously, through fasting/prayers/meditation, which brings clarity.

◆ Experience and the degree of interpreter's giftedness can influence how quickly interpretation is received.

Step 1

Listen in the spirit:

◆ Calm your soul in the Lord's presence.

◆ Use the eyes of your faith.

◆ Trust that God will give you the understanding.

◆ Allow the peace of God to rule your mind and heart.

◆ Wait for prompting of the Holy Spirit.

Put away acts of the soulish realm:

◆ Do not allow intellectualism and logic to rule the mind.

◆ Do not entertain fear and confusion.

◆ Do not be apprehensive or anxious.

◆ Do not allow emotions from the dream to cloud your judgment.

◆ Keep a clear mind.

Step 2

Allow clues as to the essence of its message to flow into your spirit from God:

The Holy Spirit lights up an aspect of the dream that grabs your attention or imagination—this could be a symbol or an action in the dream—and the rest of the storyline will hinge upon this. Therefore, be sensitive and see what stands out in the dream or vision. Here are examples of how the Holy Spirit will usually prompt you:

> *"This was the dream, and now we will interpret it to the king. You, O king, are the king of kings. The God of heaven has given you dominion and power and might and glory; in your hands He has placed mankind and the beasts of the field and the birds of the air. Wherever they live, He has made you ruler over them all. **You are that head of gold"** (Daniel 2:36-38).*

Then I wanted to know the true meaning of the fourth beast, which was different from all the others and most terrifying, with its iron teeth and bronze claws—the beast that crushed and devoured its victims and trampled underfoot whatever was left. I also wanted to know about the ten horns on its head and about the other horn that came up, before which three of them fell—the horn that looked more imposing than the others and that had eyes and a mouth that spoke boastfully (Daniel 7:19-21).

"While I was thinking about the horns, **there before me was another horn, a little one, which came up** *among them; and three of the first horns were uprooted before it. This horn had eyes like the eyes of a man and a mouth that spoke boastfully"* (Daniel 7:8).

"Then I continued to watch because of the boastful words the horn was speaking. I kept looking until the beast was slain and its body destroyed and thrown into the blazing fire" (Daniel 7:11).

God prompted Daniel by highlighting the little boastful horn.

I have found the following to be helpful in characterizing a prompting from the Holy Spirit:

♦ Every element in the dream will agree with this prompting.

♦ Its context, trends, and background will also line up with the prompting.

♦ The prompting should be capable of guiding an eventual, logical exposition of the dream's symbol and events.

♦ The plot or essence of the dream's message will hinge on this prompting.

Step 3

Allow minimal logical process:

After receiving God's prompting, allow minimal logical deductions to put the entire story into a perspective that fits correctly. Interpretation of a personal dream is often hindered by immediate progression to the logical processing without first receiving God's prompting through a rhema word. Another problem is the intrusion of mind-set or preconceived ideas, which lead to clouded judgment. Here is an example of permissible logical deduction after receiving prompting from the Holy Spirit:

After you, another kingdom will rise, inferior to yours. Next, a third kingdom, one of bronze, will rule over the whole earth. Finally, there will be a fourth kingdom, strong as iron—for iron breaks and smashes everything—and as iron breaks things to pieces, so it will crush and break all the others. Just as you saw that the feet and toes were partly of baked clay and partly of iron, so this will be a divided kingdom; yet it will have some of the strength of iron in it, even as you saw iron mixed with clay. As the toes were partly iron and partly clay, so this kingdom will be partly strong and partly brittle (Daniel 2:39-42).

Step 4

Determine who/what the dream is about:

+ A person

+ A group of persons

+ A place

Determine what aspect of the person's life is referred to in the dream:

From my experience, the aspect of a dreamer's life that is addressed in a dream is usually reflected as its background setting:

+ An office background usually represents a secular career.

+ A family setting primarily indicates issues in one's personal life, bloodline, or generation.

+ Church background relates to dreamer's ministry.

+ Money speaks of favor from God, or actual money.

Determine the timing:

Unless specified, timing is usually fairly difficult to determine in dreams. Generally, the following will determine if a dream relates to past, present, or future:

+ Old house: objects in the past influencing the present.

+ Clocks: lateness or presumption, depending on whether it indicates being late or early.

+ Dates: as relevant to the actual date.

+ Time of day, in terms of morning, afternoon, and evening.

Step 5

The interpreter intimates with the dreamer:

The interpreter should also ask the same questions that the sailors put to Jonah: *"So they asked him, '...What do you do? Where do you come from? What is your country? From what people are you?'"* (Jonah. 1:8).

Confirm if there are any preoccupations in the dreamer's mind.

Step 6

Determine the plot of the dream:

This will lead to the unraveling of the dream's superior wisdom.

Step 7

Confirm the interpretation:

Depending on the circumstance, God may speak confirmation in many ways: an audible voice; a still small voice; dreams and visions; mental pictures; and inner impressions. Confirmation can also happen in other forms of prophecies, through prophets, events (past or ongoing), and other revelatory means from God, including recurring dreams. (See previous section in Chapter 5.)

Step 8

Take responsibility for what is revealed:

We should take action on the confirmed interpretation, even if it is only to meditate and pray on what has been revealed.

Step 9

Above all, let the glory go to God:

God used Joseph and Daniel to reveal the meaning of dreams to kings. Both were very quick to acknowledge that God alone gave them ability to interpret dreams. They gave Him all the glory.

Joseph's response to Pharaoh: *"I cannot do it [interpret the dream]...but God will give Pharaoh the answer he desires"* (see Gen. 41:15-16.)

Daniel said to Nebuchadnezzar:

"No wise man, enchanter, magician or diviner can explain to the king the mystery he has asked about. But there is a God in heaven...As for me, this mystery has been revealed to me, not because I have greater wisdom than other living men, but so that you, O king, may know the interpretation and that you may understand what went through your mind" (Daniel 2:27-28,30).

UNDERSTANDING

SYMBOLS

PART III

CHAPTER 14

Understanding the
Language of Symbols

The language of the spirit is a symbolic language. No other book speaks in symbols more than the Bible. Symbolism is also the language of dreams. In several ways, the language pattern of dreams is similar to the pattern of speech used in the Bible. Because of its extensive symbolism, some people have described the Old Testament as the New Testament concealed.

The language of reason is limited, whereas the language of symbols is infinite. A symbol may be identified by one word, yet, at the same time, may take volumes to be comprehensively described. The language of symbols and symbolic actions has great depth and power. As the saying goes, "A picture is worth a thousand words." Children learn the language of pictures and symbols before learning the language of words and reason. Man thinks and processes information in pictures because the language of symbols is richer than that of words.

God Himself described His pattern of speech to the prophets:

"When a prophet of the Lord is among you, I reveal Myself to him in visions, I speak to him in dreams. But this is not true of My servant Moses; he is faithful in all My house. With him I speak face to face, clearly and not in riddles; he sees the form of the Lord. Why then were you not afraid to speak against My servant Moses?" (Numbers 12:6-8)

Key points from the above passage are:

◆ God does not speak to everyone the same way.

◆ He speaks in dreams and visions.

◆ He speaks in clear language.

◆ He speaks in riddles or parables.

◆ He speaks in dark speech.

◆ He speaks in similitude.

He may choose how to speak to us because He is God!

Jesus Christ explained why He spoke and taught in parables:

The disciples came to Him and asked, "Why do You speak to the people in parables?" He replied, "The knowledge of the secrets of the kingdom of heaven has been given to you, but not to them. Whoever has will be given more, and he will have an abundance. Whoever does not have, even what he has will be taken from him. This is why I speak to them in parables: Though seeing, they do not see; though hearing, they do not hear or understand" (Matthew 13:10-13).

With many similar parables Jesus spoke the word to them, as much as they could understand. He did not say anything to them without using a parable. But when He was alone with His own disciples, He explained everything (Mark 4:33-34).

Jesus taught in parables and used symbols to illustrate His message. But He revealed secrets of God's kingdom only to the disciples. The Lord also described the Holy Spirit's role in understanding what God says. The Holy Spirit helps us by explaining God's symbolic language of dark speeches, similitude, and parables. Without this, we will be unable to understand the mind of God on any issue.

How Symbols Derive Their Meaning

A message in symbols automatically switches us to symbolic thinking. Every parable needs symbolic interpretation, with a meaning given for each symbol. To determine a symbol's meaning, do the following: first, consult the reservoir of God's Word; second, ascertain the symbol's inherent meaning; third, determine its association to the dreamer's experience; and lastly, devise a meaning from culture and colloquial expressions in society.

However, a symbol's true meaning does not come from human reasoning, but rather by allowing it to flow into our hearts from the Holy Spirit. This process comes by being quiet and still in the inner self. The choice of symbols in a dream is very specific and purposeful, and is the prerogative of God. A dream is the truest representation of a situation, as it reflects God's perspective; therefore, it addresses the issue more frankly than human illustration.

Why God Uses Symbols

◆ It helps us to see the real situation from God's perspective because a symbol shows how He thinks about it.

  • Striking features as symbols help impartation and interpretation.

  • The hidden meaning of a symbol allows God to give clarification in stages.

  • Humility is the key, as it increases your dependence on the Holy Spirit.

◆ The Lord will relate to a person in symbols that have some personal meaning. Dreams are a form of communication—an intimate language between you and the Lord.

  • It secures the message from the enemy.

  • It makes you want to search out the meaning.

◆ The language of symbols is deep and powerful. At the same time, it is the most elementary language of man and, therefore, available to all ages.

  • The human mind understands or reads in pictures.

Those who have understood the tremendous power of symbols have gained incredible insights into God's mysteries because His ways are wrapped up in a symbolic language. As human beings tend to think in pictures, people need visual appreciation to truly grasp the essence of a concept. Symbols evoke powerful emotion and elicit strong passion, so much so that generations of politicians, philosophers, and religious leaders have used them to illustrate points. National commitment is symbolized in the pride and honor accorded to the country's symbol: a flag. Many people would be outraged to see their flag dishonored. Public hatred is often demonstrated by the burning of the enemy's national flag.

Biblical Example

Symbolism brought home the gravity of David's adulterous act to him. God could have chosen to send King David the same message through a dream. However, Nathan narrated the message to David in a dream format—of a parable—to reveal the gravity of his sin.

The Lord sent Nathan to David. When he came to him, he said, "There were two men in a certain town, one rich and the other poor. The rich man had a very large number of sheep and cattle, but the poor man had nothing except one little ewe lamb that he had bought. He raised it, and it grew up with him and his children. It shared his food, drank from his cup and even slept in his arms. It was like a daughter to him. Now a traveler came to the rich man, but the rich man refrained from taking one of his own sheep or cattle to prepare a meal for the traveler who had come to him. Instead, he took the ewe lamb that belonged to the poor man and prepared it for the one who had come to him." David burned with anger against the man and said to Nathan, "As surely as the Lord lives, the man who did this deserves to die! He must pay for that lamb four times over, because he did such a thing and had no pity" (2 Samuel 12:1-6).

At this point, the prophet Nathan reveals to King David that he is the man who has committed the crime, and that God is judging him for the murder of Uriah the Hittite and his adultery with Bathsheba.

Anatomy of Nathan's Statement to David

SYMBOL/ACTION	MEANING	THE POWER OF IMAGERY
The rich man.	David.	He represents an important personality.
The poor man.	Uriah.	A person who is vulnerable because he lacks the necessities of life.

Symbol/Action	Meaning	The Power of Imagery
A little ewe—like a daughter.	Uriah's wife, who is precious to him.	This represents something precious to the dreamer.
The arrival of traveler.	A need arises.	A potential need is imminent or at hand.
He refrains from using his own.	Selfishness.	A spirit of self-centeredness, or inconsiderate of others.
David's anger burned against the injustice of the man in Nathan's story.	Then David came to the realization that the sin was his. Therefore, he understood the true severity of his sin.	Holy anger stirred by the spirit of righteousness, or coming to one's senses after a period of being attacked with carnality.

How to Think Symbolically

A dream is God's picture language interlaced with words. No one can understand dreams in correct perspective without some understanding of the Bible's symbols, metaphors, and speech patterns. Until we can understand symbolic connotations, many elements in dreams will remain unexpressed. This comprehension consists of knowing the symbol's literal meaning and what it evokes in people's minds. Valuable information is lost if we fail to understand the symbolic meaning of elements, persons, and actions in a dream. When one comes across an image and truly switches to symbolic thinking, two questions should arise in the mind:

1. What is the literal meaning of the image? (Usually the most obvious meaning.)

2. What does the image evoke? (These are the overtones.)

If either of these aspects is not well understood, then our comprehension of the pictorial language will be limited.

An Example

Husband:

1. Ordinarily understood to mean male or man.

2. The word also evokes some lateral thinking, of father, head of a home, provider, or Jesus Christ.

Symbols From the Parables of Jesus

The Parable of the Sower

Then He told them many things in parables, saying: "A farmer went out to sow his seed. As he was scattering the seed, some fell along the path, and the birds came and ate it up. Some fell on rocky places, where it did not have much soil. It sprang up quickly, because the soil was shallow. But when the sun came up, the plants were scorched, and they withered because they had no root. Other seed fell among thorns, which grew up and choked the plants. Still other seed fell on good soil, where it produced a crop—a hundred, sixty or thirty times what was sown. He who has ears, let him hear" (Matthew 13:3-9).

The Interpretation

Listen then to what the parable of the sower means: When anyone hears the message about the kingdom and does not understand it, the evil one comes and snatches away what was sown in his heart. This is the seed sown along the path. The one who received the seed that fell on rocky places is the man who hears the word and at once receives it with joy. But since he has no root, he lasts only a short time. When trouble or persecution comes because of the word, he quickly falls away. The one who received the seed that fell among the thorns is the man who hears the word, but the worries of this life and the deceitfulness of wealth choke it, making it unfruitful. But the one who received the seed that fell on good soil is the man who hears the word and understands it. He produces a crop, yielding a hundred, sixty or thirty times what was sown (Matthew 13:18-23).

The Anatomy of the Parable of the Sower

SYMBOL	MEANING	DERIVED DREAM
Seed.	Word of God.	The Word of God is God's promise, which is capable of multiplication.

Symbol/Action	Meaning	Derived Dream
Soil.	Heart of Man.	Potential for multiplication either good or bad—the essence of life.
Farmer.	Jesus Christ.	God, pastor, spiritual leader.
"Sown along the path."	No understanding—taken away by the devil.	Unprotected—easily taken by the devil.
"Seeds fell on rocky places."	Receives the Word with joy, but lacks depth and the seed gets stolen by trouble and persecution from the world	"Walking on rocky places," equals times of trouble, persecution, and lack of depth.
"Seeds fell on thorns."	The Word of God is heard, but gets choked by worries of life or the attraction of worldly riches.	Thorns, which mean the worries of life and the distraction of worldly riches.
"Seed on good soil."	Hears the Word, understands and becomes fruitful.	Well prepared for life expectancy, conducive for growth.

The Benefits of a Parable Language

◆ Economy—a picture is worth a thousand words.

◆ The essence is shown as you apply specifics to your situation. It also gives the principle, so that the essence can be applicable at other times.

◆ A parable allows God to code messages for the dreamer.

◆ The promise is protected because the dream hides it from the enemy.

◆ Allows God to package and unfold His message according to areas of priority. Hosea 12:10 says: *"I spoke to the prophets, gave them many visions and told parables through them."*

- The language of pictures and symbols is universal and has no age barrier.

- Allows God to give the best possible picture or truest perspective of a situation.

- A dream parable often shows the present condition, and what will happen if we continue to go in the same direction.

The purpose of a parable language is explained in Proverbs 1:1-6 AMP):

> *The proverbs (truths obscurely expressed, maxims, and **parables**) of Solomon son of David, king of Israel: that people may know skillful and godly wisdom and instruction, discern and comprehend the words of understanding and insight. Receive instruction in wise dealing and the discipline of wise thoughtfulness, righteousness, justice, and integrity. That prudence may be given to the simple, and knowledge, discretion, and discernment to the youth. The wise also will hear and increase in learning, and the person of understanding will acquire skill and attain to sound counsel [so that he may be able to steer his course rightly]. That people may understand a proverb and a figure of speech or an enigma with its interpretation, and the words of the wise and their dark saying or riddles.*

A more comprehensive study of symbols is presented in the chapters preeceding the Dictionary of Dream Symbols in the second half of this book.

CHAPTER 15

Angelic Interactions in Dreams

The Bible is replete with dreams that involve angels. Most dreamers will have encountered angels in their dreams but do not actually realize this. The majority of unknown people in our dreams who were trustworthy, helpful, and protective (and not contrary to divine principles) are usually angels concealed in human form. More commonly, a faceless personality in our dreams may refer to the Holy Spirit. (However, an unknown person who is deceptive, untrustworthy, unreliable, and causes hindrance in a dream is evil and symbolic of a demonic spirit.) Angels are common in twilight dreams and are often associated with clear dream phrases that give unambiguous instructions.

Angels often bring interpretation in our dreams. These interpretations can come in numerous forms, but they are usually literal and do not require further deciphering. Remember, however, that the Bible said, *"But even if we or an angel from heaven should preach a gospel other than the one we preached to you, let him be eternally condemned"* (Gal. 1:8). Most interpretations need further study, so we should ask God for understanding of what we receive.

♦ **Most of the time, angels bring interpretation to us in dreams:**

I, Daniel, was troubled in spirit, and the visions that passed through my mind disturbed me. I approached one of those standing there and

145

asked him the true meaning of all this. So he told me and gave me the interpretation of these things (Daniel 7:15-16).

While I, Daniel, was watching the vision and trying to understand it, there before me stood one who looked like a man. And I heard a man's voice from the Ulai calling, "Gabriel, tell this man the meaning of the vision" (Daniel 8:15-16).

I asked, "What are these, my lord?" The angel who was talking with me answered, "I will show you what they are." Then the man standing among the myrtle trees explained, "They are the ones the Lord has sent to go throughout the earth" (Zechariah 1:9-10).

I asked, "Where are you going?" He answered me, "To measure Jerusalem, to find out how wide and how long it is." Then the angel who was speaking to me left, and another angel came to meet him and said to him: "Run, tell that young man, 'Jerusalem will be a city without walls because of the great number of men and livestock in it. And I myself will be a wall of fire around it,' declares the Lord, 'and I will be its glory within. Come! Come! Flee from the land of the north,' declares the Lord, 'for I have scattered you to the four winds of heaven,' declares the Lord" (Zechariah 2:2-6).

◆ **Angels can wake us up to recall and record our dreams:**

Then the angel who talked with me returned and wakened me, as a man is wakened from his sleep. He asked me, "What do you see?" I answered, "I see a solid gold lampstand with a bowl at the top and seven lights on it, with seven channels to the lights. Also there are two olive trees by it, one on the right of the bowl and the other on its left (Zechariah 4:1-3).

I, Daniel, was the only one who saw the vision; the men with me did not see it, but such terror overwhelmed them that they fled and hid themselves. So I was left alone, gazing at this great vision; I had no strength left, my face turned deathly pale and I was helpless. Then I heard him speaking, and as I listened to him, I fell into a deep sleep, my face to the ground. A hand touched me and set me trembling on my hands and knees. He said, "Daniel, you who are highly esteemed, consider carefully the words I am about to speak to you, and stand up, for I have now been sent to you." And when he said this to me, I stood up trembling (Daniel 10:7-11).

◆ **Angels bring impartation in dreams:**

*Then the voice that I had heard from heaven spoke to me once more:
"Go, take the scroll that lies open in the hand of the angel who is
standing on the sea and on the land." So I went to the angel and
asked him to give me the little scroll. He said to me, "Take it and eat
it. It will turn your stomach sour, but in your mouth it will be as
sweet as honey." I took the little scroll from the angel's hand and ate
it. It tasted as sweet as honey in my mouth, but when I had eaten it,
my stomach turned sour. Then I was told, "You must prophesy again
about many peoples, nations, languages and kings"* (Revelation
10:8-11).

*In the sixth month, God sent the angel Gabriel to Nazareth, a town in
Galilee, to a virgin pledged to be married to a man named Joseph, a
descendant of David. The virgin's name was Mary. The angel went to
her and said, "Greetings, you who are highly favored! The Lord is with
you." Mary was greatly troubled at his words and wondered what kind
of greeting this might be. But the angel said to her, "Do not be afraid,
Mary, you have found favor with God. You will be with child and give
birth to a son, and you are to give Him the name Jesus. He will be great
and will be called the Son of the Most High. The Lord God will give
Him the throne of His father David, and He will reign over the house of
Jacob forever; His kingdom will never end." "How will this be," Mary
asked the angel, "since I am a virgin?" The angel answered, "The Holy
Spirit will come upon you, and the power of the Most High will over-
shadow you. So the holy one to be born will be called the Son of God"*
(Luke 1:26-35).

◆ **Angels bring knowledge in dreams or visions:**

*Then he continued, "Do not be afraid, Daniel. Since the first day
that you set your mind to gain understanding and to humble yourself before your God, your words were heard, and I have come in
response to them. But the prince of the Persian kingdom resisted
me twenty-one days. Then Michael, one of the chief princes, came
to help me, because I was detained there with the king of Persia.
Now I have come to explain to you what will happen to your people in the future, for the vision concerns a time yet to come"*
(Daniel 10:12-14).

CHAPTER 16

Spiritual Significance
of Numbers

God speaks a great deal through numbers. The Bible is full of evidence of God's arithmetic. Numbers are a high-level form of symbolism. Here I have put together some numbers along with generally accepted scriptural relevance. The spiritual significance of numbers given is based on the Word of God.

1: Unity; the number of God; the beginning; the first.

2: Union, witnessing, or confirmation. It could also mean division, depending on the general context of the revelation.

3: Resurrection, divine completeness, and perfection; confirmation or the trinity of Godhead.

4: Creation, or rule, or reign. On the fourth day of creation, God made two great lights, the sun and the moon, to rule the day and the night (see Gen. 1:16-19).

5: Grace or the goodness of God.

6: The number of man, weakness of humanity, or the flesh. It could also mean evil or satan.

7: Completeness or spiritual perfection.

8: New birth or new beginning. The circumcision of male children of Israel on the eighth day is a type of new birth.

9: Fruit of the Spirit, harvest, or the fruit of your labor.

10: Law and responsibility. The tithe is a tenth of our earning, which belongs to God. It is also the number of the pastoral.

11: Confusion, judgment, or disorder.

12: Government, or the number of apostleship.

13: Rebellion or spiritual depravity.

14: Deliverance or salvation. The number of double anointing.

15: Rest (see Lev. 23:34-35).

16: Love.

17: Victory; immaturity.

18: Bondage (see Luke 13:16).

19: Faith (19 persons are mentioned in Hebrews 11:1-32).

20: Redemption; fit for battle.

30: Blood of Jesus, and dedication (see Matt. 26:14-15 and 27:5-8).

40: Trial, probation, or testing. Israel was in the wilderness for 40 years. Moses spent 40 years in both Egypt and Midian.

50: The number for the Holy Spirit. The Holy Spirit was poured out on the Day of Pentecost, which was 50 days after the resurrection of Christ (see Acts 2).

60: Pride or arrogance. The image set up by Nebuchadnezzar was 60 cubits high (see Dan. 3:1 NKJ).

70: Universality or restoration. The Israelites lived in exile for 70 years and were restored 70 years later.

80: Beginning of a high calling or becoming spiritually acceptable. Moses was 80 years old when he started his ministry to deliver the Israelites.

90 or 99: Fruits are ripe and ready. Abraham *"was ninety years and nine when God appeared to him"* (Gen. 17:1 KJV).

100: God's election of grace, full reward, or children of promise. *"Abraham was a hundred years old when his son Isaac* [the child of promise] *was born to him"* (Gen. 21:5).

1000: The beginning of maturity, mature service, or full status.

For multiples or complex numbers, the meaning lies in the way that the figure is pronounced, rather than as it's written. For example, 2872 is pronounced "two thousand eight hundred and seventy two." The interpretation is as follows: two thousand = confirmed spiritual maturity or mature judgment; eight hundred = new beginning into the promises; seventy-two = confirmed completed and restored.

CHAPTER 17

Animals in Dreams

Animals in dreams are mostly symbolic of circumstances, events, personality traits of people, governmental forces, evil spirits, and even the Spirit of God. Answering the following questions will help to understand what they stand for in dreams:

1. What does the Bible say about the animal?

2. What is the dreamer's experience with the animal?

3. Other specific attributes ascribable to the spirit symbolized by the animal:

   a. Can they be eaten?

      ◆ If they can be eaten, then *they represent a source of livelihood, such as cattle.*

   b. Do they pose danger to people?

      ◆ If they pose danger to people, then *they probably represent impending or existing danger to the dreamer.*

   c. Do they harm crops?

      ◆ If they harm crops, then *they probably represent limitation to source or income, reduction or destruction of harvestable resources.*

   d. Are they domesticated?

♦ If they can be domesticated, then *they may represent something that can become valuable if properly tamed.*

e. Are they tolerant of human presence?

♦ If they are tolerant of the presence of human beings, then *they probably represent something that remains innocuous unless provoked.*

Scriptural Examples of Animals in Dreams:

Pharaoh had a famous dream of the seven fat cows which came out of the Nile River only to be eaten by seven skinny cows, which also emerged from the waters of the Nile (see Gen. 41:1-4). In his interpretation, Joseph revealed the meaning behind these two sets of cows:

> **The seven good cows are seven years,** and the seven good heads of grain are seven years; it is one and the same dream. **The seven lean, ugly cows that came up afterward are seven years, and so are the seven** worthless heads of grain scorched by the east wind: They are seven years of famine. It is just as I said to Pharaoh: God has shown Pharaoh what He is about to do. **Seven years of great abundance are coming throughout the land of Egypt, but seven years of famine will follow them.** Then all the abundance in Egypt will be forgotten, and the famine will ravage the land (Genesis 41:26-30).

After having been installed into a high position in King Belshazzar's court, Daniel received a rather terrifying vision of four beasts:

> **Four great beasts, each different from the others, came up out of the sea.** The first was like a lion, and it had the wings of an eagle. I watched until its wings were torn off and it was lifted from the ground so that it stood on two feet like a man, and the heart of a man was given to it. And there before me was a second beast, which looked like a bear. It was raised up on one of its sides, and it had three ribs in its mouth between its teeth. It was told, "Get up and eat your fill of flesh!" After that, I looked, and there before me was another beast, one that looked like a leopard. And on its back it had four wings like those of a bird. This beast had four heads, and it was given authority to rule. After that, in my vision at night I looked, and there before me was a fourth beast—terrifying and frightening and very powerful. It had large iron teeth; it crushed and devoured its victims and trampled underfoot whatever was

left. It was different from all the former beasts, and it had ten horns (Daniel 7:3-7).

In the interpretation that Daniel received from an angel, he learned that *"the four great beasts are four kingdoms that will rise from the earth"* (Dan. 7:17). Each of these creatures represented a future foreign empire: The lion represented the kingdom of Babylon; the beast indicated Medo-Persia; the leopard symbolized Greece, under leadership of Alexander the Great; and the ten-horned beast was the Roman Empire.

John the Beloved experienced a multitude of visions while on the Isle of Patmos, including those displaying vicious beasts of the sea and the earth:

And the dragon stood on the shore of the sea. And I saw a beast coming out of the sea. He had ten horns and seven heads, with ten crowns on his horns, and on each head a blasphemous name. The beast I saw resembled a leopard, but had feet like those of a bear and a mouth like that of a lion. The dragon gave the beast his power and his throne and great authority. One of the heads of the beast seemed to have had a fatal wound, but the fatal wound had been healed. The whole world was astonished and followed the beast. Men worshiped the dragon because he had given authority to the beast, and they also worshiped the beast and asked, "Who is like the beast? Who can make war against him?" The beast was given a mouth to utter proud words and blasphemies and to exercise his authority for forty-two months. He opened his mouth to blaspheme God, and to slander His name and His dwelling place and those who live in heaven. He was given power to make war against the saints and to conquer them (Revelation 13:1-7).

Then I saw another beast, coming out of the earth. He had two horns like a lamb, but he spoke like a dragon. He exercised all the authority of the first beast on his behalf, and made the earth and its inhabitants worship the first beast, whose fatal wound had been healed. And he performed great and miraculous signs, even causing fire to come down from heaven to earth in full view of men. Because of the signs he was given power to do on behalf of the first beast, he deceived the inhabitants of the earth. He ordered them to set up an image in honor of the beast who was wounded by the sword and yet lived. He was given power to give breath to the image of the first beast, so that it could speak and cause all who refused to worship the image to be killed. He also forced everyone, small and great, rich and poor, free and slave, to receive a mark on his right hand or on his forehead, so that no one could buy or sell unless he had the mark, which is the name of the beast or the number of his name. This calls for wisdom. If anyone has insight, let him calculate the number of the beast, for it is man's number. His number is 666 (Revelation 13:11-18).

Interpretations of these visions reveal the beast from the sea as symbolic of an evil governmental force that may arise against the Church of Christ. The beast from the earth represents the evil conspiracy whose main task is to cause deception. This beast stands as an emblem of false religion, false prophets, and false priesthood. The beast of the earth will lead people astray by means of miraculous signs and enforce the worship of satan.

CHAPTER 18

Other Common Occurrences in Dreams

Superimpositions in Dreams

When an element is superimposed onto another in dream, it usually indicates that the two elements are very similar; they are a continuum of one to another; or they are a natural progression of one another. Superimposition can take various forms:

♦ When an element you recognize is superimposed onto an element you do not recognize, this indicates similarity.

♦ When a man and object are superimposed or used interchangeably, it indicates that one is symbolic of the other:

In the visions I saw while lying in my bed, I looked, and there before me was a messenger, a holy one, coming down from heaven. He called in a loud voice: "Cut down the tree and trim off its branches; strip off its leaves and scatter its fruit. Let the animals flee from under it and the birds from its branches. But let the stump and its roots, bound with iron and bronze, remain in the ground, in the grass of the field. Let him be drenched with the dew of heaven, and let him live with the animals among the plants of the earth. Let his mind be changed from that of a man and let him be given the mind of an animal, till seven times pass by for him" (Daniel 4:13-16).

157

♦ If a dreamer's roles of participating and observing in a dream are superimposed, then this indicates action, a consequence, or a natural progression of events.

♦ When two characters are interchangeably used in a dream—it may start off with one character, but end with the other character—such a situation usually means that what is being revealed is applicable to both characters.

♦ Seeing fulfillment of an earlier part of a dream in its later part, or seeing your thought dramatized in front of you while still in the same dream, indicates that fulfillment is imminent.

♦ A strange person acting the role of a known person in a dream may imply an approaching event, circumstance, or person that will bear resemblance to a known person from the past.

Dreaming or Recalling a Previous Dream in a Dream

Here is a practical example:

A lady dreamt that she came to me for the interpretation of a dream she had earlier; this was the outer dream. The earlier (inner) dream that she wanted to have interpreted was that she was asked to clean up bird droppings at the corners of our church; that process had become quite laborious and never ending. The interpretation that she said I gave in her dream was that she was going to get a new husband. (In the natural, she is a respectable, married woman, and her husband is my close friend.)

First, we need to interpret the inner dream and its interpretation. Getting a new husband indicates a new, higher level of relationship with Jesus Christ. The inner dream indicates that she will be privileged to see into the spirit realm. But in the process, she will see some unpleasantness that results from weaknesses in the church's leadership. As an intercessor, she will be required to continuously stand in the gap for them. If she is faithful in this assignment, then she will get a higher and new level of intimacy with Christ. The outer dream—where she sought my interpretation—represents her quest to understand the meaning of what she receives from God. I represent the prophetic ministry in this woman's life. All of this will lead to deeper revelation in the prophetic.

Bible Passages in Dreams

Bible passages that appear in dreams indicate messages from God regarding that Scripture's subject matter. This phenomenon can occur in a number of combinations:

◆ Not remembering the particular verse of a book on waking up indicates either a need to read the entire book or a faulty reception due to issues of lack of peace, anger, and unforgiveness.

◆ Not being able to locate a book or verse of the Bible while in a dream indicates a need for the dreamer to spend more time studying the Word in real life.

◆ Verbal quotes from the Bible that are twisted or controversial in a dream warn of the enemy's impending attempt to cause deception.

◆ Dramatization of a scriptural scene that is clear and correct is an instance of God's teaching solid, biblical principles to the dreamer.

Clocks or Watches in Dreams

◆ On its own, a clock or watch indicates the need to be watchful. It's a call to be alert.

◆ When a time is shown, it often indicates a Bible passage, and commonly refers to the Book of Psalms or Proverbs.

I once had a dream in which I was about to travel. I got to the bus stop, and I noticed that the time was 1:10 p.m. Yet, I was scheduled to travel with the 2:10 p.m. bus. The two buses were going to the same destination. Some people at the bus stop tried to talk me into taking the 1:10 p.m. bus, instead of waiting for the 2:10 p.m. bus. I thought that this was a good idea. However, before I could make up my mind whether or not to do so, the driver of the 1:10 p.m. bus took off in anger, as he apparently did not want me to journey with them. I watched the bus zoom off, and I felt completely embarrassed by the driver's attitude. As I watched, I noticed that the bus simply disappeared into thin air, much to everyone's amazement. No one could tell what had happened to it. The interpretation of this dream is Proverbs 1:10 (*"My son, if sinners entice you, do not give* in to them") and Proverbs 2:10 ("*For wisdom will enter your heart, and knowledge will be pleasant to your soul*").

◆ A clock that indicates lateness could mean that you are not quite as ready as you believe yourself to be. It might also mean you are at risk of missing a divine appointment.

◆ A clock that indicates being early for an appointment may signify a need to guard against being presumptuous. However, it could also be God's reassurance that you are ahead of schedule for a particular task or calling.

School or Classroom Scenes in the Dream

A scholastic environment may refer to some form of training. An inability to reach the classroom may mean that the dreamer is not in the right place or of the right attitude for required spiritual equipping. An examination often indicates standing at the verge of promotion.

Sex in Dreams

Sex in a dream suggests that you are probably making, or about to make, decisions based on a carnal nature. In Scripture, God frequently uses sexual immorality as an allegory for unfaithfulness, or deviation from spiritual truth. Frequent experience of sex in dreams speaks of carnality, but it also indicates a hidden, unbroken stronghold of lust. Rape indicates violation of the dreamer's person or integrity, and this must be averted in prayer.

Inability to Locate Otherwise Familiar Places

Inner indecision, uncertainty, or confusion in a dreamer's life often plays up as an inability to locate your room, house, office, or objects in a familiar environment. God uses this symbolism to draw that indecision and uncertainty to the dreamer's attention so that it can be addressed.

People in Your Dream

In the majority of cases, the people in my dreams are symbolic. Therefore, they often represent what I must remember about them.

◆ A man of God in your life would most probably represent a timely message from God.

♦ An untrustworthy person in your past could probably indicate an impending situation that should not be trusted.

♦ A healing evangelist would represent the healing anointing within the dream's context.

♦ Dreaming of dead people speaks of what the dreamer most remembers about them. Commonly, sentiment is attached to dreaming of deceased loved ones. These are not visitations from the dead.

♦ A husband in dreams most often represents Jesus Christ or the actual person.

♦ Getting married in dreams typically speaks of growing intimacy with Jesus Christ because the Bible speaks of Jesus Christ as the bridegroom of all Christians. Avoid the superstition of "spirit marriage."

In a minority of cases, the people in your dream are literal. If this is the case, then the following matters are important:

♦ The overall context of the dream.

♦ Your spiritual standing, in terms of the trust that God can place in you with regard to sensitive information about people. Also, how far you can take such information without jeopardizing your spiritual standing; such a dream may be followed by possible emotional backlash.

♦ An established pattern of dream-language, particularly with those in prophetic ministry.

Dreaming of One's Own Children

In these situations, what most often needs to be established is whether the dream literally refers to the child or is symbolic of a precious gift from God. To make that determination, it's worth considering:

♦ An inner witness from the Holy Spirit.

♦ What the dreamer's role is in the dream; if observatory, and the child participatory, then the child is more likely to be literal; if participatory, and the child observatory, then the dream is more likely to be symbolic.

- ◆ Who is the dream about? If it's about the child, then the child is more likely to be literal.

- ◆ What is the child's role in the dream? If the child is "out of character," then the child is more likely to be symbolic.

- ◆ In the dream, what is the relational interaction between the dreamer and the child? If it's not consistent with a real-life situation, then the child is likely to be symbolic.

- ◆ What is the child's age in real life versus in the dream? Most dreamers will find that dreaming of grownup children in their dreams often indicates a literal reference to the children.

PART IV

SYMBOLS

CHAPTER 19

INTRODUCTION TO SYMBOLS

A symbol is an image that stands for something in addition to its literal meaning. It therefore has more meaning than just its simple literal meaning on its own in the natural run of things. In practical terms, symbols are things that represent or stand for something else, or are used to typify something else, either by association, resemblance, or convention. A symbol can also mean a material object used to represent something invisible, such as an idea (e.g., the dove as a symbol of peace).

How Symbols Derive Their Meaning

A message that is given in symbols automatically switches your thinking to symbolism. Every parable needs to be symbolically interpreted and the meaning should be drawn for each symbol. (A parable language is when symbols are used to represent things.) Symbols are not real entities; they are simply representations of the real entities. The meaning of a symbol is drawn first of all from the reservoir of the Word of God, then from the inherent meaning of the symbol or its association to the dreamer's experience, or from the culture and colloquial expressions in society.

In general terms, interpretation is the deciphering of a parable language that involves:

♦ Bringing meaning to the symbols in the dream and then gaining understanding of the message in the dream. Deriving the meanings for symbols should first of all be hinged on the Word of God;

165

this process also brings understanding to the symbolic actions in the dream.

♦ Expounding on the relevance of the symbols and the message of the dream to the dreamer's life circumstance. Exposition is bringing understanding to the symbols and events as they relate to the dreamer's personal experience. Exposition centers on the dreamer's experience.

♦ The deriving of the meaning for the symbols and the exposition must go together to truly interpret a dream or vision. Therefore, the true and complete interpretation must incorporate the two phases as well as be drawn in the following order:

  * The Scriptures.

  * The inherent meaning of the symbol.

  * The dreamer's personal experience.

  * The social influences of the dreamer (the culture and the colloquial expressions the dreamer is used to).

A symbol does not mean the same thing all the time and therefore the meaning of a symbol must be drawn for each dream. Remember, the true meaning of a symbol in a dream does not come from human reasoning or intellectualism, but by allowing the meaning to flow into our hearts or subconscious mind from the Holy Spirit. This inflow into our hearts occurs by being quiet and still in the inner being. The choice of symbols in the dream is very specific and purposeful, and it is the prerogative of God. A dream is therefore the truest representation of the situation because it is God's perspective of it; a dream addresses the issue more frankly than human illustration.

Why God Uses Symbols

♦ They help us to see the real thing from God's perspective because the symbol shows God's thinking.

♦ Striking features of symbols help the impartation and interpretation.

♦ The hidden meaning of the symbol allows God to clarify things in stages.

◆ Humility is the key, as it increases your dependence on the Holy Spirit. *"To keep me from becoming conceited **because of these surpassingly great revelations,** there was given me a thorn in my flesh, a messenger of Satan, to torment me. Three times I pleaded with the Lord to take it away from me. But He said to me, 'My grace is sufficient for you, for My power is made perfect in weakness.' Therefore I will boast all the more gladly about my weaknesses, so that Christ's power may rest on me"* (2 Corinthians 12:7-9).

◆ The Lord will relate to a person in symbolism that has meaning to him/her. Dreams are a form of communication, an intimate language between the dreamer and the Lord.

◆ They secure the message from the enemies.

◆ They make you want to search out the meaning.

◆ The language of symbols is deep and powerful; at the same time it's the most elementary language of men and therefore available to all ages.

◆ The human mind understands or reads in pictures.

CHAPTER 20

THE POWER OF THE LANGUAGE OF SYMBOLS

Those who have understood the tremendous power of symbols have gained incredible insight into the mysteries of God, because God's ways are wrapped up in the language of symbolism. Human beings think in pictures and people need visual appreciation in order to grasp the essence of a concept. Symbols evoke powerful emotion and elicit strong passion; from generation to generation, politicians, philosophers, and religious leaders have used them to illustrate their points. For example, national commitment is symbolized in the pride and honor that is accorded to the national symbol in the form of a flag. Many would be outraged to see their flag dishonored, and public hatred is often demonstrated by the burning of an enemy's national flag.

David—A Biblical Example

Symbolism brought the seriousness of David's adulterous act to him. Nathan's message to King David could have easily been a perfect setting for the plotting of a dream and God could have chosen to send King David the same message through a dream. Nathan narrated the message to David in a dream format, in parable, to bring home the gravity of the sin.

The Lord sent Nathan to David. When he came to him, he said, "There were two men in a certain town, one rich and the other poor. The rich man had a very large number of sheep and cattle, but the poor man had nothing except one little ewe lamb he had bought. He raised it, and it grew up with him and his children. It shared his food, drank from his cup and even slept in his arms. It was like a daughter to him. Now a traveler came to the rich man, but the rich man refrained from taking one of his own sheep or cattle to prepare a meal for the traveler who had come to him. Instead, he took the ewe lamb that belonged to the poor man and prepared it for the one who had come to him." David burned with anger against the man and said to Nathan, "As surely as the Lord lives, the man who did this deserves to die! He must pay for that lamb four times over, because he did such a thing and had no pity." Then Nathan said to David, "You are the man! This is what the Lord, the God of Israel, says: 'I anointed you king over Israel, and I delivered you from the hand of Saul. I gave your master's house to you, and your master's wives into your arms. I gave you the house of Israel and Judah. And if all this had been too little, I would have given you even more. Why did you despise the word of the Lord by doing what is evil in His eyes? You struck down Uriah the Hittite with the sword and took his wife to be your own. You killed him with the sword of the Ammonites'" (2 Samuel 12:1-9).

Anatomy of Nathan's Statement to David

SYMBOL / ACTION	MEANING	THE POWER OF IMAGERY
Rich man.	David.	Important personality.
Poor man.	Uriah.	A person who is vulnerable because he lacks the necessities of life.
Little ewe, like a daughter.	Uriah's wife—precious to him.	Something precious to the dreamer.
Arrival of traveler.	A need arises.	A potential need is imminent or at hand.
Refrain from using his own.	Selfishness.	Spirit of self-centeredness, or inconsiderate of others.
David's anger burned against the injustice of the man in Nathan's story.	Then David came to a realization that the sin was his, therefore realizing the true gravity of the sin.	Holy anger stirred by spirit of righteousness or coming to one's senses after a period of attack of carnality.

CHAPTER 21

How to Derive Meaning from Parable Language

The Parable of the Sower

Then He told them many things in parables, saying: "A farmer went out to sow his seed. As he was scattering the seed, some fell along the path, and the birds came and ate it up. Some fell on rocky places, where it did not have much soil. It sprang up quickly, because the soil was shallow. But when the sun came up, the plants were scorched, and they withered because they had no root. Other seed fell among thorns, which grew up and choked the plants. Still other seed fell on good soil, where it produced a crop—a hundred, sixty or thirty times what was sown. He who has ears, let him hear" (Matthew 13:3-9).

The Interpretation

Listen then to what the parable of the sower means: When anyone hears the message about the kingdom and does not understand it, the evil one comes and snatches away what was sown in his heart. This is the seed sown along the path. The one who received the seed that fell on rocky places is the man who hears the word and at once receives it with joy. But since he has no root, he lasts only a short time. When trouble or persecution comes because of the word, he quickly falls away. The one who received the seed that fell among the thorns is the man who hears the word, but the worries of this life and the deceitfulness of wealth choke it, making it unfruitful. But the one who received the seed that fell on good soil is the man who hears the word and understands it. He produces a crop, yielding a hundred, sixty or thirty times what was sown (Matthew 13:18-23).

The Anatomy of the Parable of the Sower

SYMBOL	MEANING	DERIVED DREAM SYMBOL
Seed.	Word of God.	Word of God; God's promises (something capable of multiplication).
Soil.	Heart of Man.	Potential for multiplication, either good or bad; the essence of life.
Farmer.	Jesus Christ.	God, pastor, spiritual leaders.
"Sown along the paths."	No understanding, taken away by the devil.	Unprotected, easily taken by the devil.
"Seeds fell on rocky places."	Receives the Word with joy, but lacks depth and stolen by trouble and persecution of the world.	"Walking on rocky places," = times of trouble, persecution, and lack of depth in the matter.
"Seeds fell on thorns."	The Word of God is heard, but choked by worries of life or the attraction of worldly riches.	Thorns = worries of life, distraction by worldly riches.
"Seeds on good soil."	Hears the Word, understands and becomes fruitful.	Well prepared for life expectancy, conducive for growth.

Benefits of a Parable Language

◆ Economy—a picture is worth a thousand words.

◆ It shows the essence—you apply the specifics to your situation; gives the principle so that the essence can be applicable at other times.

- A parable allows God to code messages for the dreamer.

- Is protected by hiding the promise from the enemy.

- Allows God to package and unfold His message according to the areas of priority.

  The disciples came to Him and asked, "Why do You speak to the people in parables?" He replied, "The knowledge of the secrets of the kingdom of heaven has been given to you, but not to them. Whoever has will be given more, and he will have abundance. Whoever does not have, even what he has will be taken from him. This is why I speak to them in parables: 'Though seeing, they do not see; though hearing, they do not hear or understand'" (Matthew 13:10-13).

  I spoke to the prophets, gave them many visions and told parables through them (Hosea 12:10).

- The mind speaks in the language of reason and concepts, but dreams speak in the language of riddles and parables.

- The language of pictures and symbols is universal and has no age barrier.

- Allows God to give the best possible picture or the truest perspective of the situation.

- A dream parable often shows the present condition and what will happen if we continue to go in the same direction.

  *The proverbs (truths obscurely expressed, maxims, and **parables**) of Solomon son of David, king of Israel: That people may know skillful and godly wisdom and instruction, discern and comprehend the words of understanding and insight. Receive instruction in wise dealing and the discipline of wise thoughtfulness, righteousness, justice, and integrity. That prudence may be given to the simple, and knowledge, discretion, and discernment to the youth. The wise also will hear and increase in learning and the person of understanding will acquire skill and attain to sound counsel [so that he may be able to steer his course rightly]. That people may understand a proverb* **[parable]** *and a figure of speech or an enigma with its interpretation, and the words of the wise and their dark saying or riddles* (Proverbs 1:1-6 AMP).

CHAPTER 22

HOW TO USE THE DICTIONARY OF DREAM SYMBOLS

A seer receives in the language of symbols. However, in order to be relevant to the contemporary world, the seer should communicate the revelations with wisdom in language that people will understand. A seer should therefore be a student of the language of symbols and be able to communicate in simple terms with the people.

In general, when one sees a picture and switches to symbolic thinking, two questions should arise in the mind: What is the literal meaning of the picture? And what does the picture evoke? The answer to the first question will usually be the most obvious meaning for the symbol. In order to capture or broaden it to include the complete perspective of all the possible meanings, the second question must then be asked. This will help to explore the connotations and overtones in addition to the literal or most obvious meaning. If either of these two aspects is not well understood, the understanding of pictorial language is impoverished and not complete.

Example: The word *wife* is ordinarily understood to mean female, woman. This word also evokes some lateral thinking (connotations)—mother, home keeper, the Church, Bride of Christ.

Types of Symbol

A *metaphor* is a symbol with implied comparison (for example, the *tongue* as the pen of a ready writer; or *Jesus*, the Lion of the tribe of Judah). A *simile*, on the other hand, compares one thing to another and it makes the comparison explicit by using formula as "like" or "as." For example, "As the deer pants for water, so my soul pants for You." A *motif* is a pattern that appears in written text or a mental picture that has emerged from a written text. We allow the motif to develop wherever the Bible says, "Selah," i.e., pause and think.

Ezekiel—A Biblical Example

God described Ezekiel as the watchman to the house of Israel and He used extensive symbolism in most of His communications with the Prophet Ezekiel. Let us see how the above principles can help us understand the multiple dimensions to the symbolism in Ezekiel's vision of the valley of dry bones.

> *The hand of the Lord was upon me, and He brought me out by the Spirit of the Lord and set me in the middle of a valley; it was full of bones. He led me back and forth among them, and I saw a great many bones on the floor of the valley, bones that were very dry. He asked me, "Son of man, can these bones live?" I said, "O Sovereign Lord, You alone know." Then He said to me, "Prophesy to these bones and say to them, 'Dry bones, hear the word of the Lord! This is what the Sovereign Lord says to these bones: I will make breath enter you, and you will come to life. I will attach tendons to you and make flesh come upon you and cover you with skin; I will put breath in you, and you will come to life. Then you will know that I am the Lord.'" So I prophesied as I was commanded. And as I was prophesying, there was a noise, a rattling sound, and the bones came together, bone to bone. I looked, and tendons and flesh appeared on them and skin covered them, but there was no breath in them. Then He said to me, "Prophesy to the breath; prophesy, son of man, and say to it, 'This is what the Sovereign Lord says: Come from the four winds, O breath, and breathe into these slain, that they may live.'" So I prophesied as He commanded me, and breath entered them; they came to life and stood up on their feet—a vast army (Ezekiel 37:1-10).*

The interpretation given by God:

> *Then He said to me: "Son of man, these bones are the whole house of Israel. They say, 'Our bones are dried up and our hope is gone; we are cut off.' Therefore prophesy and say to them: 'This is what the Sovereign Lord says: O My people, I am going to open your graves and bring you up from them; I will bring you back to the land of Israel.*

Then you, My people, will know that I am the Lord, when I open your graves and bring you up from them. I will put My Spirit in you and you will live, and I will settle you in your own land. Then you will know that I the Lord have spoken, and I have done it, declares the Lord'" (Ezekiel 37:11-14).

The Anatomy of Ezekiel's Vision

SYMBOL	MEANING	THE POWER OF IMAGERY
A collection of dry bones littering a valley floor.	A state of hopelessness; extreme hardship; impossibility.	
Scattered.	Jews scattered in the nations.	
The bones (the hopeless situation) came together and assembled into skeletons (bone to his bones).	Coming together as predestined, each bone identified the exact skeleton to which it originally belonged.	Coming together of the Jews to a state of their own as prophesied.
As he observed flesh and skin grew on the skeleton.	This speaks of comfort and protection from God that will eventually emerge, particularly during the process.	
The bodies stayed dead, until a dramatic moment when God put breath into them.	Not filled with the spirit of God until the time appointed for this to happen.	After the restoration and recovery from the dead situation, the people remained spiritually dead. Their old souls needed to be renewed. The word "breath" also means spirit and the vision is reminiscent of Genesis 2:7 where God breathed life into the first man.

SYMBOL	MEANING	THE POWER OF IMAGERY
Come from the four winds.	The role of the four corners of the world in the eventual salvation of Israel.	God is saying that it would take a miracle to bring the remnants of Israel back together from many locations or nations where they are scattered. Israel will need an even greater miracle to be spiritually born-again with the spirit of God.
Vast army.	The eventual strength of the army of Israel, as it shall be like the army of the Lord.	

Using the Dictionary

This dictionary has been designed to assist the reader in broadening lateral thinking and to prevent or resist the tendency to become fixed on the meaning of a symbol. If you are fixed on the meaning of a symbol, you become limited in the benefits that can be obtained from a dream.

The following points are important to bear in mind when using the dictionary of symbols:

- Interpretation belongs to God. Therefore, attempting to use this dictionary without the help of the Holy Spirit is a futile exercise.

- This dictionary is not a carte blanche for dream interpretation.

- The true meaning of a symbol must be drawn within the context of each dream; do not be fixed on the meaning of a symbol as it could vary from dream to dream and from person to person.

- The Bible says that God expresses spiritual truth in spiritual words; the derived meaning for a symbol must therefore be largely dependent on the Word of God.

- The reader must bear in mind at all times that what is personally descriptive should not be taken as generally prescriptive. God deals with each one of us uniquely.

PART V

DICTIONARY

of

DREAM SYMBOLS

ACID: Something that eats from within. Keeping offense or hatred, or malice.

See to it that no one misses the grace of God and that no bitter root grows up to cause trouble and defile many (Hebrews 12:15).

ADULTERY: Unfaithfulness regarding things of the Spirit or of the natural or actual adultery; lust for the pleasures of this world; sin.

The acts of the sinful nature are obvious: sexual immorality, impurity and debauchery; idolatry and witchcraft; hatred, discord, jealousy, fits of rage, selfish ambition, dissensions, factions (Galatians 5:19-20).

You adulterous people, don't you know that friendship with the world is hatred toward God? Anyone who chooses to be a friend of the world becomes an enemy of God (James 4:4).

AIRPLANE: A personal ministry or church, capable of moving in the Holy Spirit. Flowing in high spiritual power. Holy Spirit-powered ministry.

Crashing: The end of one phase, change of direction.

High: Fully powered in the Spirit.

Low: Only partially operative in the Spirit.

Airplane Crashing

Soaring: Deep in the Spirit or moving in the deep things of God.

War plane: Call to intercessory ministry or spiritual warfare.

War Plane

AIRPORT: The ministry that sends out missionaries. High-powered spiritual church capable of equipping and sending out ministries. Preparation for ministry/provision or nourishment in readiness for service.

ALLIGATOR: Large-mouthed enemy. Verbal attacks.

Alligator

ALTAR: A place set apart for spiritual rituals or prayers/worship, whether good or bad.

David built an altar to the Lord there and sacrificed burnt offerings and fellowship offerings. Then the Lord

Altar

answered prayer in behalf of the land, and the plague on Israel was stopped (2 Samuel 24:25).

Then Noah built an altar to the Lord and, taking some of all the clean animals and clean birds, he sacrificed burnt offerings on it (Genesis 8:20).

There he built an altar, and he called the place El Bethel, because it was there that God revealed Himself to him when he was fleeing from his brother (Genesis 35:7).

Destroy completely all the places on the high mountains and on the hills and under every spreading tree where the nations you are dispossessing worship their gods. Break down their altars, smash their sacred stones and burn their Asherah poles in the fire; cut down the idols of their gods and wipe out their names from those places (Deuteronomy 12:2-3).

ANCHOR: The pillar that something or someone hangs on; something that hope is built on.

We have this hope as an anchor for the soul, firm and secure. It enters the inner sanctuary behind the curtain (Hebrews 6:19).

Anchor

ANKLES: Little faith, early stages.

As the man went eastward with a measuring line in his hand, he measured off a thousand cubits and then led me through water that was ankle-deep (Ezekiel 47:3).

ANOINT: Equipping with the Holy Spirit for service. The power of Holy Spirit to do something; sanctification; set apart for something.

Is any one of you sick? He should call the elders of the church to pray over him and anoint him with oil in the name of the Lord (James 5:14).

Also, anoint Jehu son of Nimshi king over Israel, and anoint Elisha son of Shaphat from Abel Meholah to succeed you as prophet (1 Kings 19:16).

ANT: Industrious, ability to plan ahead. Conscious of seasons of life. Unwanted guest.

Go to the ant, you sluggard; consider its ways and be wise! It has no commander, no overseer or ruler, yet it stores its provisions in summer and gathers its food at harvest (Proverbs 6:6-8).

Ants are creatures of little strength, yet they store up their food in the summer (Proverbs 30:25).

ANTIQUES: Something relating to the past. An inherited thing, whether good or bad.

This is what the Lord says: "Stand at the crossroads and look; ask for the ancient paths, ask where the good way is, and walk in it, and you will find rest for your souls." But you said, "We will not walk in it" (Jeremiah 6:16).

APPLES: Spiritual fruit, temptation; something precious like the apple of God's eyes.

When the woman saw that the fruit of the tree was good for food and pleasing to the eye, and also desirable for gaining wisdom, she took some and ate it. She also gave Apple *some to her husband, who was with her, and he ate it* (Genesis 3:6).

In a desert land He found him, in a barren and howling waste. He shielded him and cared for him; He guarded him as the apple of His eye (Deuteronomy 32:10).

For this is what the Lord Almighty says: "After he has honored Me and has sent Me against the nations that have plundered you—for whoever touches you touches the apple of His eye (Zechariah 2:8).

ARK: Something relating to God's presence. Something of strength.

Place the cover on top of the ark and put in the ark the Testimony, which I will give you. There, above the cover between the two cherubim that are over the ark of the Ark *Testimony, I will meet with you and give you all my commands for the Israelites* (Exodus 25:21-22).

ARM: Power and strength, whether good or bad.

But his bow remained steady, his strong arms stayed limber, because of the hand of the Mighty One of Jacob, because of the Shepherd, the Rock of Israel (Genesis 49:24).

Therefore, say to the Israelites: "I am the Lord, and I will Arm *bring you out from under the yoke of the Egyptians. I will free you from being slaves to them, and I will redeem you with an outstretched arm and with mighty acts of judgment* (Exodus 6:6).

"With him is only the arm of flesh, but with us is the Lord our God to help us and to fight our battles." And the people gained confidence from what Hezekiah the king of Judah said (2 Chronicles 32:8).

Who has believed our message and to whom has the arm of the Lord been revealed? (Isaiah 53:1)

ARMIES: Spiritual warriors, whether good or bad.

ARMOR: Spiritual covering that protects against attacks. Divine protection. The truth of God.

Finally, be strong in the Lord and in His mighty power. Put on the full armor of God so that you can take your stand against the devil's schemes (Ephesians 6:10-11).

Armor

ARROWS: Powerful words, whether good or bad. Word of God or curses from the devil. Spiritual children. Good or bad intentions.

Sons are a heritage from the Lord, children a reward from Him. Like arrows in the hands of a warrior are sons born in one's youth (Psalm 127:3-4).

Arrows

They sharpen their tongues like swords and aim their words like deadly arrows (Psalm 64:3).

Like a club or a sword or a sharp arrow is the man who gives false testimony against his neighbor (Proverbs 25:18).

"Open the east window," he said, and he opened it. "Shoot!" Elisha said, and he shot. "The Lord's arrow of victory, the arrow of victory over Aram!" Elisha declared. "You will completely destroy the Arameans at Aphek" (2 Kings 13:17).

He made my mouth like a sharpened sword, in the shadow of His hand He hid me; He made me into a polished arrow and concealed me in His quiver (Isaiah 49:2).

ASHES: Signs of repentance or sorrow. To humble oneself. As a memorial.

Your maxims are proverbs of ashes; your defenses are defenses of clay (Job 13:12).

My ears had heard of you but now my eyes have seen you. Therefore I despise myself and repent in dust and ashes (Job 42:5-6).

Tamar put ashes on her head and tore the ornamented robe she was wearing. She put her hand on her head and went away, weeping aloud as she went (2 Samuel 13:19).

ATOM BOMB: Something capable of great destruction. Something of great suddenness or quick in occurring.

ATTIC: The mind-zone. Thought process. The spirit-realm. Memories/past issues/stored-up materials.

Atom Bomb

About noon the following day as they were on their journey and approaching the city, Peter went up on the roof to pray. He became hungry and wanted something to eat, and while the meal was being prepared, he fell into a trance. He saw heaven opened and something like a large sheet being let down to earth by its four corners (Acts 10:9-11).

AUTOGRAPH: Prominence or fame.

AUTUMN: Transition. The close of harvest season or about to enter difficult times. End of something and beginning of another.

Autumn

They do not say to themselves, "Let us fear the Lord our God, who gives autumn and spring rains in season, who assures us of the regular weeks of harvest" (Jeremiah 5:24).

AUTOBIKE: A Spirit-powered ministry that has either one-man or two-person involvement. Single-man ministry with a lot of exhibitionism.

Autobike

AUTOMOBILE: Means of getting to a destination or achieving the desired goal.

The chariots storm through the streets, rushing back and forth through the squares. They look like flaming torches; they dart about like lightning (Nahum 2:4).

Air-condition: If in good working condition, indicates adequate comfort despite prevailing situation; but if not working, indicates faulty provision for comfort.

Brakes: Slowing down; to stop; compelled to stop; hindrance.

Convertible: Capable of open-heaven ministration; revelatory ministry.

Driver-seat: Indicates leadership.

Engine: Holy Spirit power.

Four-wheel drive: A powerful ministry; ground breaking; capable of global influence.

Junkyard: Ministries that are abandoned or in need of repairs.

Rearview mirror: Looking back, focusing on things in the past; warning to look ahead; warning to watch your back.

Seatbelt: Something that ensures safety; fastened = prepared, prayers; unfastened = prayerlessness, carelessness.

Steering: The controlling and leading part.

Tires: Symbolic of the spiritual conditions of the ministry; flat = needing spiritual enabling, needing more prayers; full = powered by the Spirit.

Topless van: Not having adequate anointing for the occasion; vulnerable, transparent.

Van: Goods = delivering, group ministering.

Vehicle key: Authority in the ministry.

Wreck: Crashing, clash, end of one phase, change of direction. Danger. Contention or confrontation or offense.

AWAKENING: To be alert, watchfulness; to be stirred into action.

Then the Lord awoke as from sleep, as a man wakes from the stupor of wine (Psalm 78:65).

Awake, awake! Clothe yourself with strength, O arm of the Lord; awake, as in days gone by, as in generations of old. Was it not you who cut Rahab to pieces, who pierced that monster through? (Isaiah 51:9)

"Awake, O sword, against My shepherd, against the man who is close to Me!" declares the Lord Almighty. "Strike the shepherd, and the sheep will be scattered, and I will turn My hand against the little ones" (Zechariah 13:7).

AXE: The Word of God. To encourage by kind word. Issue that needs to be settled.

The ax is already at the root of the trees, and every tree that does not produce good fruit will be cut down and thrown into the fire (Matthew 3:10).

Axe

BABY: The beginning of something new. Beginning to be productive. New Christians. Something in its infancy or early stages.

Like newborn babies, crave pure spiritual milk, so that by it you may grow up in your salvation (1 Peter 2:2).

Brothers, I could not address you as spiritual but as worldly—mere infants in Christ. I gave you milk, not solid food, for you were not yet ready for it. Indeed, you are still not ready (1 Corinthians 3:1-2).

BACK: Pertaining to the past. Something behind or hidden. Out of view. Concealed thing.

Answer me, O Lord, answer me, so these people will know that You, O Lord, are God, and that You are turning their hearts back again (1 Kings 18:37).

Let no one in the field go back to get his cloak (Mark 13:16).

Jesus replied, "No one who puts his hand to the plow and looks back is fit for service in the kingdom of God" (Luke 9:62).

BACKSIDE: Something in the past or behind the dreamer. Something concealed from view or understanding.

BADGER: Underground dwellers.

BAKER: One who instigates or originates something.

BAKING: Making provision for feeding people. Preparation for welfare ministry. God's provision.

BALANCES: Something reflecting both sides of the matter. Something waiting to tilt one way or the other. Judgment.

Balance

BALD HEAD: Lacking wisdom.

BALM: Healing, anointing; something to relieve pains, stress, or agony.

Is there no balm in Gilead? Is there no physician there? Why then is there no healing for the wound of My people? (Jeremiah 8:22).

Babylon will suddenly fall and be broken. Wail over her! Get balm for her pain; perhaps she can be healed (Jeremiah 51:8).

Judah and Israel traded with you; they exchanged wheat from Minnith and confections, honey, oil and balm for your wares (Ezekiel 27:17).

BANK: Heavenly account. God's favor for a future season. A place of safety/security. A dependable place or source. God's provision.

Not that I am looking for a gift, but I am looking for what may be credited to your account (Philippians 4:17).

But store up for yourselves treasures in heaven, where moth and rust do not destroy, and where thieves do not break in and steal (Matthew 6:20).

BANNER, FLAG: The covering to which everyone belongs or is committed to. Something that brings unity, love, or purpose; a unifying object or circumstance. Victory.

Moses built an altar and called it The Lord is my Banner (Exodus 17:15).

Banner

BANQUET: God's provision. A full cup. Plentiful/affluence/abundance. Satisfaction. Blessing. Celebrations. Structured teaching of the Word of God.

He has taken me to the banquet hall, and his banner over me is love (Song of Solomon 2:4).

King Belshazzar gave a great banquet for a thousand of his nobles and drank wine with them....As they drank the wine, they praised the gods of gold and silver, of bronze, iron, wood and stone. Suddenly the fingers of a human hand appeared and wrote on the plaster of the wall, near the lampstand in the royal palace. The king watched the hand as it wrote (Daniel 5:1,4-5).

BAPTIZING: A change from the natural to the spiritual. Dying to self and expression of the new man.

He went into all the country around the Jordan, preaching a baptism of repentance for the forgiveness of sins (Luke 3:3).

We were therefore buried with Him through baptism into death in order that, just as Christ was raised from the dead through the glory of the Father, we too may live a new life (Romans 6:4).

Having been buried with Him in baptism and raised with Him through your faith in the power of God, who raised Him from the dead (Colossians 2:12).

BARBERSHOP: Time, place, period of changing beliefs or customs or habits. A church where these can take place. Depending on the emphasis, either a place of vanity or correction.

BARENESS: Unproductive, difficult time or period.

Barbershop

BARN: A place of provision. A church. Stored spiritual wealth.

Let both grow together until the harvest. At that time I will tell the harvesters: First collect the weeds and tie them in

Barn

bundles to be burned; then gather the wheat and bring it into my barn (Matthew 13:30).

Is there yet any seed left in the barn? Until now, the vine and the fig tree, the pomegranate and the olive tree have not borne fruit. "From this day on I will bless you" (Haggai 2:19).

BASEMENT: The unseen part of something. Storage zone. Related to the foundation. Hidden. Bloodline related issue.

BASKET: A measure of God's provision. A measure of judgment.

Basket

This is what the Sovereign Lord showed me: a basket of ripe fruit. "What do you see, Amos?" He asked. "A basket of ripe fruit," I answered. Then the Lord said to me, "The time is ripe for My people Israel; I will spare them no longer" (Amos 8:1-2).

Then the angel who was speaking to me came forward and said to me, "Look up and see what this is that is appearing." I asked, "What is it?" He replied, "It is a measuring basket." And he added, "This is the iniquity of the people throughout the land." Then the cover of lead was raised, and there in the basket sat a woman! He said, "This is wickedness," and he pushed her back into the basket and pushed the lead cover down over its mouth. Then I looked up—and there before me were two women, with the wind in their wings! They had wings like those of a stork, and they lifted up the basket between heaven and earth. "Where are they taking the basket?" I asked the angel who was speaking to me. He replied, "To the country of Babylonia to build a house for it. When it is ready, the basket will be set there in its place" (Zechariah 5:5-11).

BAT: Creature of darkness. Satanic instrument, related to witchcraft. A nighttime creature. Could represent association with the dark side of life.

Bat

BATHING: What you do on the outside or outwardly to prevent unclean or unholy attitude. Outward repentance.

BATHROOM: A period of cleansing/entering a time of repentance. A place of voluntary nakedness or facing reality in individual life.

Bathing

BEAM: Power or illumination coming from God or the heavenly. A time of exposure. A time of spotlight.

BEAR: Danger, wicked person or spirit, vindictiveness. Evil; something that is after what you possess.

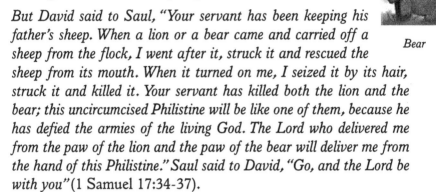

Bear

But David said to Saul, "Your servant has been keeping his father's sheep. When a lion or a bear came and carried off a sheep from the flock, I went after it, struck it and rescued the sheep from its mouth. When it turned on me, I seized it by its hair, struck it and killed it. Your servant has killed both the lion and the bear; this uncircumcised Philistine will be like one of them, because he has defied the armies of the living God. The Lord who delivered me from the paw of the lion and the paw of the bear will deliver me from the hand of this Philistine." Saul said to David, "Go, and the Lord be with you" (1 Samuel 17:34-37).

You know your father and his men; they are fighters, and as fierce as a wild bear robbed of her cubs. Besides, your father is an experienced fighter; he will not spend the night with the troops (2 Samuel 17:8).

It will be as though a man fled from a lion only to meet a bear, as though he entered his house and rested his hand on the wall only to have a snake bite him (Amos 5:19).

BEARD: To have respect for those in authority.

Messing: Insanity.

Trimmed: Sane.

BEAUTY SHOP: A place of preparation with emphasis on outward appearance, tending toward vanity.

BED: Revelations, rest, contentment. Becoming relaxed or lax.

BEDROOM: A place of intimacy. A place of rest, sleep, or dreams. A place of covenant, a place of revelation.

Bed

BEES: That which makes offensive noise. More noisy than effective. A double-edged situation capable of going bad or producing sweetness. Stinging words, gossip.

Some time later, when he went back to marry her, he turned aside to look at the lion's carcass. In it was a swarm of bees and some honey (Judges 14:8).

BELLS: Call to attention or action. To bring to alertness. To say it loudly; public warning.

BELLY: Feelings, desires, spiritual well-being, sentiment.

BICYCLE: A ministry depending on much human effort. One-man ministry.

Bell

BINOCULARS: Looking ahead, looking into the future. Prophetic ministry.

BIRD: Symbol of leader, evil or good at different levels. Agents of authority.

Binoculars

Dove: Holy Spirit. Holy Spirit—peace; a seal of approval from Heaven.

Eagle: Symbol of personality or spirit capable of soaring in the Spirit. Good focus/swiftness; powerful. A prophet of God. The nation of America.

Owl: An evil eye that monitors; spirit of craftiness.

Raven: Symbol of unclean spirit.

Sparrow: Divine provision and food. Symbol of God's desire to provide for us.

Owl

Vulture: Evil spirit, opportunistic person. Night creature or something that preys on "dead things" (human weaknesses). Unclean spirit. A loner.

Feathers: A protective covering, a shield or instrument for flying or moving in the spirit.

Wings: A place of refuge. God's presence. Safety/something that provides escape from danger.

Fowler: A person or spirit that entraps. Fowler's net.

BLACK: Lack, famine. Evil, demonic spirit. Darkness.

May darkness and deep shadow claim it once more; may a cloud settle over it; may blackness overwhelm its light (Job 3:5).

They are wild waves of the sea, foaming up their shame; wandering stars, for whom blackest darkness has been reserved forever (Jude 1:13).

I clothe the sky with darkness and make sackcloth its covering (Isaiah 50:3).

BLEEDING: Hurting. To loose spiritually. Verbal accusation. Traumatic.

BLIND: Lack of understanding, ignorance. Not able to see into the spirit world.

BLOOD: Atonement, to appease. Something that testifies.

BLOOD TRANSFUSION: Getting new life, rescuing situation.

BLUE: Heaven-related visitation from God or of the Holy Spirit. Spiritual.

BOAT: A ministry that is capable of influencing many people.

Boat

BODY ODOR: Unclean spirit, after effect of fleshy actions.

BONES: The substance of something. The main issue. Long lasting.

> *Skeleton*: Something without flesh/substance. Something without details.

Bone

BOOK: Gaining understanding/knowledge. Scriptures. Revelation. Promise from God. Message from the title of the book.

BOTTLE: Something relating to the body as the container of anointing.

Book

BOW, ARROW OR GUN: Source from which attacks come.

The power of a nation or person. Verbal attacks. The tongue.

> *But his bow remained steady, his strong arms stayed limber, because of the hand of the Mighty One of Jacob, because of the Shepherd, the Rock of Israel* (Genesis 49:24).

Bow

> *"They make ready their tongue like a bow, to shoot lies; it is not by truth that they triumph in the land. They go from one sin to another; they do not acknowledge Me," declares the Lord* (Jeremiah 9:3).

> *This is what the Lord Almighty says: "See, I will break the bow of Elam, the mainstay of their might"* (Jeremiah 49:35).

BOWL: A measure of something.

> *His offering was one silver plate weighing a hundred and thirty shekels, and one silver sprinkling bowl weighing seventy shekels, both*

according to the sanctuary shekel, each filled with fine flour mixed with oil as a grain offering (Numbers 7:13).

You drink wine by the bowlful and use the finest lotions, but you do not grieve over the ruin of Joseph (Amos 6:6).

And the Lord Almighty will shield them. They will destroy and overcome with slingstones. They will drink and roar as with wine; they will be full like a bowl used for sprinkling the corners of the altar (Zechariah 9:15).

And that is what happened. Gideon rose early the next day; he squeezed the fleece and wrung out the dew—a bowlful of water (Judges 6:38).

BRACELET: Pertaining to pride. Valuable but of the world. Identity if it has a name.

Bracelet

BRANCHES: God's people, churches. Church split.

I am the vine; you are the branches. If a man remains in Me and I in him, he will bear much fruit; apart from Me you can do nothing (John 15:5).

I am the true vine, and My Father is the gardener. He cuts off every branch in Me that bears no fruit, while every branch that does bear fruit He prunes so that it will be even more fruitful (John 15:1-2).

BRASS: Hardness, hard covering. Judgment/captivity/hard to break out from. Strength. Negative stronghold.

Do I have the strength of stone? Is my flesh bronze [brass]? (Job 6:12)

The sky over your head will be bronze [brass], the ground beneath you iron (Deuteronomy 28:23).

They killed the sons of Zedekiah before his eyes. Then they put out his eyes, bound him with bronze [brass] shackles and took him to Babylon (2 Kings 25:7).

I will break down your stubborn pride and make the sky above you like iron and the ground beneath you like bronze (Leviticus 26:19).

BREAD: Jesus Christ; Bread of life, Word of God, source of nourishment, God's provision.

Then she arose with her daughters-in-law that she might return from the country of Moab, for she had heard in the country of Moab that the Lord had visited His people by giving them bread (Ruth 1:6 NKJV).

Bread

At this the Jews began to grumble about Him because He said, "I am the bread that came down from heaven" (John 6:41).

A man ought to examine himself before he eats of the bread and drinks of the cup (1 Corinthians 11:28).

Give us today our daily bread (Matthew 6:11).

Fresh: New word from God.

Moldy: Something that is not new. Unclean.

Unleavened: Showing lack of sin.

BREAST: Source of milk for new Christians. Object of enticement. Source of sustenance.

Because of your father's God, who helps you, because of the Almighty, who blesses you with blessings of the heavens above, blessings of the deep that lies below, blessings of the breast and womb (Genesis 49:25).

Why were there knees to receive me and breasts that I might be nursed? (Job 3:12)

A loving doe, a graceful deer—may her breasts satisfy you always, may you ever be captivated by her love (Proverbs 5:19).

BREASTPLATE: God's protective shield. Covering or the anointing which covers one. Preparing to give judgment. Protective of vital human organs or issues.

He put on righteousness as his breastplate, and the helmet of salvation on his head; he put on the garments of vengeance and wrapped himself in zeal as in a cloak (Isaiah 59:17).

He placed the breastpiece on him and put the Urim and Thummim in the breastpiece (Leviticus 8:8).

Stand firm then, with the belt of truth buckled around your waist, with the breastplate of righteousness in place (Ephesians 6:14).

BREATH: Spirit of man. Breath of life. Sign of life. Revive to life.

The Lord God formed the man from the dust of the ground and breathed into his nostrils the breath of life, and the man became a living being (Genesis 2:7).

His breath sets coals ablaze, and flames dart from his mouth (Job 41:21).

Topheth has long been prepared; it has been made ready for the king. Its fire pit has been made deep and wide, with an abundance of fire and wood; the breath of the Lord, like a stream of burning sulphur, sets it ablaze (Isaiah 30:33).

Then he said to me, "Prophesy to the breath; prophesy, son of man, and say to it, 'This is what the Sovereign Lord says: Come from the four winds, O breath, and breathe into these slain, that they may live'" (Ezekiel 37:9).

BRICK: Something that is manmade; designed to be durable. Personality building.

They said to each other, "Come, let's make bricks and bake them thoroughly." They used brick instead of stone, and tar for mortar (Genesis 11:3).

The bricks have fallen down, but we will rebuild with dressed stone; the fig trees have been felled, but we will replace them with cedars (Isaiah 9:10).

A people who continually provoke Me to My very face, offering sacrifices in gardens and burning incense on altars of brick (Isaiah 65:3).

BRIDE: The Church relationship to Jesus. Special to Jesus. Covenant or relationship.

"Lift up your eyes and look around; all your sons gather and come to you. As surely as I live," declares the Lord, "you will wear them all as ornaments; you will put them on, like a bride" (Isaiah 49:18).

Bride

The bride belongs to the bridegroom. The friend who attends the bridegroom waits and listens for him, and is full of joy when he hears the bridegroom's voice. That joy is mine, and it is now complete (John 3:29).

One of the seven angels who had the seven bowls full of the seven last plagues came and said to me, "Come, I will show you the bride, the wife of the Lamb" (Revelation 21:9).

BRIDGE: Something that takes you across an obstacle, e.g. faith. The connection between two things/circumstances. Something that holds you up in times of difficulty.

Bridge

BRIDLE: Put control over, e.g. self-control over the use of the tongue. Something imposed by some higher authority to effect control—good or bad.

A whip for the horse, a bridle for the donkey, and a rod for the fool's back (Proverbs 26:3 NKJV).

If anyone among you thinks he is religious, and does not bridle his tongue but deceives his own heart, this one's religion is useless (James 1:26 NKJV).

I said, "I will watch my ways and keep my tongue from sin; I will put a muzzle [bridle] on my mouth as long as the wicked are in my presence" (Psalm 39:1).

Because your rage against Me and your tumult have come up to My ears, therefore I will put My hook in your nose and My bridle in your lips, and I will turn you back by the way which you came (Isaiah 37:29 NKJV).

BRIERS: Something "wild and thorny" that needs to be trimmed. Something uncultivated or false.

BRIGHTNESS: Presence of God. Revelation. Solution. End of difficult period.

I looked, and I saw a figure like that of a man. From what appeared to be his waist down he was like fire, and from there up his appearance was as bright as glowing metal (Ezekiel 8:2).

Those who are wise will shine like the brightness of the heavens, and those who lead many to righteousness, like the stars for ever and ever (Daniel 12:3).

You looked, O king, and there before you stood a large statue—an enormous, dazzling statue, awesome in appearance (Daniel 2:31).

The Son is the radiance (brightness) of God's glory and the exact representation of His being, sustaining all things by His powerful word. After He had provided purification for sins, He sat down at the right hand of the Majesty in heaven (Hebrews 1:3).

BRIMSTONE: Judgment of God. Punishment. Trail period.

BROKEN: Loss of strength, authority, or influence. Open. Heart, wounded.

Like a city whose walls are broken down is a man who lacks self-control (Proverbs 25:28).

I will seek what was lost and bring back what was driven away, bind up the broken and strengthen what was sick; but I will destroy the fat and the strong, and feed them in judgment (Ezekiel 34:16 NKJV).

BROOK: A provision of God. Something that brings refreshment, wisdom, prosperity from God. If dirty, means corrupted or contaminated. A source of defense.

Brook

The rivers will turn foul; the brooks of defense will be emptied and dried up; the reeds and rushes will wither (Isaiah 19:6 NKJV).

Get away from here and turn eastward, and hide by the Brook Cherith, which flows into the Jordan. And it will be that you shall drink from the brook, and I have commanded the ravens to feed you there (1 Kings 17:3-4 NKJV).

My brothers have dealt deceitfully like a brook, like the streams of the brooks that pass away (Job 6:15 NKJV).

BROOM: Something, or in the process of, getting rid of sins. Symbol of witchcraft.

Broom

BROTHER: Christian brother (spiritual brother). Your brother. Someone with similar qualities.

Whoever does God's will is my brother and sister and mother (Mark 3:35).

BROTHER-IN-LAW: Same as a brother but under special obligation. Spiritual brother without in-depth love. A person of another church who is also Christian. Actual brother-in-law. Someone with similar qualities.

BROWN/TAN: Life; change of season; born again.

BRUISE: Event or circumstance that leaves a hurt feeling with one. In need for healing. Suffering of Jesus on our behalf.

This is what the Lord says: "Your wound is incurable, your injury (bruise) beyond healing" (Jeremiah 30:12).

But He was wounded for our transgressions, He was bruised for our iniquities; the chastisement for our peace was upon Him, and by His stripes we are healed (Isaiah 53:5 NKJV).

BUCKET: A measure of something. Used for service. Supplies life.

Bucket

Surely the nations are like a drop in a bucket; they are regarded as dust on the scales; he weighs the islands as though they were fine dust (Isaiah 40:15).

Water will flow from their buckets; their seed will have abundant water. Their king will be greater than Agag; their kingdom will be exalted (Numbers 24:7).

BUILDING: Symbolic of the spiritual and emotional being of the place, person, or church. Life of the person, church, or office.

And I tell you that you are Peter, and on this rock I will build My church, and the gates of Hades will not overcome it (Matthew 16:18).

He is like a man building a house, who dug down deep and laid the foundation on rock. When a flood came, the torrent struck that house but could not shake it, because it was well built (Luke 6:48).

Therefore everyone who hears these words of Mine and puts them into practice is like a wise man who built his house on the rock. The rain came down, the streams rose, and the winds blew and beat against that house; yet it did not fall, because it had its foundation on the rock. But everyone who hears these words of Mine and does not put them into practice is like a foolish man who built his house on sand (Matthew 7:24-26).

BULL: Threatening situation. Warfare. Opposition. A source of economy.

BUNDLE: Measure of harvest. Grouping for judgment or reward. Fullness.

Bull

Then it happened as they emptied their sacks, that surprisingly each man's bundle of money was in his sack; and when they and their father saw the bundles of money, they were afraid (Genesis 42:35 NKJV).

Even though someone is pursuing you to take your life, the life of my master will be bound securely in the bundle of the living by the Lord your God. But the lives of your enemies He will hurl away as from the pocket of a sling (1 Samuel 25:29).

BURIAL: Memorial to mark the end of something.

Uzziah rested with his fathers and was buried near them in a field for burial that belonged to the kings, for people said, "He had leprosy." And Jotham his son succeeded him as king (2 Chronicles 26:23).

He will have the burial of a donkey—dragged away and thrown outside the gates of Jerusalem (Jeremiah 22:19).

When she poured this perfume on My body, she did it to prepare Me for burial (Matthew 26:12).

BURIED: A permanent end to something.

We were therefore buried with Him through baptism into death in order that, just as Christ was raised from the dead through the glory of the Father, we too may live a new life (Romans 6:4).

Having been buried with Him in baptism and raised with Him through your faith in the power of God, who raised Him from the dead (Colossians 2:12).

BURN: To consume. To heat up or strip up. To set aflame. To kindle. Sign of fervency.

Now the people complained about their hardships in the hearing of the Lord, and when He heard them His anger was aroused. Then fire from the Lord burned among them and consumed some of the outskirts of the camp (Numbers 11:1).

Burn

I will enslave you to your enemies in a land you do not know, for My anger will kindle a fire that will burn against you (Jeremiah 15:14).

Command the Israelites to bring you clear oil of pressed olives for the light so that the lamps may be kept burning (Exodus 27:20).

BUS: A big ministry.

School bus: A teaching ministry.

Bus

BUTTER: Something that brings soothing, smooth words. Encouragement.

He will eat curds [butter] *and honey when he knows enough to reject the wrong and choose the right* (Isaiah 7:15).

His speech is smooth as butter, yet war is in his heart; his words are more soothing than oil, yet they are drawn swords (Psalm 55:21).

BUY: To prepare, take, acquire, or obtain something good or bad.

Fields will be bought for silver, and deeds will be signed, sealed and witnessed in the territory of Benjamin, in the villages around Jerusalem, in the towns of Judah and in the towns of the hill country, of the western foothills and of the Negev, because I will restore their fortunes, declares the Lord (Jeremiah 32:44).

Buy the truth and do not sell it; get wisdom, discipline and understanding (Proverbs 23:23).

For a hundred pieces of silver, he bought from the sons of Hamor, the father of Shechem, the plot of ground where he pitched his tent (Genesis 33:19).

CAFETERIA: A place or period of spiritual nourishment/good or bad. A church. Structural teaching of the Word of God. Celebration.

CAGE: To restrict. Limited mobility. Negatively—captivity. Positively—to guard or watch.

Like cages full of birds, their houses are full of deceit; they have become rich and powerful (Jeremiah 5:27).

Cage

CAKE, BREAD: Provisions from Heaven. Nourishment from God.

The people went around gathering it, and then ground it in a handmill or crushed it in a mortar. They cooked it in a pot or made it into cakes. And it tasted like something made with olive oil (Numbers 11:8).

Cake

CALF: A young cow or bull. Increase in prosperity.

CAMEL: Having a servant heart. Capable of bearing other people's burdens. Intercessory spirit.

CAMP: Temporary settlement; a transit situation. Something intended for traveling or for temporary residence, not permanent building.

Jacob also went on his way, and the angels of God met him. When Jacob saw them, he said, "This is the camp of God!" So he named that place Mahanaim (Genesis 32:1-2).

They left the Red Sea and camped in the Desert of Sin. They left the Desert of Sin and camped at Dophkah. They left Dophkah and camped at Alush. They left Alush and camped at Rephidim, where there was no water for the people to drink. They left Rephidim and camped in the Desert of Sinai. They left the Desert of Sinai and camped at Kibroth Hattaavah. They left Kibroth Hattaavah and camped at Hazeroth. They left Hazeroth and camped at Rithmah (Numbers 33:11-18).

CANDLE: Word of God.

The lamp of the Lord searches the spirit of a man; it searches out his inmost being (Proverbs 20:27).

At that time I will search Jerusalem with lamps and punish those who are complacent, who are like wine left on its dregs, who think, "The Lord will do nothing, either good or bad" (Zephaniah 1:12).

Candle

Lamp and electricity: Symbolic of man's spirit. If not lit, it could mean lack of God's presence. (Jesus is also source of light.) Conscience.

CANDLESTICK: People who carry the light of God. The lamp stand, Spirit of God. Church.

CARPENTER: Jesus. Someone who makes or amends things. A preacher.

CAT: A personal pet. Deceptive situation/person. Something or a person who is self-willed. Not a teachable spirit. A sneaky, crafty, and deceptive spirit. Witchcraft, waiting to attack—a precious habit that could be dangerous.

Cat

CAVE: Safe hiding place. Secret place of encountering God.

CHAIN: Symbolic of bondage or captivity. To be bound in the spirit or in the natural.

Chain

CHAIR: Authority over something; coming to position of authority. Throne of God.

CHANNEL: A way out. A process of time. Difficult period leading to the next stage.

Chair

CHASE: Cause to flee. Get rid of something. To pursue. To go after something.

CHEQUE: The seal of promise. Promise that is guaranteed.

CHEEK: Vulnerable part, beauty.

CHEESE: To comfort. To soothe.

Cheese

CHEETAH: Unclean spirit.

CHEW: To meditate. To ruminate. To cut off.

CHICKEN: An evangelist. Gifting, caring spirit. Gathering.

Cheetah

O Jerusalem, Jerusalem, you who kill the prophets and stone those sent to you, how often I have longed to gather your children together, as a hen gathers her chicks under her wings, but you were not willing (Matthew 23:37, Luke 13:34).

Roaster: Boasting.

Chick: Defenseless.

CHILDHOOD home: Influence from the distant past, good or bad.

CHOKING: Biting more than you can chew. Too fast, too much in the wrong way.

CHRISTMAS: New thing in Christ. Tradition of men. Spiritual gift. Season of gifts/love. A period of joy and humanitarianism.

CIRCLE, RING/ROUND: Something endless; signifies agreement or covenant. Hunting, if making a circle. Relating to the universe.

He sits enthroned above the circle of the earth, and its people are like grasshoppers. He stretches out the heavens like a canopy, and spreads them out like a tent to live in (Isaiah 40:22).

CIRCUMCISION: Cutting off fleshy things/coming to liberty. Covenanting with God. Blood relationship. New levels of spiritual walk—born again.

You are to undergo circumcision, and it will be the sign of the covenant between Me and you (Genesis 17:11).

Circumcise yourselves to the Lord, circumcise your hearts, you men of Judah and people of Jerusalem, or My wrath will break out and burn like fire because of the evil you have done—burn with no one to quench it (Jeremiah 4:4).

Then He gave Abraham the covenant of circumcision. And Abraham became the father of Isaac and circumcised him eight days after his birth. Later Isaac became the father of Jacob, and Jacob became the father of the twelve patriarchs (Acts 7:8).

CITY: The makeup of the person. All that has been input into the person or people. The city or what the city is known for. Group, church.

City

CLASSROOM: A time of spiritual preparation. A person with a gifting to teach others.

CLAY: Something that refers to frailty of man. Delicate and fragile. Not secure.

I am just like you before God; I too have been taken from clay (Job 33:6).

Its legs of iron, its feet partly of iron and partly of baked clay. While you were watching, a rock was cut out, but not by human hands. It struck the statue on its feet of iron and clay and smashed them....As the toes were partly iron and partly clay, so this kingdom will be partly strong and partly brittle (Daniel 2:33-34,42).

CLEAN: To make holy, purity. To make righteous. To make ready and acceptable.

CLEANSE: To put something right. To put away what is bad.

CLEAR: To bring light to the situation. To bring understanding. To be set free from something.

CLOCK: Timing is important in the situation. The time to do it is revealed. May refer to Bible passages. Running out of time.

Clock

CLOSE: To shut up, to keep silent, or to be hedged or walled up.

For the Lord has poured out on you the spirit of deep sleep, and has closed your eyes, namely, the prophets; and He has covered your heads, namely, the seers (Isaiah 29:10 NKJV).

For this people's heart has become calloused; they hardly hear with their ears, and they have closed their eyes. Otherwise they might see with their eyes, hear with their ears, understand with their hearts and turn, and I would heal them (Matthew 13:15).

CLOSET: Hidden, confidential, personal, or exclusive. A place of prayer. A place of fellowship with God.

Gather the people, consecrate the assembly; bring together the elders, gather the children, those nursing at the breast. Let the bridegroom leave his room and the bride her chamber [closet] (Joel 2:16).

But when you pray, go into your room [closet], *close the door and pray to your Father, who is unseen. Then your Father, who sees what is done in secret, will reward you* (Matthew 6:6).

What you have said in the dark will be heard in the daylight, and what you have whispered in the ear in the inner rooms [closet] *will be proclaimed from the roofs* (Luke 12:3).

CLOTHING: Covering, whether pure or impure. Your standing or authority in a situation. Covering, God is providing us with.

Tearing clothes: Signifies grief, sorrow.

CLOUDS: Heavenly manifestation; glory presence of God. Dark time of travel, fear, trouble, or storms of life.

By day the Lord went ahead of them in a pillar of cloud to guide them on their way and by night in a pillar of fire to give them light, so that they could travel by day or night (Exodus 13:21).

Clouds

The Lord said to Moses: "Tell your brother Aaron not to come whenever he chooses into the Most Holy Place behind the curtain in front of the atonement cover on the ark, or else he will die, because I appear in the cloud over the atonement cover (Leviticus 16:2).

At that time the sign of the Son of Man will appear in the sky, and all the nations of the earth will mourn. They will see the Son of Man coming on the clouds of the sky, with power and great glory (Matthew 24:30).

Dark clouds: A time of storm.

White clouds: Glory of God.

CLOWN: Not a serious person. Not taking God seriously. Childish.

COAT: Protective, covering, mantle.

Clown

The Lord God made garments [coat] of skin for Adam and his wife and clothed them (Genesis 3:21).

He is to put on the sacred linen tunic, with linen undergarments next to his body; he is to tie the linen sash around him and put on the linen turban. These are sacred garments [coats]; so he must bathe himself with water before he puts them on (Leviticus 16:4).

Take the garments [coats] and dress Aaron with the tunic, the robe of the ephod, the ephod itself and the breastpiece. Fasten the ephod on him by its skillfully woven waistband (Exodus 29:5).

Clean: Righteousness.

Dirty: Not righteous, unclean.

COLLEGE: Promotion in the Spirit. Pertaining to the equipping season.

COLUMNS: Spirit of control and manipulation or obsessive orderliness.

CONCEIVE: In process of preparation. To add. To multiply.

CONGREGATION: An appointed meeting. An assembly. Called together.

CORD: Something that holds things together. Enhances unity/love.

COUCH: Rest, relaxation, peace.

COUNTRYSIDE: A time of peace/tranquillity. A potential that is yet unexplored.

Couch

COURTHOUSE: Time of being judged or persecution; trial.

COW: Food/source of enrichment. Potential source of sin.

CRAWLING: Humility or to be humiliated.

CROOKED: Distorted, not straight.

> *Every valley shall be raised up, every mountain and hill made low; the rough ground* [crooked] *shall become level* [straight]*, the rugged places a plain* (Isaiah 40:4).

> *But those who turn to crooked ways the Lord will banish with the evildoers. Peace be upon Israel* (Psalm 125:5).

CROSSING STREET: Changing perspective.

CROSSROADS: Vital choice to make or change in position. Options.

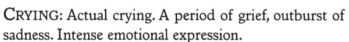

Crossing street

CROWN: Symbol of authority. Seal of power. Jesus Christ. To reign. To be honored.

CRYING: Actual crying. A period of grief, outburst of sadness. Intense emotional expression.

Crown

CULTURAL CLOTHES: Call to nation.

CUP: Your portion in life, provision or responsibility.

CYMBALS: Instrument to praise God with. Could be used without genuine love.

Cup

DAM: The power of unity or gathering resources. Obstacle to flow. Reserve sustenance. Stillness.

DANCING, WORSHIP: Worshiping something—God or idol. A time of joy or rejoicing.

Dam

DARKNESS: Lack of light. Without spiritual direction.

DAUGHTER: Gift of God. Ministry that is your child in the Spirit. The child herself. Someone with similar qualities.

DAYTIME: The opportune time. A time of light. Season of good deeds. Season when things are revealed or understanding is gained.

DEAF: Not spiritually attentive. Not paying attention.

DEATH: What the Bible says more frequently about death is dying to self. Some measure of dying to self in an area. Separation from things of evil; actual physical death. The end of life on earth. Death is also overcoming the work of the flesh to resume communion with God.

DEER: Spiritual longing. Symbol of hunger for the things of God. Ability to take great strides. Grace. Divine enabling.

Deer

> *As the deer pants for streams of water, so my soul pants for You, O God. My soul thirsts for God, for the living God. When can I go and meet with God?* (Psalm 42:1-2)
>
> *A loving doe, a graceful deer—may her breasts satisfy you always, may you ever be captivated by her love* (Proverbs 5:19).
>
> *The Sovereign Lord is my strength; He makes my feet like the feet of a deer, He enables me to go on the heights. For the director of music. On my stringed instruments* (Habakkuk 3:19).

DEN: Busy doing the wrong thing.

DESERT: Training, lack or testing. A place of reliance on God.

Desert

DEW: Blessings. Condensed, moisturised air formed in drops during still, cloudless night indicates divine blessing on the earth. The Word of God.

> *May God give you of heaven's dew and of earth's richness—an abundance of grain and new wine* (Genesis 27:28).
>
> *It is as if the dew of Hermon were falling on Mount Zion. For there the Lord bestows His blessing, even life forevermore* (Psalm 133:3).
>
> *Let my teaching fall like rain and my words descend like dew, like showers on new grass, like abundant rain on tender plants* (Deuteronomy 32:2).
>
> *Therefore, because of you the heavens have withheld their dew and the earth its crops* (Haggai 1:10).

DIAMOND: Something to engrave with, something hard, and something that is sharp at cutting. Diamond as a pen nib. Something valuable.

Diamond

DIFFICULT WALKING: Difficult times of life. Facing opposition.

DINING ROOM: Feeding on the Word of God. A place of spiritual food. Table of the Lord.

DINOSAUR: Something in the distant past. Something big and terrible but something God has dealt with.

Dinosaur

DIRTY CLOTH: False doctrine. Of a sinful nature.

> *Now Joshua was dressed in filthy clothes as he stood before the angel. The angel said to those who were standing before him, "Take off his filthy clothes." Then he said to Joshua, "See, I have taken away your sin, and I will put rich garments on you." Then I said, "Put a clean turban on his head." So they put a clean turban on his head and clothed him, while the angel of the Lord stood by* (Zechariah 3:3-5).

DIRTY/DRY: Not pure spiritual things.

DIRTY/NEGLECTED: A place in need of attention.

DISEASE: Emotional upset. Bondage from the devil.

DITCH: Deception, a trap; fleshy desire.

DOCTOR: Jesus—the healer. A person with healing anointing. Someone with caring service, minister. Symbol of healing anointing.

DOG: A gift that could be harnessed to do good, but should not be too trusted. Could be versatile in function but unpredictable. Man's best friend. A pet sin.

DONKEY: An enduring spirit, useable by the Lord. A spirit that God could use if surrendered to Him.

DOOR: An opening. Jesus Christ. The way, a possibility, grace. Something to do with Jesus.

> *Set a guard over my mouth, O Lord; keep watch over the door of my lips* (Psalm 141:3).

Door

Therefore Jesus said again, "I tell you the truth, I am the gate [door] *for the sheep. All who ever came before Me were thieves and robbers, but the sheep did not listen to them. I am the gate* [door]; *whoever enters through Me will be saved. He will come in and go out, and find pasture* (John 10:7-9).

After this I looked, and there before me was a door standing open in heaven. And the voice I had first heard speaking to me like a trumpet said, "Come up here, and I will show you what must take place after this" (Revelation 4:1).

DOWN: Spiritual descent/backslide. Falling away. Humiliation. Failure.

DRAGON: Satan. High demonic spirit. Great level of wickedness. Antichrist.

Dragon

Then another sign appeared in heaven: an enormous red dragon with seven heads and ten horns and seven crowns on his heads (Revelation 12:3).

The great dragon was hurled down—that ancient serpent called the devil, or Satan, who leads the whole world astray. He was hurled to the earth, and his angels with him (Revelation 12:9).

DRAWING: Conceptualization.

Artist's paint: A means or method of illustration. To be fluent in expression.

Paint: Doctrine, truth, or deception.

DREAMING: Deeply spiritual message. A futuristic message.

DRINKING: Receiving from the spiritual realm, good or bad. Receiving your portion in life. Bearing your cross.

DRIVER: The one in command or control. The one that makes the decisions.

DRIVING IN REVERSE: Not going in correct direction with anointing.

DROUGHT: A period of lack without God.

DROWNING: Overcome by situation leading to depression. Overwhelmed to the point of self-pity.

DRUGS: Medication. Illicit drugs = counterfeit anointing.

DRUNKARD: Influenced by counterfeit source of anointing. Self-indulgence error. Uncontrolled lust.

Drugs

DUST: Temporary nature of humanity. Frailty of man. Curse. Numerous. Humiliation.

The Lord God formed the man from the dust of the ground and breathed into his nostrils the breath of life, and the man became a living being (Genesis 2:7).

Your descendants will be like the dust of the earth, and you will spread out to the west and to the east, to the north and to the south. All peoples on earth will be blessed through you and your offspring (Genesis 28:14).

Shake off your dust; rise up, sit enthroned, O Jerusalem. Free yourself from the chains on your neck, O captive Daughter of Zion (Isaiah 52:2).

DYNAMITE: Holy Spirit "dynamos"—power/great spiritual power, good or bad.

Dynamite

EAR: Symbolic of the prophet—not the seer. Hearing spiritual things that either build up or tear down. Lack of hearing or need to be paying more attention.

EARTHQUAKE: Sudden release of great power. Judgment. Ground-shaking changes. Great shock. A time of trial. Release from prison.

As when fire sets twigs ablaze and causes water to boil, come down to make Your name known to Your enemies and cause the nations to quake before You! For when You did awesome things that we did not expect, You came down, and the mountains trembled before You. Since ancient times no one has heard, no ear has perceived, no eye has seen any God besides You, who acts on behalf of those who wait for Him (Isaiah 64:2-4).

EAST: God's glory—the sun rising. East wind brings judgment/hardship.

East

EATING: Feeding on something, e.g. Word of God or evil things. Meditation and gaining greater understanding.

ECHO: Word coming back. Word sphere against living revealed. Repercussions.

EGG, SEED: Delicate seed or promise. Sustenance. The possibility for growth—potential and development in any manner, revelation.

EGYPT: Bondage/slavery. Refuge—was refuge for Jesus. Old sin. Pre-Christian life.

Egypt

EIGHT: A new beginning. Circumcision of flesh.

EIGHTEEN: Bondage. God gave Israelites to Philistine for eighteen years.

> *He became angry with them. He sold them into the hands of the Philistines and the Ammonites, who that year shattered and crushed them. For eighteen years they oppressed all the Israelites on the east side of the Jordan in Gilead, the land of the Amorites* (Judges 10:7-8).

> *And a woman was there who had been crippled by a spirit for eighteen years. She was bent over and could not straighten up at all. When Jesus saw her, He called her forward and said to her, "Woman, you are set free from your infirmity." Then He put His hands on her, and immediately she straightened up and praised God. Indignant because Jesus had healed on the Sabbath, the synagogue ruler said to the people, "There are six days for work. So come and be healed on those days, not on the Sabbath." The Lord answered him, "You hypocrites! Doesn't each of you on the Sabbath untie his ox or donkey from the stall and lead it out to give it water? Then should not this woman, a daughter of Abraham, whom Satan has kept bound for eighteen long years, be set free on the Sabbath day from what bound her?"* (Luke 13:11-16)

ELECTRICITY: Spiritual power of God; potential for God's flow.

Outlet for electricity: Possibility of being connected into the flow of the Holy Spirit.

Unplugged cord: Not connected to the power of the Spirit.

ELEMENTARY: The infant stage, not yet mature.

ELEVATOR: Moving up and down in levels of godly authority.

Elevator

ELEVEN: Disorder, confusion, lawlessness.

EMPLOYEE/SERVANTS: The one who is submitted to the authority. The actual person.

EMPLOYER/MASTER: Jesus. The authority, good or bad. Pastor. Evil leadership.

EXPLOSION: Quick outburst, generally positive. Sudden expansion or increase. Quick work or devastating change.

Explosion

EYES: Seer's anointing.

Eyes

> **Winking**: Concealed intention or cunning person.
>
> **Closed**: Ignorance, spiritually blind, mostly self-imposed.

FACE: Identity or characteristics. Image expression.

Face

FACTORY: Structured service in God's vineyard.

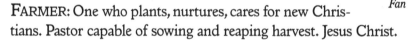

Factory

FALLING: Loss of support. Falling out of favor. Entering a time of trial/darkness/sin.

FAMILY: The Christian or spiritual family. Group of people in covenant or spirit of oneness; unified fellowship.

FAN: Stirring up of gifting. Something that brings relief or comfort. Make fire hotter. Increasing circulation.

Fan

FARMER: One who plants, nurtures, cares for new Christians. Pastor capable of sowing and reaping harvest. Jesus Christ.

FATHER: Father God, supplier of needs. Natural father of the bloodline. One who provides. The head of home or place.

FATHER-IN-LAW: Father figure within the organization. An advisor, spirit of delegation, head of another organization.

FEATHERS: Protective spiritual covering. Weightless. Something with which to move in the spiritual realm. Presence of God.

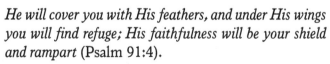

Feathers

> *He will cover you with His feathers, and under His wings you will find refuge; His faithfulness will be your shield and rampart* (Psalm 91:4).
>
> *Say to them, "This is what the Sovereign Lord says: A great eagle with powerful wings, long feathers and full plumage of varied colors came to Lebanon. Taking hold of the top of a cedar, he broke off its topmost shoot and carried it away to a land of merchants, where he planted it in a city of traders. He took some of the seed of your land and put it in fertile soil. He planted it like a willow by abundant*

water, and it sprouted and became a low, spreading vine. Its branches turned toward him, but its roots remained under it. So it became a vine and produced branches and put out leafy boughs. But there was another great eagle with powerful wings and full plumage. The vine now sent out its roots toward him from the plot where it was planted and stretched out its branches to him for water" (Ezekiel 17:3-7).

FEEDING: To partake in a spiritual provision, good or evil.

FEET: A spiritual walk, heart attitude.

Barefoot: Humble before the presence of God.

Diseased: Spirit of offense.

Kicking: Not under authority or working against authority.

Lame: Crippled with unbelief, mind-set, negative stronghold.

Washing: Humble; duty of Christians.

Overgrown nails: Lack of care, not in proper order.

FENCE: Protection. Security. Self-imposed. Limitation. Stronghold.

Fence

How long will you assault a man? Would all of you throw him down—this leaning wall, this tottering fence? (Psalm 62:3)

Then the king of the North will come and build up siege ramps and will capture a fortified [fenced] city. The forces of the South will be powerless to resist; even their best troops will not have the strength to stand (Daniel 11:15).

FIELD: Life situation, things to do and accomplish. (Depends on the field and context.)

He gives rain on the earth, and sends waters on the fields (Job 5:10 NKJV).

FIFTEEN: Mercy, grace, liberty, rest, freedom.

FIFTY: Period or time of outpouring such as Pentecost. Number of Holy Spirit/jubilee/freedom/liberty.

FIGHT: To struggle with, to agonize, to war or resist something.

Contend, O Lord, with those who contend with me; fight against those who fight against me (Psalm 35:1).

Fight the good fight of the faith. Take hold of the eternal life to which you were called when you made your good confession in the presence of many witnesses (1 Timothy 6:12).

Remember those earlier days after you had received the light, when you stood your ground in a great contest [fight] *in the face of suffering* (Hebrews 10:32).

FINGER: Means of discernment. Spiritual sensitivity—feelings.

Pointed finger: Accusations, persecution, instructions, direction.

Finger of God: Work of God, authority of God.

Clenched: Pride.

Thumb: Apostle.

Index: Prophet.

Middle: Evangelist.

Small: Pastor.

FIRE: God's presence. Trial, persecution, burning fervency, emotion, longing, aching, and craving. Power. Holy Spirit. Anger or judgment/punishment. Lake of fire, very different from tongue of fire.

Fire

Then the Lord rained down burning sulphur on Sodom and Gomorrah—from the Lord out of the heavens (Genesis 19:24).

FISH: New converts to the Lord. Newly recreated spirit of man. Miraculous provision of food.

"Come, follow Me," Jesus said, "and I will make you fishers of men" (Mark 1:17).

Fish

FIVE: Grace related to the fivefold ministry.

FLASH: Revelation or insight.

FLEA: Not plentiful. Inconvenience. Subtlety.

FLOOD: Judgment on those who use whatever power they have to inflict violence on others. Sin judged. Overcome. To be overcome and unable to recover.

From the west, men will fear the name of the Lord, and from the rising of the sun, they will revere His glory. For He will come like a pent-up flood that the breath of the Lord drives along (Isaiah 59:19).

I am going to bring floodwaters on the earth to destroy all life under the heavens, every creature that has the breath of life in it. Everything on earth will perish (Genesis 6:17).

FLOWERS: Man's glory of the flesh that is passing away. An offering. Glory of God. Beautiful expression of love. Renewal. Spring.

Flower

That fading flower, his glorious beauty, set on the head of a fertile valley, will be like a fig ripe before harvest—as soon as someone sees it and takes it in his hand, he swallows it (Isaiah 28:4).

But the one who is rich should take pride in his low position, because he will pass away like a wild flower (James 1:10).

For, "All men are like grass, and all their glory is like the flowers of the field; the grass withers and the flowers fall" (1 Peter 1:24).

Lily of the valley: Jesus.

Rose: Love, courtship, romance.

FLY: Evil spirits. Corruption. To possess by evil spirit. Results of unclean actions.

As dead flies give perfume a bad smell, so a little folly outweighs wisdom and honor (Ecclesiastes 10:1).

In that day the Lord will whistle for flies from the distant streams of Egypt and for bees from the land of Assyria (Isaiah 7:18).

FLYING: Highly powered by the Holy Spirit.

Who are these that fly along like clouds, like doves to their nests? (Isaiah 60:8)

Like birds hovering overhead, the Lord Almighty will shield Jerusalem; He will shield it and deliver it, He will "pass over" it and will rescue it (Isaiah 31:5).

He mounted the cherubim and flew; He soared on the wings of the wind (Psalm 18:10, 2 Samuel 22:11).

FOG: Not clear, uncertainty, concealed, vagueness. Wrath of God.

FOOD: Spiritual and physical nourishment, good or evil. To bring increase.

Food

They should collect all the food of these good years that are coming and store up the grain under the authority of Pharaoh, to be kept in the cities for food (Genesis 41:35).

FOREIGNER: A person outside the Christian faith (not a citizen of Heaven). Someone to be taught and cared for, and brought into the covenant.

FOREHEAD: Thought process and reasoning. Revelations. Retaining and recalling ability. Commitment to God.

FOREST: Growth in life (depending on the context). Place of danger and darkness where one can be easily lost and harmed. Confusion and lack of direction, uncultivated. A land covered with trees that are naturally planted is different from a park where man's hand is more evident.

Forest

The battle spread out over the whole countryside, and the forest claimed more lives that day than the sword (2 Samuel 18:8).

FORTY: Testing period, season of trial.

Moses was there with the Lord forty days and forty nights without eating bread or drinking water. And he wrote on the tablets the words of the covenant—the Ten Commandments (Exodus 34:28).

I brought you up out of Egypt, and I led you forty years in the desert to give you the land of the Amorites (Amos 2:10).

Where for forty days he was tempted by the devil. He ate nothing during those days, and at the end of them he was hungry (Luke 4:2).

FOUR: Worldly creation; four corners of the world; four seasons. Global implication or the four Gospels.

FOURTEEN: Double anointing. Recreation. Reproduction. Passover.

FOX: A cunning spirit. Craftiness, secretly or counter-productive.

Tobiah the Ammonite, who was at his side, said, "What they are building—if even a fox climbed up on it, he would break down their wall of stones!" (Nehemiah 4:3)

Catch for us the foxes, the little foxes that ruin the vineyards, our vineyards that are in bloom (Song of Solomon 2:15).

Your prophets, O Israel, are like jackals [foxes] among ruins (Ezekiel 13:4).

He replied, "Go tell that fox, 'I will drive out demons and heal people today and tomorrow, and on the third day I will reach My goal'" (Luke 13:32).

FREEZER: Storing spiritual food for future time.

FRIEND: Brother or sister in Christ. Yourself. Showing to have similar qualities. Faithful person.

FROG: Evil spirit. Makes a lot of noise, boastful. Sorcery. Lying nature. Issuing curses.

Frog

If you refuse to let them go, I will plague your whole country with frogs (Exodus 8:2).

He sent swarms of flies that devoured them, and frogs that devastated them (Psalm 78:45).

Then I saw three evil spirits that looked like frogs; they came out of the mouth of the dragon, out of the mouth of the beast and out of the mouth of the false prophet (Revelation 16:13).

FRONT SIDE: Looking ahead, something in the future.

FRUITS: Source of nourishment. Means of increase. Reward of labor. To bear something or child. Harvest. Come to fullness. Gifts of the Spirit. Fruit of our labor. Fruit of the womb. Fruit of the Holy Spirit, consisting of all the Christian virtues.

Fruits

FUEL: Source of energy. Source of food for the Spirit. Capable of reviving.

FURNACE: Source of heat, the heart, heated and painful experiences. Period of trial. Source of pruning. Center of holy activities.

Whoever does not fall down and worship will immediately be thrown into a blazing furnace (Daniel 3:6).

But as for you, the Lord took you and brought you out of the iron-smelting furnace, out of Egypt, to be the people of His inheritance, as you now are (Deuteronomy 4:20).

See, I have refined you, though not as silver; I have tested you in the furnace of affliction (Isaiah 48:10).

GALLOWS: A place of severe punishment. A place of nemesis or a place of death.

Gallows

So they hanged Haman on the gallows he had prepared for Mordecai. Then the king's fury subsided (Esther 7:10).

GAP: Breach. A weak spot. A loophole. An opening.

You have not gone up to the breaks in the wall to repair it for the house of Israel so that it will stand firm in the battle on the day of the Lord (Ezekiel 13:5).

I looked for a man among them who would build up the wall and stand before Me in the gap on behalf of the land so I would not have to destroy it, but I found none (Ezekiel 22:30).

GARAGE: Symbolic of storage. Potential or protection.

GARBAGE: Abandoned things. Corruption. Reprobate or unclean. Unclean spirit; departure from all that is godly. Something that is thrown away. Opinion of life without Jesus.

GARDEN: A piece of land that is cultivated, signifying the life situation as planned by God. Field of labor in life. A place of increase, fruitfulness, and productivity. A place of rest or romance. Life of believer as a garden mastered by the Holy Spirit.

Now the Lord God had planted a garden in the east, in Eden; and there He put the man He had formed (Genesis 2:8).

The Lord will guide you always; He will satisfy your needs in a sunscorched land and will strengthen your frame. You will be like a well-watered garden, like a spring whose waters never fail (Isaiah 58:11).

The woman said to the serpent, "We may eat fruit from the trees in the garden" (Genesis 3:2).

Then the man and his wife heard the sound of the Lord God as He was walking in the garden in the cool of the day, and they hid from the Lord God among the trees of the garden (Genesis 3:8).

GARDENING: An area of labor. A place of reward, increase, or harvest.

GARMENT: Covering.

Clean: Honor or mantle.

Dirty: The glory of God upon a person. Stained with sin.

GASOLINE: Source of energy. Faith filled/prayer. Danger. Sinful motives.

GATE: Doors, opening. Salvation. Entrance to something such as building, grounds, or cities. In biblical days, business bargaining negotiations were conducted at the gates. Passage into or out of a place.

Gate

All these cities were fortified with high walls and with gates and bars, and there were also a great many unwalled villages (Deuteronomy 3:5).

For He breaks down gates of bronze and cuts through bars of iron (Psalm 107:16).

I will go before you and will level the mountains; I will break down gates of bronze and cut through bars of iron (Isaiah 45:2).

The twelve gates were twelve pearls, each gate made of a single pearl. The great street of the city was of pure gold, like transparent glass (Revelation 21:21).

The Lord loves the gates of Zion more than all the dwellings of Jacob (Psalm 87:2).

GIANT: A powerful spiritual being e.g. an angel or demon. A challenging situation that needs to be overcome. Something that arouses fear.

We saw the Nephilim there (the descendants of Anak come from the Nephilim). We seemed like grasshoppers in our own eyes, and we looked the same to them (Numbers 13:33).

GIRDLE: To prepare for use; might potency. To strengthen for readiness. Gathering together of the strength within you.

GLOVES: Something that protects the means of service. Something that fits. Something that protects the means of productivity.

GOAT: Pertaining to foolishness. Carnal, fleshly. Not submitting to authority. Walking into sin. Need for repentance. Miscarriage of judgment, i.e. scapegoat.

Goat

GOLD: Of God. Seal of divinity. Honorable. God's glory. Faithful; endurance; holiness that endures. Symbol of honor; of high valor. Something valuable that endures.

I turned around to see the voice that was speaking to me. And when I turned I saw seven golden lampstands (Revelation 1:12).

Overlay it with pure gold, both inside and out, and make a gold molding around it (Exodus 25:11).

Make a table of acacia wood—two cubits long, a cubit wide and a cubit and a half high. Overlay it with pure gold and make a gold molding around it. Also make around it a rim a handbreadth wide and put a gold molding on the rim. Make four gold rings for the table and fasten them to the four corners, where the four legs are. The rings are to be close to the rim to hold the poles used in carrying the table. Make the poles of acacia wood, overlay them with gold and carry the table with them. And make its plates and dishes of pure gold, as well as its pitchers and bowls for the pouring out of offerings. Put the bread of the Presence on this table to be before Me at all times (Exodus 25:23-30).

In a large house there are articles not only of gold and silver, but also of wood and clay; some are for noble purposes and some for ignoble (2 Timothy 2:20).

GOVERNOR: The person who has the power in the place. Spiritual leader in the church, to a geographical region or evil principality. Authority; rulership; reigning.

GRANDCHILD: Blessing passed on from a previous generation. Spirit passed on from the past generation. Generation inheritance, good or bad. Heir. Spiritual offspring of your ministry.

GRANDMOTHER: Generational authority over the person. Spiritual inheritance. Past wisdom or gifting.

GRAPES: Fruit of the promised land. Successful agriculture or success in life. Pleasant to the eyes. Evidence of fertility.

Grapes

When I found Israel, it was like finding grapes in the desert; when I saw your fathers, it was like seeing the early fruit on the fig tree. But when they came to Baal Peor, they consecrated themselves to that shameful idol and became as vile as the thing they loved (Hosea 9:10).

"The days are coming," declares the Lord, "when the reaper will be overtaken by the plowman and the planter by the one treading grapes. New wine will drip from the mountains and flow from all the hills" (Amos 9:13).

Still another angel, who had charge of the fire, came from the altar and called in a loud voice to him who had the sharp sickle, "Take your sharp sickle and gather the clusters of grapes from the earth's vine, because its grapes are ripe" (Revelation 14:18).

When they reached the Valley of Eshcol, they cut off a branch bearing a single cluster of grapes. Two of them carried it on a pole between them, along with some pomegranates and figs (Numbers 13:23).

GRASS: Divinely provided; something meant to be maintained. Life. God's Word in seed form. Word of God.

Dried: Death of the flesh through repentance.

Mowed: Disciplined obedience.

GRASSHOPPER/LOCUST: A devastating situation. Instrument of God's judgment. Low self-esteem.

GRAVEYARD/GRAVE: Old tradition. Cultural reserve. Death. Demonic influence from the past. Buried potentials.

Let's swallow them alive, like the grave, and whole, like those who go down to the pit (Proverbs 1:12).

Grave

All your pomp has been brought down to the grave, along with the noise of your harps; maggots are spread out beneath you and worms cover you (Isaiah 14:11).

They came out of the tombs, and after Jesus' resurrection they went into the holy city and appeared to many people (Matthew 27:53).

GREY: Uncertainty, compromise, consisting of good and bad mixture.

GREEN: Life—can be good or evil life. Provision. Rest and peace.

GROOM: Christ. Marriage. Headship.

GUARD: Ability to keep on the right path. Spirit of protection/to be vigilant.

GUEST: Spiritual messenger. An angel or evil presence.

GUN: Instrument of demonic affliction. Spoken words that wound. Power of words in prayer. Dominion through speaking the Word of God.

Gun

HAIL: Means of judgment against God's enemies. Something that can cause considerable damage to crops, property, and life. Means of punishment for the wicked.

Therefore, at this time tomorrow I will send the worst hailstorm that has ever fallen on Egypt, from the day it was founded till now (Exodus 9:18).

> *When Moses stretched out his staff toward the sky, the Lord sent thunder and hail, and lightning flashed down to the ground. So the Lord rained hail on the land of Egypt; hail fell and lightning flashed back and forth. It was the worst storm in all the land of Egypt since it had become a nation* (Exodus 9:23-24).

> *I will execute judgment upon him with plague and bloodshed; I will pour down torrents of rain, hailstones and burning sulfur on him and on his troops and on the many nations with him* (Ezekiel 38:22).

HAMMER: Living Word. Preaching the Word hard and fast. Capable of breaking something to pieces. Something that smooths strong things such as metal or rocks. For building.

Hammer

> *The craftsman encourages the goldsmith, and he who smooths with the hammer spurs on him who strikes the anvil. He says of the welding, "It is good." He nails down the idol so it will not topple* (Isaiah 41:7).

> *"Is not My word like fire," declares the Lord, "and like a hammer that breaks a rock in pieces?"* (Jeremiah 23:29)

HANDS: Means of service. Means of expressing strength.

Clapping: Joy and worship.

Fist: Pride in one's strength; anger.

Covering face: Guilt or shame.

Holding hands: In agreement.

Left hand: Something spiritual.

Raised hands: Surrender or worshiping.

Right hand: Oath of allegiance. Means of power, of honor. Natural strengths.

Shaking hands: Coming to an agreement.

Stretched out hands: Surrender.

Trembling: To fear; spirit of fear; anxiety. Awe at God's presence.

Under thighs: In oaths.

Washing: Declaring innocence; to dissociate oneself.

HARLOT, PROSTITUTE: A tempting situation. Something that appeals to your flesh. Worldly desire. Pre-Christian habit that wants to resurrect. Enticement.

HARP: If used for God, praise and worship in Heaven and in the earth. Instrument for praise and worship. Could be used for idolatry.

Harp

HARVEST: Seasons of grace. Opportunities to share the gospel. Fruitfulness. Reward of labor and action.

HAT: Covering, protection, mantle, crown. Protection of the head.

Hat

HEAD: Lordship, authority. Jesus/God. Husband. Master/boss. Pastor. Mind, thoughts.

Anointed: Set apart for God's service.

Hands on head: Signifying sorrow.

HEDGE: God's safeguard, security, safety. Literally—loose stonewall without mortar. Protection. Supernatural or prophetic protection. God as hedge around His people. Where the very poor find shelter.

Why have you broken down its walls [hedge] *so that all who pass by pick its grapes?* (Psalm 80:12)

He then began to speak to them in parables: "A man planted a vineyard. He put a wall around it, dug a pit for the winepress and built a watchtower. Then he rented the vineyard to some farmers and went away on a journey (Mark 12:1).

HEEL: The crushing power.

HELICOPTER: Spirit-powered for spiritual warfare. One-man ministry.

Helicopter

HELMET: The awareness and inner assurance of salvation. God's promise.

HIGH SCHOOL: Moving into a higher level of walk with God. Capable of giving the same to others.

HIGHWAY: Holy way; the path of life. Truth of God, Christ. Predetermined path of life, or path of life that enjoys high volume usage. May lead to good or evil destinations.

Dead end: A course of action that will lead to nothing.

Gravel: Way; God's Word; stony ground.

Muddy: Difficult path; not clear; uncertain path.

Construction: In preparation, change.

HILLS: A place of exaltation. Uplift high above the natural. Throne of God. Mount Zion.

HIPS: Reproduction. Relating to reproduction or supporting structure.

HONEY: Sweet; strength; wisdom. Spirit of God. The abiding anointing. The sweet Word of our Lord. Standard of measure for pleasant things. The best product of the land. Abundance. A land flowing with milk and honey. Food in times of scarcity.

> *Then their father Israel said to them, "If it must be, then do this: Put some of the best products of the land in your bags and take them down to the man as a gift—a little balm and a little honey, some spices and myrrh, some pistachio nuts and almonds* (Genesis 43:11).

> *He will not enjoy the streams, the rivers flowing with honey and cream* (Job 20:17).

> *So I have come down to rescue them from the hand of the Egyptians and to bring them up out of that land into a good and spacious land, a land flowing with milk and honey—the home of the Canaanites, Hittites, Amorites, Perizzites, Hivites and Jebusites* (Exodus 3:8).

> *Honey and curds, sheep, and cheese from cows' milk for David and his people to eat. For they said, "The people have become hungry and tired and thirsty in the desert"* (2 Samuel 17:29).

HORNS: The source of anointed power. The power of the kings.

HORSE: Of great strength; powerful in warfare. Spirit of tenaciousness, not double-minded. A ministry that is powerful and capable of competing. Strength under control, such as meekness. God's judgment.

Horse that kicks: Threatening, or opposition to the agreed terms.
Black: Lack.
Bay (flame-colored): Power, fire.
Pale: Spirit of death.
Red: Danger; passion; blood of Jesus.
White: Purity or righteousness.
Blue: Spiritual.
Brown: Repented, born-again.
Green: Life, mortal.
Grey: In between black and white. Vague, hazy.

Orange: Danger, evil.

Pink: Flesh. Relating to desire and decision based on the mind.

Purple: Something related to royalty. Noble in character. Riches.

Yellow: Gift from God or cowardliness, fear.

HOSPITAL: A gift of healing/anointing or caring or love. Edifying others.

HOTEL: A place of gathering, a temporary place of meeting. A transit place of meeting, church; a transit situation.

HOUSE: One's spiritual and emotion house. Personality. Church.

House

HUSBAND: Jesus Christ. Actual person.

HUSBAND, EX-HUSBAND: Previous head over you—something that had control over you in the past.

INCENSE: Prayer, worship, praise. Acceptable unto God.

IRON: Something of strength, powerful. Strict rules/powerful strongholds.

IRONING: The process of correction by instructions, teaching. To talk things over. Working out problem relationships. Turning from sin.

ISLAND: Something related to the island. What the island is known for, or its name.

ISRAEL: The nation of Israel. The Christian community; the redeemed ones. Authority that comes from God over men. People of God.

JERUSALEM: The establishment of peace. Chosen place by God. The city of God.

JEWELRY: Valuable possessions. God's people. Gifted person who has received abilities from the Lord. Something or some-one valued by the dreamer.

Jewelry

JUDGE: Father God. Authority. Anointed to make decisions. Jesus Christ. Unjust ruler.

KANGAROO: Something that is not based on the truth. Prej-udiced. Rushing to conclusion.

Judge

KEY: The authority to something, claim to ownership. Prophetic authority. Kingdom authority.

KISS: Coming to agreement, covenant. Seductive process. Enticement. Deception or betrayal. Betrayal from a trusted friend or brother/sister in Christ.

KITCHEN: A place of preparing spiritual food. Hunger for the word of God.

KNEELING: Surrender; praying; art of submission.

KNEES: Reverence; prayerfulness; submission.

KNIVES, SWORD: Word of God. Speaking against someone.

Knife

LADDER: A means of change in spiritual position. Means of escape from captivity.

LAMB/SHEEP: Jesus. Believer. Gentleness. Blamelessness.

LAME: Shortcomings. A flaw in one's walk with God. Limitation.

LAMP: Source of light. Inward part of man or spirit. Holy Spirit.

LAND: Inheritance. Promise given by God.

Newly cleared land: Newly revealed area of God's promise.

Lamp

Ripe on the land: Fruitful work of the ministry.

Bare earth or dust: Curse, bareness.

Neglected, unwanted land: Neglected promise or inheritance.

LAUGH: Rejoicing. Joy or sarcasm.

LAUGHING: Outburst of excitement or joy.

LAVA: Enemy.

LAWYER: Jesus Christ. The accuser of brethren. Pertaining to legalism. Mediator.

LEAD (METAL): Heavy burden; heavy thing.

LEAVEN: Sin that spreads to others. False belief system.

LEAVES: Trees with healthy leaves are planted by the rivers of life; healing of the nation.

Dry leaves: Pressures of life.

Leaf

LEFT: That which is of the Spirit. That which is not natural with man. God manifested through the flesh of man.

> *Who has gone into heaven and is at God's right hand—with angels, authorities and powers in submission to Him* (1 Peter 3:22).

LEGS: Means of support. Spiritual strength to walk in life.

> *Legs, female*: Power to entice.

LEOPARD: Powerful, either good or bad. Permanent. Unchanging character.

LEMON: Something gone sour; bitter doctrine.

LEVIATHAN: Ancestral spirit of demonic nature; difficult to eliminate—only God can deal with it.

Lemon

LIBRARY: A place of knowledge. Schooling. Wisdom.

Library

LICE: Concerted attempt to smear you. Accusation, shame.

LIFTING HANDS: Total surrender. Giving worship to God.

LIGHT: Illumination on the established truth. No longer hidden; to show forth.

> *Dim light*: Showing the need for the fullness of the knowledge of the Word.
>
> *Absence of light*: Lack of understanding; absence of God.
>
> *Small lamp or flashlight*: Walking in partial founding of the Word.

LIGHTNING: God's voice; the Lord interrupting an activity to get man's attention. Something happening very quickly.

LIMOUSINE: Call of God. Pride or exhibitionism.

Lightning

LION: Conquering nature of Jesus (majority of the time). A powerful spirit, good or bad.

LIPS: Word of God. Enticement. Means of testifying. Offering. Speak falsehood/accusation.

LIVING ROOM: Part of your personality that is opened to others to see.

LOST IN WHAT IN THE NATURAL IS A FAMILIAL ENVIRONMENT (DIRECTION): Indicating inner confusions or indecision in the dreamer.

MACHINES: Power and mechanism of the Spirit.

MAGGOT: Filthiness or the lust of the flesh. Corruption.

MAN (UNKNOWN): A spiritual messenger, either God's messenger or evil. Jesus.

MANNA: God's miraculous provision. Coming directly from God. Glory of God. Bread of life.

MAP: Word of God. Instruction. Direction.

MARBLE: Beauty. Majesty of God.

MARK: Something that distinguishes. Symbol. To set apart. Mark of God or devil.

Map

MARRIAGE: Going deeper into things of God (intimacy). A covenant process. Actual marriage. Jesus Christ's union with the Church.

MEAT: Something meant for the spiritually mature. Strong doctrine.

> *I gave you milk, not solid food, for you were not yet ready for it. Indeed, you are still not ready* (1 Corinthians 3:2).

Meat

> *But strong meat belongeth to them that are of full age, even those who by reason of use have their senses exercised to discern both good and evil* (Hebrews 5:14 KJV).

MERCY SEAT: Indicating the mercy of God. Kingship of the Lord. The throne of God. God's love.

MICE: Something that eats up valuables secretly. Devourer. Spirit of timidity or fear. Evil that can multiple rapidly.

MICROPHONE: Amplification of the Word of God. Preaching. The prophetic ministry. Ability to influence many people.

Microphone

MICROSCOPE: Need to look more carefully. Obtaining clearer vision. To magnify something, whether good or bad.

Microscope

MICROWAVE OVEN: May indicate lack of patience. Looking for easy option. Quick acting process.

MIDDLE/JUNIOR HIGH: Medium level equipping by God.

MILK: Good nourishment. Elementary teaching.

MIRROR: Something that enables you to look more closely. Reflecting on something. Word of God revealing the need for change. Self-consciousness; vanity.

MISCARRIAGE: To lose something at the preparatory stage, whether good or bad. Plans aborted.

MONEY: God's favor. Spiritual and natural wealth. Spiritual authority, power. Man's strength. Greed.

Money

MOON: Indicating the rulership. To reign in the night seasons. Light of God at dark season of life.

> *God made two great lights—the greater light to govern the day and the lesser light to govern the night. He also made the stars* (Genesis 1:16).

MOON TO BLOOD: The Church being prosecuted. Something bright in darkness.

MORNING: The beginning of something. Light of God after dark season of life. Sins being revealed. Rejoicing.

MOTH: Insect that dwells in dark places. Causes loss by deceitfulness. Corruption and deterioration.

Moth

MOTHER: The Church. Jerusalem. Actual person. Spiritual mother. Carer/teacher.

MOTHER-IN-LAW: A church that is not your actual church. Actual person. False teacher.

MOTOR, ENGINE AND BATTERY: The source of power and of the anointing.

MOTORCYCLE: Spirit-powered personal ministry. Loner. Show-off pride or exhibitionism.

MOUNTAIN: Great power and strength, whether good or bad. A place of revelation or meeting with God or God's glory. Obstacle, difficulty.

MOUTH: Instrument of witnessing, good or bad. Speaking evil or good words. Something from which come the issues of life. Words coming against you.

MOVING: Change in spiritual and emotional well-being. Changing situation; a change is imminent.

MOVING VAN: A time or period of change, either in the natural or in the spirit.

MUSIC: Praise and worship, good or bad. Flowing in spiritual gift. Teaching. Admonishing. A message.

MUSTARD SEED: Faith. Value or power of faith. Sowing is faith; Word of God. God's promise.

> *He replied, "Because you have so little faith. I tell you the truth, if you have faith as small as a mustard seed, you can say to this mountain, 'Move from here to there' and it will move. Nothing will be impossible for you"* (Matthew 17:20).

NAILS: Makes something more permanent. The way Jesus dealt with our sins.

NAME: The identity of something; designate; rank or status. Meaning of the name.

NATION: Could represent the characteristics of the nation. The calling related to the nation. The actual nation.

> *America*: Cowboy.
> *France*: Romance.
> *Germany*: Hardworking. World war.
> *Jews*: Business minded.

NECK: Stubborn, strong willed.

> *Stiff-necked*: Rebellious.

NEST: Security that is not real; God's place of rest.

NET: To trap, ensnare. The plans of the enemy. To win souls.

Nest

NEW: New condition.

NEWSPAPER: Proclamation. Bringing something to the public. Prophetic utterance.

NIGHT: Time of trial or difficulty. Lack of God's lights or understanding. Without involvement of the Spirit.

NINE: Fruit of the Spirit or gift of the Spirit; harvest.

NINETEEN: Faith, repentance.

NOISE: Irritation that is intrusive. Sound that draws attention.

NORTH: Refers to great powers that will come.

NOSE: Discerning spirit. Intruding into people's privacy. Discernment, good or bad. Gossiper.

NOSEBLEED: Strife. Need to strengthen your discerning.

Nose

OCEAN: Masses of people.

OIL: The anointing. Prosperity. Holy Spirit. Grace/mercy of God. Medicine. Joy.

OLD: Old ways.

OLD MAN: Pre-Christian self. Spirit of wisdom.

ONE: New beginning. Unity (divinity). Deity.

ONE HUNDRED: Fullness. One hundred-fold reward. The promise.

Isaac planted crops in that land and the same year reaped a hundred-fold, because the Lord blessed him (Genesis 26:12).

ONE HUNDRED FIFTY: The promise and the Holy Spirit.

ONE HUNDRED TWENTY: The beginning of the work of the Holy Spirit.

In those days Peter stood up among the believers (a group numbering about a hundred and twenty) (Acts 1:15).

ORANGE: Warning, danger ahead, caution needed.

OVEN: The heart of the matter. Of high intensity. Fervency.

OVERSLEPT: There is a chance of missing a divine appointment.

Oven

PAINTING: Creating a new image. Renew or revamp.

PARACHUTING: Bail out, escape and flee.

PARK: A place of rest, worship, tranquillity. A temporary place. A place of peace. A place of romance. A place of meditation, exercise, and leisure.

Parachuting

PARROT: Something that mimics. Not the original.

PATH: The path of life. Personal walk with God. Directions in life.

PEACOCK: Something of pride. Generally adornment of royal courts.

PEARL: Something of value. Established truth of God. Glory of Heaven.

PEN/PENCIL: Pertaining to writing. Words that are written. To make permanent.

PERFUME: Aroma of something. The glory of God. Fragrance of Holy Spirit or anointing.

Perfume

PICTURE: Something relating to images. To keep in memory. To honor.

Frames: Mind-set; mentality.

Golden frames: Divine seal.

Old frame: Outdated.

PIG: Unclean spirit. Spirit of religion. Caged by mind-set. Phoney, not trustworthy. Selfish, hypocritical.

PILLAR: The main support of something. Spiritual and natural. Foundational truths.

Pillar

PINK: Flesh or natural desire. Not showing great passion for the things of God.

PIT: Enticement, trap; a hole on the pathway.

PLATTER: Something on which to present things.

PLAY: Life competition. Spiritual warfare/contention.

PLAYING: Reflective of true-life situation. The game of life.

PLOW: Preparing the heart to receive the Word of God. Cracking fallow grounds hardened by sin.

POISON: Evil and deadly teaching or doctrine.

POLICE: Spiritual authority. Having power to enforce purpose, whether good or bad. Pastor, elders. Angels or demons. Enforcer of a curse or of the law.

PORCH: Public part of the building, exhibition. Easily seen and openly displayed.

POSTAGE STAMP: The seal of authority. Authorization. Empowered.

POST-MORTEM: Examination of what has happened. Giving testimony.

POT: The vessel or container, e.g. tradition. A person.

PREGNANCY: In the process of reproducing; preparatory stage. The promise of God. The Word of God as seed. Prophetic word.

PREGNANCY, LABOR PAINS: Process of birthing something, whether good or bad. Final stages of trial or preparation; wilderness period.

PREACHER/PASTOR (PRIEST AND PROPHET): A person who represents God. Timely message from God. Spiritual authority.

PRISON: A place where a person is restricted and where human rights are limited. A place of bondage or confinement. Often indicates a place of depression; areas of stronghold bondage.

PRISONER: The lost soul.

PURPLE: Related to royalty. Kingly anointing or authority.

> *One of those listening was a woman named Lydia, a dealer in purple cloth from the city of Thyatira, who was a worshiper of God. The Lord opened her heart to respond to Paul's message* (Acts 16:14).

PURSE/WALLET: Treasure, heart, personal identity; precious and valuable.

Empty: Bankrupt.

RABBIT: Evil spirit. Something capable of carnal multiplication.

RADIO: Continuous broadcasting of news, nuisance. Prophetic utterance. Teaching gospel.

Radio

RAFT: Without purpose or direction.

RAGS: Poverty; humility or lack.

RAILROAD TRACK: Tradition; unchanging habit. Stubborn. Caution, danger.

RAIN: Blessings, God's Word. Outpouring of the Spirit. Hindrance, trial or disappointment.

> *Drought*: Lack of blessing. Absence of the presence of God.

RAINBOW: Sign of God's covenant. Sign of natural agreement.

RAINING: The blessing from God. Testing time or trial.

RAM: Satanic occult.

RAT: Rubbish (sin), left out to eat. A passion that is unclean or something that feeds it.

REAP: Harvest. Reward of effort, good or bad.

REAPING: Reward of labor.

RED: Passion. Blood of Jesus. Strong feeling, danger, anger. Heated emotion and bloody. Jesus. Zeal, enthusiasm.

REED: Weakness: spiritual or natural. Too weak to be relied on.

REFRIGERATOR: Where "issues" are kept. Heart issues. Motivation. Thoughts. Storing up spiritual food for the right time.

> *Stored food*: Things stored in the heart.
> *Spoiled food:* To harbor a grudge, unclean thoughts, or desires.

Refrigerator

REFUGE: The place of protection, safety, or security.

REINS: A means of control or to restrain.

RENDING: Sorrow or disagreement. To tear apart as sign of anger. Grief, repentance, sorrow, disagreement.

REST: A state of stillness or inactivity, tranquility. A place where you can receive from God. Laziness.

RESTAURANT: A place of choice regarding the spiritual food you need. A place where the fivefold ministry is taught.

RESTING: Not in activity; lax.

RIGHT: Natural inclination, authority, or power. What you are naturally able to do.

RIGHT TURN: Natural change.

RING: Never-ending, unchanging, uninterrupted. Unity of purpose in a place. Covenant relationship. Relating to God's authority.

Wedding ring: Symbol of our covenant with God. Marriage between man and woman.

Engagement ring: Promise. Sign of commitment.

Ring worn as jewelry: Vanity, worldliness.

RIVER: Movement of God. Flow of the Spirit. River as an obstacle. Trial.

Deep: Deep things of God.

Muddy: Operating in mixtures, flesh, and spirit.

Dangerous currents: Difficulty in moving in the flow of the Spirit. Danger ahead.

Dried up: Lack of the presence of God; traditions or legalism. Empty of spiritual power.

ROACHES: Unclean. Something that can cause and thrive on sin.

ROBE: The true covering from God. Righteousness; right standing with God.

ROCK: Jesus Christ; solid foundation. Obstacle. A place of refuge. Stumbling block.

And drank the same spiritual drink; for they drank from the spiritual rock that accompanied them, and that rock was Christ (1 Corinthians 10:4).

He is the Rock, His works are perfect, and all His ways are just. A faithful God who does no wrong, upright and just is He (Deuteronomy 32:4).

ROCKET: A ministry or person with great power or potential for deep things of the Spirit. Capable of quick take-off and great speed.

Rocket

ROCKING: Reflective.

ROCKING CHAIR: Long standing in nature, intercession, recollection, prayer, relaxation, old age.

ROD: Staff or scepter of authority. To guard. Discipline.

The rod of correction imparts wisdom, but a child left to himself disgraces his mother (Proverbs 29:15).

Even though I walk through the valley of the shadow of death, I will fear no evil, for You are with me; Your rod and Your staff, they comfort me (Psalm 23:4).

ROLLER COASTER: Something that moves up and down. Swings of season or moods. Faith needing more faith.

ROLLER SKATES: Skillful walk with God. Speedy progress. Fast but may be dangerous.

ROOF: Zone of mind, thinking, meditation. Spiritual rather than the natural. Revelations from above; covering.

ROOT: The origin of something. The source of something. The heart of the matter, good or bad. The motives.

A shoot will come up from the stump of Jesse; from his roots a Branch will bear fruit (Isaiah 11:1).

In the morning, as they went along, they saw the fig tree withered from the roots (Mark 11:20).

ROPE/CORD: Something used in binding either. In covenant or in bondage.

ROUND (SHAPE): Never-ending. Favor, love, or mercy.

ROWBOAT: A ministry that intervenes for others. Offering earnest prayers.

ROWING: Working at something, to labor in spirit. Travailing in the spirit. Hard work.

RUG: To cover up something. Protection.

RUNNING: Trying to catch up with something. Hard work. Race.

SACRIFICE: To give up something. To lay down one's life for another. Something to cover up or wash away.

But King David replied to Araunah, "No, I insist on paying the full price. I will not take for the Lord what is yours, or sacrifice a burnt offering that costs me nothing" (1 Chronicles 21:24).

SALT: Something that adds value. Something that preserves. Something that purifies. To make to last.

You are the salt of the earth. But if the salt loses its saltiness, how can it be made salty again? It is no longer good for anything, except to be thrown out and trampled by men (Matthew 5:13).

Let your conversation be always full of grace, seasoned with salt, so that you may know how to answer everyone (Colossians 4:6).

SALT WATER: To add flavor. To cleanse.

SANCTUARY: A sacred place. A place set apart for spiritual offering, sacrifices. A place of immunity or rest. An asylum, a refuge.

Observe my Sabbaths and have reverence for my sanctuary. I am the Lord (Leviticus 26:2).

On the contrary, it is to be a witness between us and you and the generations that follow, that we will worship the Lord at His sanctuary with our burnt offerings, sacrifices and fellowship offerings. Then in the future your descendants will not be able to say to ours, "You have no share in the Lord" (Joshua 22:27).

SAND: Symbolic of work of flesh. Not suitable for foundation. Numerous. Seeds. Promises.

But You have said, "I will surely make you prosper and will make your descendants like the sand of the sea, which cannot be counted" (Genesis 32:12).

But everyone who hears these words of mine and does not put them into practice is like a foolish man who built his house on sand (Matthew 7:26).

SCEPTER: Staff of authority. Office. Staff of sovereignty.

The scepter will not depart from Judah, nor the ruler's staff from between his feet, until He comes to whom it belongs and the obedience of the nations is His (Genesis 49:10).

Scepter

Your throne, O God, will last for ever and ever; a scepter of justice will be the scepter of your kingdom (Psalm 45:6).

SCHOOL, CLASSROOM: Training period, a place of teaching. A ministry with teaching anointing.

SCORPION: Highly demonic spirit or any evil spirit. Something that could be poisonous.

SEA: Great multitude of people. Nations of the world. Unsettled, as the mark of a sea. Something by which to reach the nations. Great obstacle.

Four great beasts, each different from the others, came up out of the sea (Daniel 7:3).

SEACOAST: Transition phase. Borderland.

SEAL: Confirmation or authenticity or guarantee. Mark of God's approval or belonging. Mark of evil.

SEA OF GLASS: Peaceful and clear. Symbol of revelation. Stillness/transparency.

SEAT: The power base. Rulership. Authority. Coming to rest. A place of mercy.

SEED: Word of God. Promise. Something capable of giving rise to many or greater things, whether good or bad.

SERPENT: Symbol of satan. Kingdom of the world. An accursed thing or cunning.

> *Snake (if hung on a pole, stick, tree)*: Emblem of Christ on the cross.
>
> *Viper*: Gossip or persecution.
>
> *Python*: Spirit of divination.
>
> *Rattles*: Evil words against the dreamer.
>
> *Fangs*: Dangerous intentions coming against the dreamer.
>
> *Cobra*: Venous, capable of forming hooded neck, and can send off poison from a distance. Evil words that can spread far.
>
> *Anaconda*: Kills by squeezing out air (spiritual life) from the victim.

SEVEN: The number of perfection, completion, or finished work. Rest. A time of blessing or holy time. Freedom.

> *Remember the Sabbath day by keeping it holy. Six days you shall labor and do all your work, but the seventh day is a Sabbath to the Lord your God. On it you shall not do any work, neither you, nor your son or daughter, nor your manservant or maidservant, nor your animals, nor the alien within your gates. For in six days the Lord made the heavens and the earth, the sea, and all that is in them, but He rested on the seventh day. Therefore the Lord blessed the Sabbath day and made it holy (Exodus 20:8-11).*
>
> *These are the laws you are to set before them: If you buy a Hebrew servant, he is to serve you for six years. But in the seventh year, he shall go free, without paying anything (Exodus 21:1-2).*

SEVENTEEN: Spiritual process of maturation. Not yet matured.

This is the account of Jacob. Joseph, a young man of seventeen, was tending the flocks with his brothers, the sons of Bilhah and the sons of Zilpah, his father's wives, and he brought their father a bad report about them (Genesis 37:2).

SEVENTY: Impartation of God's Spirit/increase/restoration.

The Lord said to Moses: "Bring me seventy of Israel's elders who are known to you as leaders and officials among the people. Have them come to the Tent of Meeting, that they may stand there with you. I will come down and speak with you there, and I will take of the Spirit that is on you and put the Spirit on them. They will help you carry the burden of the people so that you will not have to carry it alone (Numbers 11:16-17).

SEVENTY-FIVE: Period for purification and separation. Abraham was 75 when he set out from Haran.

So Abram left, as the Lord had told him; and Lot went with him. Abram was seventy-five years old when he set out from Haran (Genesis 12:4).

SEWAGE: Something that carries away waste. Good appearance but carrying waste within. Waste that could defile flesh.

SEWING: Putting together something. Amendment; union; counselling.

SEXUAL ENCOUNTER: Soulish desires.

Sexual encounter with old lover: You desire your old life.

SHADOW: Reflection of something. The spiritual cover. A place of safety, security. Only partially illuminated. Poor resemblance of. Delusion or imitation. Imperfect or lacking the real substance.

He who dwells in the shelter of the Most High will rest in the shadow of the Almighty (Psalm 91:1).
Dark shadows: Demons.

SHEPHERD: Jesus Christ, God. Leader, good or bad. Ability to separate goat from sheep. Selfless person.

Then he blessed Joseph and said, "May the God before whom my fathers Abraham and Isaac walked, the God who has been my shepherd all my life to this day" (Genesis 48:15).
I am the good shepherd. The good shepherd lays down his life for the sheep (John 10:11).

Wherever I have moved with all the Israelites, did I ever say to any of their rulers whom I commanded to shepherd My people Israel, "Why have you not built Me a house of cedar?" (2 Samuel 7:7)

SHIELD: A protective thing. God's truth. Faith in God.

Shield

After this, the word of the Lord came to Abram in a vision: "Do not be afraid, Abram. I am your shield, your very great reward" (Genesis 15:1).

In addition to all this, take up the shield of faith, with which you can extinguish all the flaming arrows of the evil one (Ephesians 6:16).

The Lord is my strength and my shield; my heart trusts in Him, and I am helped. My heart leaps for joy and I will give thanks to Him in song (Psalm 28:7).

SHIP: A big ministry capable of influencing large numbers of people.

Battleship: Built for effective spiritual warfare.

Crashing: End of the ministry or end of one phase.

Fast: Operating in great power.

Large: Large area of influence.

Sinking: Out of line with the purpose of God, losing spiritual control.

Small: Small or personal.

On dry ground: Without the move of the Spirit. Moving more with the work of the flesh. (A miracle, if moving on dry ground.)

SHOES: Readiness to spread the gospel. Knowledge of the Word of God.

Shoes

And with your feet fitted with the readiness that comes from the gospel of peace (Ephesians 6:15).

Boots: Equipped for spiritual warfare.

Does not fit: Walking in something you're not called to.

Giving away: Depending on the context, equipping others.

High heels: Seduction/discomfort.

Need of shoes: Not dwelling on the Word of God. In need of comfort or protection.

New shoes: Getting new understanding of the gospel. Fresh mandate from God.

Putting on: Preparation for a spiritual journey.

Slippers: Too comfortable or too lax.

Snowshoes: Faith, walking in the Spirit, supported by faith in the Word of God.

Taking off: Honoring God, ministering to the Lord.

Taking someone else's shoes off: To show respect.

Tennis shoes: Spiritual giftedness. Running the race of life.

SHOPPING CENTER, MARKETPLACE: Ministry that has multifaceted giftedness within its midst. Coming to a place of choices that may lead to not being single-minded. Could also indicate the various methods of the enemy strategies.

SHOULDER: The responsibility; the authority.

Broad shoulders: Capable of handling much responsibility.

Bare female shoulders: Enticement.

Drooped shoulders: Defeated attitude. Overworked; over tired. Burned-out.

SHOVEL: Digging up something. To smear someone.

Shovel

SICKLE: Reaping. Word of God. The harvest.

SIEVE: To separate the impure from the pure. Trial or testing.

Sickle

For I will give the command, and I will shake the house of Israel among all the nations as grain is shaken in a sieve, and not a pebble will reach the ground (Amos 9:9).

SIFT: Separation by testing.

Simon, Simon, Satan has asked to sift you as wheat (Luke 22:31).

SIGN: A witness of something. A foreshadow. To draw attention to something.

Crossroad/intersection: A place for decision. Time for change.

Stop sign: Stop and pray for guidance.

Yield: A sign of submission.

SIGNATURE: Commitment and ownership or take responsibility for.

SILVER: Symbol of redemption. Understanding, knowledge. Something of valor, worldly knowledge, betrayal. Furnace of affliction.

SINGING: The words of the song = message from God. Rejoicing. Heart overflow.

SISTER: Sister in Jesus Christ. Actual person. Similar qualities in you.

SISTER-IN-LAW: Same as sister. A Christian in another fellowship. A relationship without much depth. Actual person. Person with similar qualities.

SITTING: A place of authority, position in power. Throne of God or seat of satan.

SIX: The number of man. Symbol of satan. Pride in the work of man.

SIX-SIX-SIX: Number of satan. Mark of the beast. Number of human hubris.

> *This calls for wisdom. If anyone has insight, let him calculate the number of the beast, for it is man's number. His number is 666* (Revelation 13:18).

SIXTEEN: Set free by love. The power of love or salvation. Sixteen characteristics of love mentioned in First Corinthians 13.

SKIING: Stepping out in faith. The power of faith. Smooth riding in God is provision. Making rapid process.

SKINS: The covering of.

SKY: Above the natural. God's presence. Related to God or high things of the Spirit.

SKYSCRAPER: A ministry or person who has a built-up structure to function on multilevels. A church or person with prophetic giftedness. High level of spiritual experience. Revelation.

Skyscraper

SLEEPING: Being overtaken. Not being conscious of something. Hidden. Laziness. State of rest; danger. Out of control.

Overslept: In danger of missing a divine appointment.

SMILE: Sign of friendliness. Act of kindness. To agree with.

SMILING: Sign of friendship. Seductive process.

SMOKE: The manifested glory of God. Prayers of saints. Praise; worship. Sign of something. Hindrance.

SNAKE: Backbiting; divination; false accusations; false prophecies. Gossip; long tales; slander.

Snake

SNARE: A trap. The fear of man. Bring into bondage.

SNOW: Favor of God. Totally pure.

> *He spreads the snow like wool and scatters the frost like ashes* (Psalm 147:16).
>
> *As the rain and the snow come down from heaven, and do not return to it without watering the earth and making it bud and flourish, so that it yields seed for the sower and bread for the eater* (Isaiah 55:10).
>
> *As I looked, thrones were set in place, and the Ancient of Days took His seat. His clothing was as white as snow; the hair of His head was white like wool. His throne was flaming with fire, and its wheels were all ablaze* (Daniel 7:9).

Dirty snow: No longer pure.

SOAP: Something that cleans. Forgiveness. Interceding for others.

SOCKS: Reflective of the state of the heart as the fertile ground for the Word of God. Peace. Protection of the feet.

White socks: Heart and walk before God that is unblemished.

Dirty or torn socks: Heart and walk before God that is blemished.

SOLDIER: Spiritual warfare. Call for more prayers, fasting, worship. A period of trial or persecution.

SON: A ministry or gifting from God. Actual child who has similar traits to you. Child of God.

SOUR: Corrupted. False.

SOUTH: A place of peace. Source of refreshment. The natural inclination.

SOWING: Planning for the future, good or bad. Spreading the Word of God.

SPEAKING: Revealing the contents of your heart. Proclamation.

SPEAR: Words, whether good or bad. Word of God. Evil words, curses.

SPIDER: An evil spirit that works by entrapping people. False doctrine.

Spider

SPOT: A fault. Contamination.

Without spot: Glorious Church.

SPRINKLING: Spiritual change by washing away dirt. Cleansing, purifying, consecrating.

SQUARE: Tradition. Mind-set. Worldly and blind to the truth.

STADIUM: Tremendous impact.

STAFF: Symbol of authority. Part of authority.

STAIRS: Means of bringing about changes.

Down: Demotion; backslide; failure.

Guardrail: Safety; precaution; warning to be careful.

Staff

STANDING: Firmness in faith. Committed to the belief. Not finished.

Straight: No crookedness but in the correct direction.

STARS: Important personality. Great number. Descendant. Supernatural. Jesus Christ.

Falling star: Apostate Church.

STONE: Jesus Christ—chief cornerstone. Hard and sturdy foundation. Word of God. Defiance.

STONING SOMEONE: Involved in malicious accusation of others. Unforgiveness. Act of wickedness.

Dragged him out of the city and began to stone him. Meanwhile, the witnesses laid their clothes at the feet of a young man named Saul (Acts 7:58).

STORM: Trial. Testing period. Satanic attacks.

Before very long, a wind of hurricane force, called the "northeaster," swept down from the island. The ship was caught by the storm and could not head into the wind; so we gave way to it and were driven along (Acts 27:14-15).

White storm: God's power, revival.

STRAIGHT: To be fixed in attitude. Going in the right direction.

STUMBLING: To make mistakes, to fail, in error. Lack of the truth.

SUICIDE: Act of self-destruction, foolishness. Sinful behavior. Pride. Lack of hope.

SUITCASE: On the move. Transition. Private walk with God.

SUMMER: Time of harvest. The opportune time. Fruits of the Spirit.

SUN: The light of God. The truth. Glory of God.

Suitcase

SUPPER: The body and blood of Jesus. Marriage supper. God's provision. God's enabling power.

SWEATING: Signs of intense work of the flesh. Much work without Holy Spirit. Difficult and agonizing time.

SWEEPING: Getting rid of sinful things. Cleaning the place from evil. The process of making clean. Repentance. Correcting process.

SWEET: Something gratifying. Reflection in the Word of God. Communion with the Spirit.

SWIMMING: Moving in spiritual gifts. Prophetic utterance.

SWIMMING POOL: Church, place or provision available for moving in the Spirit.

Dirty or dry: Corrupt or apostate.

SWING: Moving in ups and downs of life.

SWINGING: Full flow of peace.

High: Overindulgence. Taking unnecessary risks.

SWORD: Word of God. Evil words.

TABLE: A place of agreement or covenant. To iron issues out. Altar. Community, fellowship.

Sword

You prepare a table before me in the presence of my enemies. You anoint my head with oil; my cup overflows (Psalm 23:5).

TAIL: The end of something. The least of something. The last time.

TAR: Covering; bitterness.

TARES: Children of darkness. Evil ones. Degenerates. Deceptive, e.g. grains.

TASTING: To experience something good or bad. Judging something. Try something out.

TEA: A place or time of rest. Revelation or grace of God. Soothing.

TEACHER: Jesus Christ. Holy Spirit. Gift of God.

Tea

TEARS: Emotional sowing; mostly distress but could represent brokenness. Joy.

TEETH: Wisdom, gaining understanding; to work something out.

Baby teeth: Childish. Without wisdom or knowledge.

Broken teeth: Inexperienced. Difficulty in coming to understanding.

Brushing teeth: Gaining wisdom or understanding.

False teeth: Full of reasoning of this world instead of pure spiritual understanding.

Toothache: Tribulation coming; heartache.

TELEPHONE: Spiritual communication, good or evil. Godly counsel.

TELESCOPE: Looking or planning for the future. To make a problem appear bigger and closer.

Telephone

TELEVISION: Visionary revelations or prophetic dreams. Prophetic utterance.

TEMPLE: A place of meeting with God. A place of refuge. God's habitation. Human body.

TEN: Law, government order and obligation. Testing trial.

TENT: Temporary covering. Flexible.

TEN THOUSAND: Army of the Lord. Battle readiness.

Tent

And he said: "The Lord came from Sinai, and dawned on them from Seir; He shone forth from Mount Paran, and He came with ten thousands of saints; from His right hand came a fiery law for them"(Deuteronomy 33:2 NKJV).

Now Enoch, the seventh from Adam, prophesied about these men also, saying, "Behold, the Lord comes with ten thousands of His saints"(Jude 1:14 NKJV).

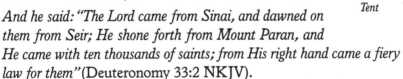

TERMITES: Something that can cause hidden destruction.

THIEF: Satan. Deceiver. Secret intruder. Unexpected loss.

THIGH: Strength; flesh. To entice. Oath taken.

THIRTEEN: Rebellion; backsliding.

THIRTY: Beginning of ministry. Mature for God's work. Jesus was thirty when He began His ministry; Joseph was thirty when he became prime minister.

THORNS: Evil disturbance. Curse. Gossip.

THOUSANDS: Maturity approved.

THREE/THIRD: Witness; divine fullness; Godhead. Triumph over sin. Resurrection. Conform.

THREE HUNDRED: Chosen by God. Reserve of the Lord.

The Lord said to Gideon, "With the three hundred men that lapped I will save you and give the Midianites into your hands. Let all the other men go, each to his own place." So Gideon sent the rest of the Israelites to their tents but kept the three hundred, who took over the provisions and trumpets of the others. Now the camp of Midian lay below him in the valley (Judges 7:7-8).

THRONE: A seat of power. A place of authority. God's throne. Evil throne.

At once I was in the Spirit, and there before me was a throne in heaven with someone sitting on it. And the one who sat there had the appearance of jasper and carnelian. A rainbow, resembling an emerald, encircled the throne" (Revelation 4:2-3).

THUMB: Apostolic; authority; soul power.

THUNDER: Loud signal from God. God speaking, touching. Warning or blessing.

TIN: Something of low valor. Not original, an imitation.

TITANIC: Big plan that is not going to work out.

TITLE/DEED: Ownership seal. Potential to possess something.

TONGUE: Powerful. National language. Something that cannot be tamed.

TORNADO: Distressing situation. Great trouble. Spiritual warfare.

TOWER: High spiritual thing. Supernatural experience. Great strength. Pride, i.e. the tower of Babel.

TRACTOR: Groundbreaking ministry. Prepare the mind to receive.

TRAILER: An equipping ministry. A caring service. A ministry that is migrating.

TRAIN: A large ministry that influences a lot of people. Move or send people out. Movement of God.

TREE: Leader, good or bad. Person or organization. Nations or kingdom.

Christmas: Celebrations.

Evergreen: Long-lasting, everlasting.

Oak: Great strength. Durable.

Olive: Anointed of God. Israel. Church. Anointing oil.

Palm: A leader that is fruit producing.

Tree stump: Tenacity or stubbornness. Retaining hope despite circumstances. Keeping the root in place.

Willow: Indicating sadness; defeat.

And provide for those who grieve in Zion—to bestow on them a crown of beauty instead of ashes, the oil of gladness instead of mourning, and a garment of praise instead of a spirit of despair. They will be called oaks of righteousness, a planting of the Lord for the display of His splendor (Isaiah 61:3).

These are the visions I saw while lying in my bed: I looked, and there before me stood a tree in the middle of the land. Its height was enormous (Daniel 4:10).

A shoot will come up from the stump of Jesse; from his roots a Branch will bear fruit (Isaiah 11:1).

But let the stump and its roots, bound with iron and bronze, remain in the ground, in the grass of the field. Let him be drenched with the dew of heaven, and let him live with the animals among the plants of the earth (Daniel 4:15).

TROPHY: Victory.

TRUCK: A personal ministry that brings provision.

TRUMPET: Voice of the prophet. The second coming of Christ. Proclaiming the good news. Blessing; promise.

To gather the assembly, blow the trumpets, but not with the same signal (Numbers 10:7).

For the Lord Himself will come down from heaven, with a loud command, with the voice of the archangel and with the trumpet call of God, and the dead in Christ will rise first (1 Thessalonians 4:16).

TUNNEL: A passage. A time or place of transition. Troubled or dark seasons of life.

He tunnels through the rock; his eyes see all its treasures (Job 28:10).

TWELVE: Government of God. Divine order. Discipleship. Government by election, theocracy.

TWENTY: Holiness and redemption.

TWENTY-FOUR: Completed order of God. Maturity; perfect government. Elders in the throne room.

Surrounding the throne were twenty-four other thrones, and seated on them were twenty four elders. They were dressed in white and had crowns of gold on their heads (Revelation 4:4).

TWO: Witnessing; confirmation. Division. Whole in marriage.

TWO HUNDRED: Fullness confirmed. Promise guaranteed.

TWO STORY: Multilevel giftedness. Symbolic of flesh and spirit. Multitalented church.

UPSTAIRS: Pertaining to the Spirit. Pentecost. Zone of thought; great balance. Spiritual realm.

UPWARD MOTION: Moving onto higher spiritual things.

URINATING: Releasing pressure. Compelling urge or temptation. Repentance.

VAN, MOVING: A time or period of change, either in the natural or in the spirit. To walk.

VAPOR: Something temporary. Presence of God. Evidence of something.

VEIL: To conceal. To conceal glory or sin. To deceive. Blind to the truth. Lack of understanding.

Even to this day when Moses is read, a veil covers their hearts. But whenever anyone turns to the Lord, the veil is taken away (2 Corinthians 3:15-16).

And even if our gospel is veiled, it is veiled to those who are perishing (2 Corinthians 4:3).

VESSEL: People as instrument of use, for good or bad purposes. The Christian believers.

VINE: Jesus Christ. Christian believers.

I had planted you like a choice vine of sound and reliable stock. How then did you turn against Me into a corrupt, wild vine? (Jeremiah 2:21)

I am the true vine, and My Father is the gardener (John 15:1).

VINEYARD: A place of planting; harvest. Heavenly Kingdom.

The vineyard of the Lord Almighty is the house of Israel, and the men of Judah are the garden of His delight. And He looked for justice, but saw bloodshed; for righteousness, but heard cries of distress (Isaiah 5:7).

VOICE: Message from God or devil. The Word of God. Godly instruction.

VOLCANO: Something sudden and explosive. Out of control and unstable; unpredictable. Judgment.

WALKING: Walking the path of life; life in the Spirit. Progress, living in the Spirit.

Difficulty: Trials or opposition; evil opposition to destiny.

Unable: Hindrance to doing what you are called to do.

WALL: Obstacle, barrier, defense, limitation. Great hindrance. Blocking the view of presenting spiritual signs.

WAR: Spiritual warfare.

WASHING: To clean.

WASHBASIN: Means of cleansing. Prayers and intercession.

WASHCLOTH: Something that enhances the cleansing process.

WATCH: Need to be watchful. Time for something. Watch what's about to happen.

WATERMELON: Spirit-ruled soul. Fruitfulness.

WATERS: Move of the Spirit; Holy Spirit. Nations of the world.

Stagnant: Instability.

Muddy or polluted: Corrupted spiritual moves, sin, false doctrine.

Troubled water: Healing pool. Troubled mind.

Water fountain: God's Spirit welling up in man. Salvation. Revival coming. Time of refreshing.

WEEDS: Sinful nature or acts.

WEIGHT: Great responsibility, load, or burden.

WHEEL: Pertaining to life cycle. Long-lasting. Continuously.

WHIRLWIND: Powerful move in the spirit, good or bad.

WHITE: Something that is pure, righteousness. God's glory, light of God. Innocence, blamelessness.

WIFE: Actual person. Someone joined to you in covenant. Spirit of submission. The Church. Israel. The work of Christ in the dreamer.

WILDERNESS: Hard times. Place of trial/testing. Distant from God. Place of training. Place of provision.

WIND, BLOWING: Movement of the spirit, usually good, but may be evil. Disappears quickly. Unstable. Difficult to understand.

WINDOW: Prophetic gifting. Revelation knowledge. Gaining insight.

WINE: Holy Spirit. Counterfeit spirit. Communion. Teaching; blessing.

Then I will send rain on your land in its season, both autumn and spring rains, so that you may gather in your grain, new wine and oil (Deuteronomy 11:14).

No, new wine must be poured into new wineskins (Luke 5:38).

Likewise, teach the older women to be reverent in the way they live, not to be slanderers or addicted to much wine, but to teach what is good (Titus 2:3).

WINEPRESS: True doctrine.

WINESKINS: The Body. The Church.

WINGS: Prophetic. Under the protection of God.

You yourselves have seen what I did to Egypt, and how I carried you on eagles' wings and brought you to Myself (Exodus 19:4).

Have mercy on me, O God, have mercy on me, for in You my soul takes refuge. I will take refuge in the shadow of Your wings until the disaster has passed (Psalm 57:1).

Each of the four living creatures had six wings and was covered with eyes all around, even under his wings. Day and night they never stop saying: "Holy, holy, holy is the Lord God Almighty, who was, and is, and is to come" (Revelation 4:8).

O Jerusalem, Jerusalem, you who kill the prophets and stone those sent to you, how often I have longed to gather your children together, as a hen gathers her chicks under her wings, but you were not willing! (Luke 13:34)

WINTER: Season of unfruitfulness. Latent period.

Pray that your flight will not take place in winter or on the Sabbath (Matthew 24:20).

Do your best to get here before winter. Eubulus greets you, and so do Pudens, Linus, Claudia and all the brothers (2 Timothy 4:21).

WITCH: Spirit of rebellion. Non-submission. Manipulative person. Spirit of control.

For rebellion is as the sin of witchcraft (1 Samuel 15:23a NKJV).

WOLF: A tendency to destroy God's work. False minister. Opportunistic person.

WOMAN (UNKNOWN): A messenger from God or satan. An angel or demonic spirit. Seducing spirit.

WOOD: Life. Dependence on flesh. Humanity. Carnal reasoning. Lust.

WORK AREA: The place or time of your service.

WORM: Something that eats from the inside, often secretly. Not obvious on the surface. Disease; filthiness.

WRESTLING: Struggling with something in the spirit or real life. To battle. Perseverance. To contend with, struggle.

YARD: The opened part of your personality. Behind or past.

YEAR: Time of blessing or judgment.

YELLOW: Hope; fear; mind.

YOKE: Bondage. Tied to something; usually evil but sometimes good. Enslaved.

ZION: A place of strength. A place of protection. God's Kingdom.

Here am I, and the children the Lord has given me. We are signs and symbols in Israel from the Lord Almighty, who dwells on Mount Zion (Isaiah 8:18).

Their bloodguilt, which I have not pardoned, I will pardon. The Lord dwells in Zion! (Joel 3:21).

But on Mount Zion will be deliverance; it will be holy, and the house of Jacob will possess its inheritance (Obadiah 1:17).

PART VI

OTHER

Symbolic

OVERTONES

ACTIONS AND FEELINGS

FEELINGS OR EMOTIONS: Feelings in dreams are expressions of what the truest situation is in the life of the dreamer. They come without the moderating effect of social norms, mind-sets, prejudices, or pretences. Sometimes, the feeling expressed by the dreamer may be incongruous to what the dreamer thinks he or she is. If this happens, it is often because there are suppressed desires or hidden hurts, wounds, or scars in the life of the dreamer that could resurrect. By and large, most feelings in dreams are usually the reflection of the degree or intensity with which an actual event will eventually happen. However, in my experience, in over 80 percent of cases, the following feelings are symbolized as indicated below.

Anger: Anger.

Bitterness: Bitterness.

Hatred: Hatred.

Joy: Happiness.

Love: Love.

Sadness: Lack of joy.

Tears: Deep emotional move, could either be for a pleasant or unpleasant reason.

FLYING: The dreamer has the potential to soar high in the things of the Spirit. Divine miraculous intervention, especially the provision of escape from danger or acceleration toward destiny.

HUNGRY: Inspiration to desire spiritual food. Lack of adequate spiritual nourishment.

INABILITY TO MOVE: This may indicate hindrances to the divine purposes in the life of the dreamer. Call for intensification of spiritual warfare.

INDIFFERENT: Not considerate. Resistant. Perseverance. Carefree.

RUNNING: (Consider the context of the dream.) Accelerated pace of events is approaching—either toward or away from something.

SLEEP: To be overtaken by something beyond your control.

THINKING: A time of study, reflection, meditation, and intellectual exercise.

WALKING: The normal routine or run of life events; the expected pace of progression.

On gravel, on stones: Hard times.

On sand: May indicate not having sound foundation on the aspect of life the dream addresses.

On swampy, moldy path: May indicate sticky situation, hard times, or hindrances.

On clear waters: Moving in the Spirit and grace of God.

On dirty waters: Dabbling in wrong doctrines.

On a straight path with near infinite view: Many places to go in life.

WORRYING: Uncertain times, insecurity. Consider the context of its occurrence.

SCHOOLS/SCHOOLING

*Note the level of school education in the dream.

SCHOOL BUILDING: May indicate a place of learning, church, or professional institute.

PRIMARY SCHOOL: Indicates the fundamental things of life.

SECONDARY SCHOOL: Indicates the equipping period of life.

TERTIARY SCHOOL: Indicates the definite place of specialized call on the dreamer's life.

HIGH SCHOOL: Moving into a higher level of walking with God. Capable of giving same to others.

DELAY/HINDRANCES OR DISTURBANCES DURING EXAMINATIONS: May be indications of negative influences that are at play in deciding the desired placement. It could represent personal weaknesses that are standing in the way of the dreamer.

END OF SCHOOL SEASON: Indicates the completion of the equipping season.

EXAMINATION: At the verge of a promotion.

FAILING EXAMINATIONS: May mean one is not meeting the requirement for the desired placement.

INABILITY TO GET TO THE SCHOOL PREMISES: Indicates you are not in the right place for the required equipping. Extraneous hindrances to the dreamer's drive to achieve required equipping.

INABILITY TO LOCATE A CLASSROOM: May indicate inner uncertainty about definite vocation or call of God in the dreamer.

LATENESS: May indicate inadequate preparation for a time of equipping.

OLD SCHOOL TIME OR PLACE: May indicate similar time or season of experience and importance is at hand or imminent.

NOT FINISHING A TEST: Could mean inadequate preparation.

PASSING EXAMINATIONS: Confirms divine approval for the promotion.

PREPARING FOR EXAMINATION: A season preceding a promotion.

RECEIVING OR GIVING A LECTURE: The theme of the lecture is the message for the dreamer, or for the people or occasion.

RUNNING OUT OF PAPER, INK, OR PEN: Could indicate inadequate knowledge for the desired placement.

Parts of the Human Body

BEARD: To have respect for authority.

So Hanun seized David's men, shaved off half of each man's beard, cut off their garments in the middle at the buttocks, and sent them away. When David was told about this, he sent messengers to meet the men, for they were greatly humiliated. The king said, "Stay at Jericho till your beards have grown, and then come back" (2 Samuel 10:4-5).

Messy: Insanity.

Trimmed: Respectable or sane.

BELLY: Feelings, desires. Spiritual well-being. Sentiment. Humiliation.

They conceive trouble and give birth to evil; their womb [belly] *fashions deceit* (Job 15:35).

Whoever believes in Me, as the Scripture has said, streams of living water will flow from within [from his belly] *him* (John 7:38).

For such people are not serving our Lord Christ, but their own [belly] *appetites. By smooth talk and flattery they deceive the minds of naive people* (Romans 16:18).

BONES: The substance of something. The main issue. Long lasting.

Moses took the bones of Joseph with him because Joseph had made the sons of Israel swear an oath. He had said, "God will surely come to your aid, and then you must carry my bones up with you from this place" (Exodus 13:19).

Once while some Israelites were burying a man, suddenly they saw a band of raiders; so they threw the man's body into Elisha's tomb. When the body touched Elisha's bones, the man came to life and stood up on his feet (2 Kings 13:21).

BONES, SKELETON: Something without substance or flesh. Something without details.

EYES: The means of seeing. To want something. The seer's anointing.

Closed eyes: Spiritual blindness. Ignorance, mostly self-imposed.

Winking: Concealed intention or cunning person.

FACE: Who the person is. The identity of the person. The reflection of the heart of the person. Identity or characteristics. Image expression.

FEET: Symbol of the heart or thought pattern. The part of the body that comes in contact with the earth. The lower members of the Church. Not to be ignored. Have tendency to be ignored.

And with your feet fitted with the readiness that comes from the gospel of peace (Ephesians 6:15).

"Do not come any closer," God said. "Take off your sandals, for the place where you are standing is holy ground" (Exodus 3:5).

If the foot should say, "Because I am not a hand, I do not belong to the body," it would not for that reason cease to be part of the body (1 Corinthians 12:15).

Bare foot: Humble before the presence of God. Lack of studying the Word of God. Lack of preparation.

Diseased: Spirit of offense.

Lame feet: Crippled with unbelief, mind-set. Negative stronghold.

Kicking: Not under authority or working against authority.

Overgrown nails: Lack of care or not in proper order.

Washing: Humility or Christian duty.

FINGERS: Image of activity, whether human or divine. Image of sensitivity. Denoting power or authority. Assigning blame. Unit of measure. For battle.

Then Pharaoh took his signet ring from his finger and put it on Joseph's finger. He dressed him in robes of fine linen and put a gold chain around his neck (Genesis 41:42).

The magicians said to Pharaoh, "This is the finger of God." But Pharaoh's heart was hard and he would not listen, just as the Lord had said (Exodus 8:19).

Then you will call, and the Lord will answer; you will cry for help, and He will say: Here am I. If you do away with the yoke of oppression, with the pointing finger and malicious talk (Isaiah 58:9).

For your hands are stained with blood, your fingers with guilt. Your lips have spoken lies, and your tongue mutters wicked things (Isaiah 59:3).

Each of the pillars was eighteen cubits high and twelve cubits in circumference; each was four fingers thick, and hollow (Jeremiah 52:21).

The young men who had grown up with him replied, "Tell these people who have said to you, 'Your father put a heavy yoke on us, but make our yoke lighter'—tell them, 'My little finger is thicker than my father's waist'" (1 Kings 12:10).

Praise be to the Lord my Rock, who trains my hands for war, my fingers for battle (Psalm 144:1).

Clenched: Pride or boastfulness.

Finger of God: Work of God or authority of God.

Fourth: Teacher.

Index: Prophet.

Little: Pastor.

Middle: Evangelist.

Pointed finger: Accusations or persecutions. Instruction or direction.

Thumb: Apostle.

FOREHEAD: That which is prominent and determines the identity of something or someone.

Therefore the showers have been withheld, and there has been no latter rain. You have had a harlot's forehead; you refuse to be ashamed (Jeremiah 3:3 NKJV).

They will see His face, and His name will be on their foreheads (Revelation 22:4).

HAIR: Cover, or something numerous, or man's glory. Protection, beauty, and identification. Mark of beauty or pride. Uncut hair is symbol of covenant. Long hair is a shame for men but glory for women. Sign of good age or dignity.

Whenever he cut the hair of his head—he used to cut his hair from time to time when it became too heavy for him—he would weigh it, and its weight was two hundred shekels by the royal standard (2 Samuel 14:26).

Because you will conceive and give birth to a son. No razor may be used on his head, because the boy is to be a Nazirite, set apart to God from birth, and he will begin the deliverance of Israel from the hands of the Philistines (Judges 13:5).

Does not the very nature of things teach you that if a man has long hair, it is a disgrace to him, but that if a woman has long hair, it is her glory? For long hair is given to her as a covering. If anyone wants to be contentious about this, we have no other practice—nor do the churches of God (1 Corinthians 11:14-16).

As I looked, thrones were set in place, and the Ancient of Days took His seat. His clothing was as white as snow; the Hair of his head was white like wool. His throne was flaming with fire, and its wheels were all ablaze (Daniel 7:9).

Grey hair is a crown of splendor; it is attained by a righteous life (Proverbs 16:31).

Baldness: Grief and shame.

Haircut: Getting something in correct shape or cutting off evil or bad habit or tradition.

Long and well maintained: Covenant and strength.

Long on a man: Probably rebellious behavior or covenant relationship.

Long on a woman: Glory of womanhood. Wife or submissive church.

Long and unkempt: Out of control.

Losing hair: Loss of wisdom or glory.

Out of shape: Not in order.

Shaving: Getting rid of things that hinder or things that are dirty.

Short on a woman: Probably lack of submission or manliness.

HANDS: Power. Personal service, taking action on behalf of someone. A person in action. Means of service. Means of expressing strength.

The fear and dread of you will fall upon all the beasts of the earth and all the birds of the air, upon every creature that moves along the ground, and upon all the fish of the sea; they are given into your hands (Genesis 9:2).

So they called together all the rulers of the Philistines and said, "Send the ark of the god of Israel away; let it go back to its own place, or it will kill us and our people."' For death had filled the city with panic; God's hand was very heavy upon it (1 Samuel 5:11).

My Father, who has given them to Me, is greater than all; no one can snatch them out of My Father's hand (John 10:29).

Stretch out your hand to heal and perform miraculous signs and wonders through the name of your holy servant Jesus (Acts 4:30).

The Lord rewards every man for his righteousness and faithfulness. The Lord delivered you into my hands today, but I would not lay a hand on the Lord's anointed (1 Samuel 26:23).

The Lord says to my Lord: "Sit at my right hand until I make your enemies a footstool for your feet" (Psalm 110:1).

But Israel reached out his right hand and put it on Ephraim's head, though he was the younger, and crossing his arms, he put his left hand on Manasseh's head, even though Manasseh was the firstborn (Genesis 48:14).

Do not neglect your gift, which was given you through a prophetic message when the body of elders laid their hands on you (1 Timothy 4:14).

For this reason I remind you to fan into flame the gift of God, which is in you through the laying on of my hands (2 Timothy 1:6).

Clapping: Joy and worship.

Fist: Pride in one's strength.

Covering face: Anger. Guilt or shame.

Holding: In agreement.

Left hand: Something spiritual.

Place on the right hand: Position of honor.

Put hand on the head: Blessings. Ordination.

Raised: Surrender or worshiping.

Right hand: Oath of allegiance; means of power of honor, natural strengths.

Shaking hands: Coming to an agreement. Surrender.

Stretched out hands: In security or anger.

Striking: Demonstrating strength or anger.

Trembling: To fear; spirit of fear; anxiety/awe at God's presence.

Under thighs: In oaths.

Washing: Declaring innocence or to dissociate oneself.

HEAD: Leader. To take responsibility. Be proud of something. God-ordained authority—husband. Christ. Christ as head of all people. God as the Father and head of Christ.

And Moses chose able men out of all Israel, and made them heads over the people: rulers of thousands, rulers of hundreds, rulers of fifties, and rulers of tens (Exodus 18:25 NKJ).

If anyone goes outside your house into the street, his blood will be on his own head; we will not be responsible. As for anyone who is in the house with you, his blood will be on our head if a hand is laid on him (Joshua 2:19).

Now I want you to realize that the head of every man is Christ, and the head of the woman is man, and the head of Christ is God (1 Corinthians 11:3).

For the husband is the head of the wife as Christ is the head of the church, His body, of which He is the Savior (Ephesians 5:23).

Instead, speaking the truth in love, we will in all things grow up into Him who is the Head, that is, Christ (Ephesians 4:15).

And He is the head of the body, the church; He is the beginning and the firstborn from among the dead, so that in everything He might have the supremacy (Colossians 1:18).

He has lost connection with the Head, from whom the whole body, supported and held together by its ligaments and sinews, grows as God causes it to grow (Colossians 2:19).

And you have been given fullness in Christ, who is the head over every power and authority (Colossians 2:10).

Anointed: Set apart for God's service.

Covered with the hand: Signifying sorrow.

HEART: Most mentioning of the heart in Scripture is almost never in literal terms. The seat of affection. The seat of intellect. Innermost being.

Do not trust in extortion or take pride in stolen goods; though your riches increase, do not set your heart on them (Psalm 62:10).

The Lord saw how great man's wickedness on the earth had become, and that every inclination of the thoughts of his heart was only evil all the time (Genesis: 6:5).

Blessed are they who keep His statutes and seek Him with all their heart (Psalm 119:2).

The Lord was grieved that He had made man on the earth, and His heart was filled with pain (Genesis 6:6).

HEEL: The crushing power.

HIPS: Reproduction. Relating to reproduction or supporting structure.

KNEES: Sign of expression of relationship. Submission, blessing, or fear. Submission to Christ. Blessing. A measure of faith.

Then, at the evening sacrifice, I rose from my self-abasement, with my tunic and cloak torn, and fell on my knees with my hands spread out to the Lord my God (Ezra 9:5).

That at the name of Jesus every knee should bow, in heaven and on earth and under the earth, and every tongue confess that Jesus Christ is Lord, to the glory of God the Father (Philippians 2:10-11).

Why were there knees to receive me and breasts that I might be nursed? (Job 3:12)

Your words have supported those who stumbled; you have strengthened faltering knees (Job 4:4).

They are brought to their knees and fall, but we rise up and stand firm (Psalm 20:8).

Strengthen the feeble hands, steady the knees that give way (Isaiah 35:3).

Trembling knees: Weakness or fear.

LEGS: Means of support. Spiritual strength to walk in life. Symbol of strength. Object of beauty. Something you stand on—your foundational principles.

His pleasure is not in the strength of the horse, nor His delight in the legs of a man (Psalm 147:10).

Then I saw another mighty angel coming down from heaven. He was robed in a cloud, with a rainbow above his head; his face was like the sun, and his legs were like fiery pillars (Revelation 10:1).

His legs are pillars of marble set on bases of pure gold. His appearance is like Lebanon, choice as its cedars (Song of Solomon 5:15).

How beautiful your sandaled feet, O prince's daughter! Your graceful legs are like jewels, the work of a craftsman's hands (Song of Solomon 7:1).

His face turned pale and he was so frightened that his knees knocked together and his legs gave way (Daniel 5:6).

I heard and my heart pounded, my lips quivered at the sound; decay crept into my bones, and my legs trembled. Yet I will wait patiently for the day of calamity to come on the nation invading us (Habakkuk 3:16).

Legs giving way: Giving up on the issue.

Female legs: Power to entice.

LIPS: Reflects the quality of the heart. Lying lips. Can determine out-come in life. Issuing deception. Object of seduction.

Let their lying lips be silenced, for with pride and contempt they speak arrogantly against the righteous (Psalm 31:18).

He who guards his lips guards his life, but he who speaks rashly will come to ruin (Proverbs 13:3).

Words from a wise man's mouth are gracious, but a fool is consumed by his own lips (Ecclesiastes 10:12).

The Lord says: "These people come near to Me with their mouth and honor Me with their lips, but their hearts are far from Me. Their wor-ship of Me is made up only of rules taught by men (Isaiah 29:13).

His cheeks are like beds of spice yielding perfume. His lips are like lilies dripping with myrrh (Song 5:13).

MOUTH: Instrument of witnessing. Speaking evil or good words. Some-thing from which comes the issues of life. Words coming against you.

NECK: Associated with beauty. A place to secure something valuable. Capture and subjection. Cut off or break.

Outstretched: Arrogance.

Long neck: Noisy.

Risk the neck: To take risk.

Stiff-necked: Stubbornness.

Are they not finding and dividing the spoils: a girl or two for each man, colorful garments as plunder for Sisera, colorful garments embroidered, highly embroidered garments for my neck—all this as plunder? (Judges 5:30)

They will be a garland to grace your head and a chain to adorn your neck (Proverbs 1:9).

Let love and faithfulness never leave you; bind them around your neck, write them on the tablet of your heart (Proverbs 3:3).

In His great power God becomes like clothing to me; He binds me like the neck of my garment (Job 30:18).

The Lord has appointed you priest in place of Jehoiada to be in charge of the house of the Lord; you should put any madman who acts like a prophet into the stocks and neck-irons (Jeremiah 29:26).

Therefore in hunger and thirst, in nakedness and dire poverty, you will serve the enemies the Lord sends against you. He will put an iron yoke on your neck until He has destroyed you (Deuteronomy 28:48).

Who risked their own necks for my life, to whom not only I give thanks, but also all the churches of the Gentiles (Romans 16:4 NKJ).

NOSE: Discerning spirit. Discernment, good or bad. Intruding into people's privacy. Gossiper.

SHOULDERS: The responsibility, the authority. Something, person or animal on which burden or load is laid or can be placed. Something that can be of good for work. Governmental responsibility. Sign of unity—shoulder to shoulder. Captivity.

For as in the day of Midian's defeat, you have shattered the yoke that burdens them, the bar across their shoulders, the rod of their oppressor (Isaiah 9:4).

For to us a child is born, to us a son is given, and the government will be on His shoulders. And He will be called Wonderful Counselor, Mighty God, Everlasting Father, Prince of Peace (Isaiah 9:6).

Then will I purify the lips of the peoples, that all of them may call on the name of the Lord and serve Him shoulder to shoulder (Zephaniah 3:9).

He says, "I removed the burden from their shoulders; their hands were set free from the basket" (Psalm 81:6).

They tie up heavy loads and put them on men's shoulders, but they themselves are not willing to lift a finger to move them (Matthew 23:4).

Bare female shoulders: Enticement.

Broad: Capable of handling much responsibility.

Drooped: Defeated attitude, overworked, overtired, burnt-out.

TEETH: Primary symbol of strength. Image of good consumption by breaking down into tiny bits. To simplify into its smallest bits for easy processing for wisdom. Power.

And there before me was a second beast, which looked like a bear. It was raised up on one of its sides, and it had three ribs in its mouth between its teeth. It was told, "Get up and eat your fill of flesh!" (Daniel 7:5)

Like the ungodly they maliciously mocked; they gnashed their teeth at me (Psalm 35:16).

But the subjects of the kingdom will be thrown outside, into the darkness, where there will be weeping and gnashing of teeth (Matthew 8:12).

Baby teeth: Immaturity.

Breaking of teeth: Defeat and/or losing wisdom.

Brushing teeth: Gaining understanding.

False teeth: Wisdom of this world.

Gnashing of teeth: Sign of taunt, division or regret and sorrow.

Toothache: Trial, problems.

BUILDINGS

Personalities or Structure of an Organization

I will show you what he is like who comes to Me and hears My words and puts them into practice. He is like a man building a house, who dug down deep and laid the foundation on rock. When the flood came, the torrent struck that house but could not shake it, because it was well built (Luke 6:47-48).

CHURCH BUILDING: Pertaining to church, ministry, or the call of God.

COURTROOM: Being judged. Under scrutiny. Persecution, trial.

CURRENT HOUSE: The dreamer's make-up.

FACTORY: A place of putting things together. A place of protection. A church.

Foundation: Something on which the person or object stands on.

Idle: Not put into proper use.

Factory in good state: Good standing.

Factory ruins: Needing attention.

FAMILY HOME: Related to the past. Something from the past influencing the present. Something from the bloodline.

House:

High-rise: Multitalented ministry; multiple ministries in one place.

Mobile home: A transitory situation. Character in transition. Temporary place.

Moving home: Changes in personality.

New: New personality, either natural or spiritual.

Old: Past or something inherited. If in good state, then it is righteous or good from the past. If in bad state, then it is sin or weakness that runs in a family.

Shop: A place of choices. Business-related venue.

Under construction: In process of formation.

LIBRARY: Time or place of knowledge; education.

OFFICE BUILDING: Relates to secular jobs, the dreamer's office life.

Parts of a Building

BACK: Something in the past or unexpected.

BATHROOM: A period of cleansing; entering a time of repentance. A place of voluntary nakedness. Facing reality in individual life.

BEDROOM: A place of intimacy. A place of rest or where you sleep and dream. A place of covenant or a place of revelation.

FRONT: Something in the future.

KITCHEN: A plea of nourishment; heart. The mind or intellect, where ideas are muted in the natural realm. The heart (Spirit). Where revelations are received and nurtured for the equipping of others.

ROOF: The covering.

SITTING ROOM: That which is easily noticed by the public. The revealed part.

States of a Building

CRACKED WALL: Faulty protective measures. Not adequately protected.

LEAKING ROOF: Inadequate spiritual cover.

MODERN: Current doctrine up-to-date.

NEGLECTED: Lack of maintenance.

OLD-FASHIONED: Tradition or old belief.

SPIRITUAL SIGNIFICANCE OF NUMBERS

God speaks through numbers a great deal, and the Bible is full of evidence of God's arithmetic. Numbers are high-level forms of symbolism. I have put together some numbers and their generally accepted scriptural relevance or meaning. The spiritual significance of numbers given here is based on the Word of God, and I have found it very useful in my personal experience.

ONE: Unity. The number of God. The beginning, the first. Precious.

> There is one body and one Spirit—just as you were called to one hope when you were called—one Lord, one faith, one baptism; one God and Father of all, who is over all and through all and in all (Ephesians 4:4-6).

> I and the Father are one (John 10:30).

> That all of them may be one, Father, just as You are in Me and I am in You. May they also be in Us so that the world may believe that You have sent Me. I have given them the glory that You gave Me, that they may be one as We are one (John 17:21-22).

> Make every effort to keep the unity of the Spirit through the bond of peace (Ephesians 4:3).

> And I will pour out on the house of David and the inhabitants of Jerusalem a spirit of grace and supplication. They will look on Me, the one they have pierced, and they will mourn for Him as one mourns for an only child, and grieve bitterly for Him as one grieves for a firstborn son (Zechariah 12:10).

> A mediator, however, does not represent just one party; but God is one (Galatians 3:20).

TWO: Union, witnessing or confirmation. It could also mean division depending on the general context of the events or revelation.

> The man said, "This is now bone of my bones and flesh of my flesh; she shall be called 'woman,' for she was taken out of man." For this reason a man will leave his father and mother and be united to his wife, and they will become one flesh (Genesis 2:23-24).

But if he will not listen, take one or two others along, so that every matter may be established by the testimony of two or three witnesses (Matthew 18:16).

He is a double-minded man, unstable in all he does (James 1:8).

So God made the expanse and separated the water under the expanse from the water above it. And it was so. God called the expanse "sky." And there was evening, and there was morning—the second day (Genesis 1:7-8).

Then the king said, "Bring me a sword." So they brought a sword for the king. He then gave an order: "Cut the living child in two and give half to one and half to the other" (1 Kings 3:24-25).

THREE: Resurrection, divine completeness and perfection. Confirmation. The trinity of Godhead. Restoration.

Therefore go and make disciples of all nations, baptizing them in the name of the Father and of the Son and of the Holy Spirit (Matthew 28:19).

For as Jonah was three days and three nights in the belly of a huge fish, so the Son of Man will be three days and three nights in the heart of the earth (Matthew 12:40).

Jesus answered them, "Destroy this temple, and I will raise it again in three days" (John 2:19).

FOUR: Creation or to rule or to reign. On the fourth day of creation, God made two great lights—the sun and the moon—to rule the day and the night.

And God said, "Let there be lights in the expanse of the sky to separate the day from the night, and let them serve as signs to mark seasons and days and years, and let them be lights in the expanse of the sky to give light on the earth." And it was so. God made two great lights—the greater light to govern the day and the lesser light to govern the night. He also made the stars. God set them in the expanse of the sky to give light on the earth, to govern the day and the night, and to separate light from darkness. And God saw that it was good. And there was evening, and there was morning—the fourth day (Genesis 1:14-19).

Also before the throne there was what looked like a sea of glass, clear as crystal. In the center, around the throne, were four living creatures, and they were covered with eyes, in front and in back. The first living creature was like a lion, the second was like an ox, the third had a face like a man, the fourth was like a flying eagle. Each of the four living creatures had six wings and was covered with eyes all around, even under his wings. Day and night they never stop saying: 'Holy, holy, holy is the Lord God Almighty, who was, and is, and is to come"(Revelation 4:6-8).

FIVE: Grace or the goodness of God. Fivefold ministry.

It was He who gave some to be apostles, some to be prophets, some to be evangelists, and some to be pastors and teachers (Ephesians 4:11).

SIX: The number of man. Weakness of humanity or the flesh. Can mean evil or satan. God created man on the sixth day.

Then God said, "Let us make man in Our image, in Our likeness, and let them rule over the fish of the sea and the birds of the air, over the livestock, over all the earth, and over all the creatures that move along the ground." So God created man in His own image, in the image of God He created him; male and female He created them (Genesis 1:26-27).

Nebuchadnezzar the king made an image of gold, whose height was sixty cubits and its width six cubits. He set it up in the plain of Dura, in the province of Babylon (Daniel 3:1 NKJV).

SEVEN: Completeness or spiritual perfection. Rest. Blessing. Redemption.

Thus the heavens and the earth were completed in all their vast array. By the seventh day God had finished the work He had been doing; so on the seventh day He rested from all His work. And God blessed the seventh day and made it holy, because on it He rested from all the work of creating that He had done (Genesis 2:1-3).

But in the days when the seventh angel is about to sound his trumpet, the mystery of God will be accomplished, just as He announced to His servants the prophets (Revelation 10:7).

The seventh angel poured out his bowl into the air, and out of the temple came a loud voice from the throne, saying, "It is done!" (Revelation 16:17)

At the end of every seven years you must cancel debts. This is how it is to be done: Every creditor shall cancel the loan he has made to his fellow Israelite. He shall not require payment from his fellow Israelite or brother, because the Lord's time for cancelling debts has been proclaimed (Deuteronomy 15:1-2).

EIGHT: New birth or new beginning. The circumcision of male children of Israel on the eighth day is a type of new birth.

On the eighth day, when it was time to circumcise Him, He was named Jesus, the name the angel had given Him before He had been conceived. When the time of their purification according to the Law of Moses had been completed, Joseph and Mary took Him to Jerusalem to present Him to the Lord (as it is written in the Law of the Lord, "Every firstborn male is to be consecrated to the Lord") (Luke 2:21-23).

For the generations to come every male among you who is eight days old must be circumcised, including those born in your household or bought with money from a foreigner—those who are not your offspring (Genesis 17:12).

NINE: Fruit of the Spirit. Harvest or the fruit of your labor. Nine gifts of the Spirit.

But the fruit of the Spirit is love, joy, peace, patience, kindness, goodness, faithfulness, gentleness and self-control. Against such things there is no law (Galatians 5:22-23).

To one there is given through the Spirit the message of wisdom, to another the message of knowledge by means of the same Spirit, to another faith by the same Spirit, to another gifts of healing by that one Spirit, to another miraculous powers, to another prophecy, to another distinguishing between spirits, to another speaking in different kinds of tongues, and to still another the interpretation of tongues (1 Corinthians 12:8-10).

TEN: Law and responsibility. Tithe is a tenth of our earning, which belongs to God. It is also the number for the pastoral. Judgment. Ten plagues upon Egypt.

ELEVEN: Confusion, judgment, or disorder.

TWELVE: Government. The number of apostleship.

One of those days Jesus went out to a mountainside to pray, and spent the night praying to God. When morning came, He called His disciples to Him and chose twelve of them, whom He also designated apostles (Luke 6:12-13).

Jesus said to them, "I tell you the truth, at the renewal of all things, when the Son of Man sits on His glorious throne, you who have followed Me will also sit on twelve thrones, judging the twelve tribes of Israel" (Matthew 19:28).

THIRTEEN: Thirteen evil thoughts from the heart listed. Rebellion or spiritual depravity.

For from within, out of men's hearts, come evil thoughts, sexual immorality, theft, murder, adultery, greed, malice, deceit, lewdness, envy, slander, arrogance and folly (Mark 7:21-22).

FOURTEEN: Deliverance or salvation. The number of double anointing.

Thus there were fourteen generations in all from Abraham to David, fourteen from David to the exile to Babylon, and fourteen from the exile to the Christ (Matthew 1:17).

FIFTEEN: Rest, mercy.

Mordecai recorded these events, and he sent letters to all the Jews throughout the provinces of King Xerxes, near and far, to have them celebrate annually the fourteenth and fifteenth days of the month of Adar as the time when the Jews got relief from their enemies, and as the month when their sorrow was turned into joy and their mourning into a day of celebration. He wrote them to observe the days as days of feasting and joy and giving presents of food to one another and gifts to the poor (Esther 9:20-22).

Say to the Israelites: "On the fifteenth day of the seventh month the Lord's Feast of Tabernacles begins, and it lasts for seven days. The first day is a sacred assembly; do no regular work" (Leviticus 23:34-35).

SIXTEEN: Love—sixteen things are said of love.

Love is patient, love is kind. It does not envy, it does not boast, it is not proud. It is not rude, it is not self-seeking, it is not easily angered, it keeps no record of wrongs. Love does not delight in evil but rejoices with the truth. It always protects, always trusts, always hopes, always perseveres. Love never fails. But where there are prophecies, they will cease; where there are tongues, they will be stilled; where there is knowledge, it will pass away (1 Corinthians 13:4-8).

SEVENTEEN: Immaturity. Transition. Victory.

Joseph, a young man of seventeen, was tending the flocks with his brothers, the sons of Bilhah and the sons of Zilpah, his father's wives, and he brought their father a bad report about them (Genesis 37:2).

Jacob lived in Egypt seventeen years, and the years of his life were a hundred and forty-seven (Genesis 47:28).

And on the seventeenth day of the seventh month the ark came to rest on the mountains of Ararat (Genesis 8:4).

EIGHTEEN: Bondage.

Then should not this woman, a daughter of Abraham, whom Satan has kept bound for eighteen long years, be set free on the Sabbath day from what bound her? (Luke 13:16)

The Israelites were subject to Eglon king of Moab for eighteen years (Judges 3:14).

He became angry with them. He sold them into the hands of the Philistines and the Ammonites, who that year shattered and crushed them. For eighteen years they oppressed all the Israelites on the east side of the Jordan in Gilead, the land of the Amorites (Judges 10:7-8).

NINETEEN: Faith. Nineteen persons mentioned in Hebrews chapter 11.

Now faith is being sure of what we hope for and certain of what we do not see. This is what the ancients were commended for... (Hebrews 11:1-32).

TWENTY: Redemption (silver money in the Bible).

THIRTY: Blood of Jesus. Dedication. The beginning of service. Salvation.

Then one of the Twelve—the one called Judas Iscariot—went to the chief priests and asked, "What are you willing to give me if I hand Him over to you?" So they counted out for him thirty silver coins (Matthew 26:14-15).

Count all the men from thirty to fifty years of age who come to serve in the work in the Tent of Meeting. This is the work of the Kohathites in the Tent of Meeting: the care of the most holy things (Numbers 4:3-4).

Joseph was thirty years old when he entered the service of Pharaoh king of Egypt. And Joseph went out from Pharaoh's presence and traveled throughout Egypt (Genesis 41:46).

David was thirty years old when he became king, and he reigned forty years (2 Samuel 5:4).

FORTY: Trial. Probation. Testing or temptation.

Remember how the Lord your God led you all the way in the desert these forty years, to humble you and to test you in order to know what was in your heart, whether or not you would keep His commands. He humbled you, causing you to hunger and then feeding you with manna, which neither you nor your fathers had known, to teach you that man does not live on bread alone but on every word that comes from the mouth of the Lord. Your clothes did not wear out and your feet did not swell during these forty years. Know then in your heart that as a man disciplines his son, so the Lord your God disciplines you (Deuteronomy 8:2-5).

Jesus, full of the Holy Spirit, returned from the Jordan and was led by the Spirit in the desert, where for forty days He was tempted by the devil. He ate nothing during those days, and at the end of them He was hungry (Luke 4:1-2).

So he got up and ate and drank. Strengthened by that food, he traveled forty days and forty nights until he reached Horeb, the mountain of God (1 Kings 19:8).

On the first day, Jonah started into the city. He proclaimed: "Forty more days and Nineveh will be overturned" (Jonah 3:4).

FIFTY: Number of the Holy Spirit. Jubilee, liberty. The number for the Holy Spirit: He was poured out on the day of Pentecost which was fifty days after the resurrection of Christ.

Consecrate the fiftieth year and proclaim liberty throughout the land to all its inhabitants. It shall be a jubilee for you; each one of you is to return to his family property and each to his own clan (Leviticus 25:10).

SIXTY: Pride or arrogance. The image that Nebuchadnezzar set up was sixty cubits high.

Nebuchadnezzar the king made an image of gold, whose height was sixty cubits and its width six cubits. He set it up in the plain of Dura, in the province of Babylon (Daniel 3:1 NKJV).

SEVENTY: Universality or restoration. Israel lived in exile for seventy years after which they were restored.

In the first year of his reign, I, Daniel, understood from the Scriptures, according to the word of the Lord given to Jeremiah the prophet, that the desolation of Jerusalem would last seventy years (Daniel 9:2).

EIGHTY: Beginning of a high calling or becoming spiritually acceptable.

Moses was eighty years old when he started his ministry to deliver the Israelites.

NINETY OR NINETY-NINE: Fruits are ripe and ready. Abraham was ninety-nine years old when God appeared to him.

When Abram was ninety-nine years old, the Lord appeared to him and said, "I am God Almighty; walk before Me and be blameless" (Genesis 17:1 NKJV).

ONE HUNDRED: God's election of grace. Children of promise. Full reward. Abraham was one hundred years old when his son Isaac (child of promise) was born.

Abraham was a hundred years old when his son Isaac was born to him (Genesis 21:5).

ONE THOUSAND: The beginning of maturity; mature service or full status.

Multiples or Complex Numbers

For these numbers, the meaning lies in the way it is pronounced rather than as it is written.

Example:

2872 is pronounced "Two thousand, eight hundred, seventy-two."

Two thousand = confirmed spiritual maturity or mature judgment.

Eight hundred = new beginning into the promises.

Seventy-two = confirmed, completed, and restored.

GLOSSARY OF TERMS

APOSTOLIC DOCTRINE: A principle of acceptable beliefs by Christians, as based on teachings of the apostles of Jesus Christ.

APPARITIONS: Supernatural happenings in the natural realm as perceptible to the natural eyes.

BLIND SPOT: Any part of an issue that a person cannot directly observe with his natural rationalism. An area where perception is weak, or a subject about which one is markedly ignorant or prejudiced.

CAPTURING YOUR DREAM: The process of remembering your dreams.

CARRY-OVER: A thought pattern carried over into or from a dream.

CHRISTIAN DOCTRINE: A system of principles of acceptable beliefs practiced by Christians.

CLOSED VISION: A vision perceived by the spiritual eyes while the natural eyes are closed.

COMMUNION: Sharing of thoughts, feelings, and close rapport in a spiritual atmosphere.

CONCEPTUALIZATION: The process of forming concepts, theories, or ideas.

CONFIRMATION: The process of ascertaining a dream's true interpretation that reveals the dream as sent by God.

CORRECTIVE DREAMS: Dreams that bring correction to a dreamer's life.

COVERT KNOWLEDGE: Knowledge available but concealed to immediate awareness of a person's rational mind.

DARK SPEECH: Speeches with concealed meaning.

DECREED EVENTS: Events settled in Heaven that will happen in the natural realm despite human effort.

DEMONIC DREAM: Dream dominated by demonic activities.

DIALOGUING DREAMS: Dreams on the same subject, as separated by an interlude in which the dreamer wakes up and intercedes on the issue.

DISPENSATIONAL PATTERN: Divine ordering of worldly affairs, or a system of commands or specific arrangement by which something is administered, and considered to have been divinely revealed or appointed.

DIVINE INSIGHTS: An in-depth revelation from God.

DIVINE MESSENGER: One who brings a message from God.

DIVINE PREMIUMS: The measure of God-given motivation to seek a dream's meaning.

DIVINE SIGHT: An open vision where natural surroundings blend into the scene, so one cannot tell if it is real or spiritual.

DIVINE CODE: A system of symbols, letters, numbers, or words that conceal the meaning of a message that requires secrecy by God.

DREAM: A pictorial revelation received in the spirit when one is sleeping. True dreams are Holy Spirit-inspired.

DREAM CLUSTERING: Dreams on related subjects received by different people, either within the same geographic location or in the same field of interest. Usually, this indicates a divine message for the group.

DREAM ESSENCE: The quality of a dream's main message that gives it substance.

DREAM INTERPRETATION: The study of understanding symbols and elements in dreams for the purpose of interpretation.

DREAMLAND: The atmosphere and capabilities under which a dream encounter occurs.

DREAMLIFE: The pattern and extent to which the dreamer can receive revelation in dream form.

DREAM MESSAGE: The essential message of a dream.

DREAM PHRASES: Statements of truth in a dream that are either profound or have relevance to a dreamer's life situation.

DREAM PROMISE: A promise revealed in a dream.

ELEMENTS: Objects or persons in a dream or vision.

EMOTIONAL BACKLASH: A strong and adverse reaction to an occurrence, which is often delayed and was construed as a threat or danger.

EXPERIENTIAL KNOWLEDGE: The imbibed nature, attributes, or knowledge of God, as derived from direct experience of His presence.

EXTRA-BIBLICAL EXPERIENCE: Experience without Bible precedence or example justifying subsequent similar cases.

FALSE DREAM: A dream not sent by God—a made-up story or delusion of the person's mind.

FEELERS IN THE DREAM: Elements in a dream that God uses to fill gaps in the storyline of a dream message to add to a conclusion.

FELLOWSHIP: The condition of being together for sharing similar interests and experiences that leads to mutual concern and trust among Christians.

HEALING DREAM: A dream in which healing occurs to the dreamer's physical or soul realm.

HEART CONNECTION: The intents or outworking of the dreamer's heart as revealed by the dream.

HUMANIST IDEOLOGY: Pertaining to that which concerns the interest and needs of human beings, as opposed to divine or supernatural concerns. Ideology often associated with a belief that man is capable of reaching self-fulfillment without divine aspect.

HUMAN REASONING: Reasoning at human level, which is usually not dependent on divine input.

IMAGE CENTER: Part of the imagination that handles imagery, pictures, dreams, and visions (memory).

IMPARTATION: To bestow anointing upon a person by transference.

INBUILT DIVINE DRIVE: Divine motivation to seek the meaning of a dream.

INNER DREAM: A dream within a dream.

INNER VOICE: The gentle intrusion into your consciousness of birthing within your spirit, or evidence from your inner witness.

INNER WITNESS: A verification of truth that arises from within the dream's spirit realm.

INTERACTIVE DREAM: A dream encounter that includes exchange between the dreamer and God.

INTERNAL COMPONENT: Aspects of a dreamer's emotional make-up that God plays up in dramatization of a dream to bring it to his attention.

INTERPRETATION: The process of deciphering symbols within a dream and simplifying the meaning of a parable illustration.

LOVE TEST: A test that ascertains the presence or absence of the love of God. The ultimate love test is the respect for human life.

MEANING OF A DREAM: The true meaning as to why God sent the dream.

MENTAL PICTURES: Images present in your mind.

METAPHOR: A symbol with implied comparison, such as: Jesus is the lion of the tribe of Judah.

MIND-SET: Preconceived ideas, or prejudiced point of view.

MULTIPLE DREAMS: More than two dreams in a single night. Each dream often refers to an aspect of the same message. This is a common occurrence in the life of a high-volume dreamer.

MYSTERIES OF GOD: Unexplained, inexplicable, or secret truth divinely revealed, which one could not know through reason.

NATURAL CONSCIOUSNESS: A critical awareness of one's own identity and situations.

NIGHTMARE: A dream arousing feelings of acute fear, dread, or anguish. Nightmare is a subjective term depending on the dreamer's perception.

NIGHT SEASONS: Related to nighttime, or periods in life full of difficulties.

OPEN HEAVEN: Access between the earth and the third Heaven.

OPEN VISION: Vision received with natural eyes wide open, but perceived with spiritual eyes.

OUTER DREAM: A dream that contains another dream within it.

PANORAMIC VISION: A vision in motion (as in a movie).

PARABLE: A story illustrating a lesson by using one element to represent another element.

PERSONAL TRAITS: Attributes specific to a person.

PHYSICAL REALM: The sphere of the natural.

PICTORIAL DEPOSITORY: Center in the mind where issues relating to imagery and pictures are processed.

PICTORIAL VISION: A vision of pictures without motion.

PLANT DREAM IN THE SPIRIT: Handling a dream's message in accordance with dictates of the Spirit of God and in line with His Word and His manifest presence.

POTENTIAL EVENT: Events likely to occur in the future.

PREDICTIVE DREAM: A dream that foretells future events.

PROGRESSIVE REVELATION: Revelation received in bits and pieces, in an increasingly unfolding manner.

PROPHET: A person who speaks by divine inspiration, or as the interpreter through whom divine will is expressed.

PROPHETIC DECLARATION: A proclamation under divine inspiration that is supernaturally revealed.

PURE DREAM: A dream without a visionary component or superimposition.

REALM OF THE SPIRIT: The sphere or arena of the spirit.

RECURRING DREAMS: Dreams repeated more than twice over a long period of time. They may indicate issues that need to be resolved or are in the process of being resolved.

REPEATED DREAMS: Dreams repeated more than once within a short time, often in one single night. There may be minor variations in elements or symbolic action, but the dream's storylines are essentially the same.

SECOND HEAVEN: The abode of spiritual warfare—the zone of conflict between good and evil forces from which satan exerts his influence.

SECURITY CONTENT: The measure of sensitivity of information in a dream as coupled with its liability to cause damage if not maturely handled.

SEER: One who sees and receives insights by divine inspiration through pictures, dreams, visions, and utterance on a constant basis.

SIMILITUDE: An element that closely resembles another element.

SLEEP: A temporary suspension in the exercise of the power of body and soul.

SOUL DREAM: Dream dominated by issues emanating from a dreamer's soulish realm.

SOUL REALM: The sphere of the soul or the act of handling decisions in the realm of emotion, feeling, or will.

SPIRITUAL ATMOSPHERE: Impact or influence of the spirit that envelopes surroundings of an event or occurrence.

SPIRITUAL CONNOTATIONS: The reason beyond the obvious, which touches on deeper meanings from a supernatural point of view.

SPIRITUAL ENCOUNTER: An experience in the spirit.

SPIRITUAL IMPARTATION: To bestow spiritual equipping from God upon a person.

BEST SELLERS BY DR. JOE IBOJIE

Dreams and Visions: How to Receive, Interpret and Apply Your Dreams

The Illustrated Bible-Based Dictionary of Dream Symbols

How to Live the Supernatural Life in the Here and Now

For more details visit: www.the-fathers-house.org.uk

Order Now from Destiny Image Europe
Telephone: +39 085 4716623 - Fax +39 085 4716622
E-mail: ordini@eurodestinyimage.com

Internet: www.eurodestinyimage.com.

DREAM COURSES

Dreams are the parable language of God in a world that is spiritually distancing itself from experiencing the reality of His Presence. They are personalized, coded messages from God. Through dreams, God breaks through our thought processes, mind-sets, prejudices, and emotions to connect with the spirit of man. In this way He shows us what we might have missed or not heard or what our natural mind was incapable of comprehending. We all dream. He speaks to us at our individual levels and leads us further in Christ. God's ultimate purpose in dreams and visions is to align us to His plan and purposes in our lives!

The purpose of these courses is to equip the saints for the end-time move of God by learning the art of hearing Him and understanding how he speaks through dreams at an individual level.

Each dream course builds on the knowledge gained in the previous course. Attendees are strongly encouraged to take the courses in order for maximum effectiveness.

Topics to be covered include

COURSE 1

* Introduction to dreams and visions.

* Biblical history of dreams and visions.

* How dreams are received.

* Hindrances to receiving and remembering your dreams.

* How to respond to your dreams.

* Differences between dreams and visions.

* Introduction to interpreting your dreams.

* Understanding the ministry of angels.

Course 2

* Introduction to the language of symbols (the language of the spirit).

* Different levels of interpretation of dreams.

* Why we seek the meaning of our dreams.

* What to do with dreams you do not immediately understand.

* Maintaining and developing your dreamlife.

* Expanding the scope of your dreams.

* Improving your interpretative skill.

* Visions and the Third Heaven.

Course 3

* Responding to revelations.

* Interpreting the dreams of others.

* Guidelines for setting up a corporate dream group.

* Prophetic symbolism.

* How to organize Dream Workshops.

* The Seer's anointing.

* The ministry of a Watchman.

* Spiritual warfare (fighting the good fight).

* Understanding the roles of angels and the different categories of angelic forces.

* How to work with angels.

Course 4

* Living the supernatural in the natural.

* Understanding the spiritual senses.

* Maintaining balance while blending the natural and the spiritual senses.

* Security and information management in revelatory ministry.

* Understanding the anointing.

* Dialoguing with God.

* An anatomy of Scriptural dreams.

WEEKEND COURSES

FRIDAY:

* Registration begins at 5:00 PM.

* Teaching begins at 6:00 PM.

SATURDAY:

* Registration begins at 9:00 AM.

* Sessions begin at 10:30 AM, 1:30 PM and 7:00 PM.

ONE WEEK COURSE (MONDAY TO FRIDAY)

Courses begin Monday morning and end Friday evening.

* Registration begins each day at 9:00 AM.

* Sessions begin at 10:00 AM and end at 5:00 PM.

There are breaks for lunch and tea.

The contents of each Dream Course will be covered in two weekend courses or a single one-week course (Monday to Friday).

To request a DREAM COURSE in your area,
please call to arrange a program to fit your needs:

Dr Joe Ibojie
jcnibojie@hotmail.com
Phone: 44-77 6583 4253

Order Now from Destiny Image Europe
Telephone: +39 085 4716623 - Fax: +39 085 9431270
E-mail: ordini@eurodestinyimage.com

Internet: www.eurodestinyimage.com.

Additional copies of this book and other book titles from DESTINY IMAGE™ EUROPE are available at your local bookstore.

We are adding new titles every month!

To view our complete catalog online, visit us at:
www.eurodestinyimage.com.

Send a request for a catalog to:

**Via Acquacorrente, 6
65123 - Pescara - ITALY
Tel: +39 085 4716623 - Fax: +39 085 9431270**

"Changing the world, one book at a time."

Are you an author?

Do you have a "today" God-given message?

CONTACT US

We will be happy to review your manuscript for the possibility of publication:

publisher@eurodestinyimage.com
http://www.eurodestinyimage.com/pages/AuthorsAppForm.htm

Ingram Content Group UK Ltd.
Milton Keynes UK
UKHW012314210623
423834UK00003B/41